The Problem
of Truth
in Applied Psychoanalysis

THE GUILFORD PSYCHOANALYSIS SERIES

Robert S. Wallerstein, Editor

Associate Editors
Leonard Shengold
Neil J. Smelser
Albert J. Solnit
Edward M. Weinshel

THE PROBLEM OF TRUTH IN APPLIED PSYCHOANALYSIS
Charles Hanly

HALO IN THE SKY
Observations on Anality and Defense
Leonard Shengold

FROM SAFETY TO SUPEREGO
Selected Papers of Joseph Sandler
Joseph Sandler

THE TEACHING AND LEARNING OF PSYCHOANALYSIS
Selected Papers of Joan Fleming, M.D.
Stanley S. Weiss, Editor

FORTY-TWO LIVES IN TREATMENT
A Study of Psychoanalysis and Psychotherapy
Robert S. Wallerstein

The Problem of Truth in Applied Psychoanalysis

CHARLES HANLY, PhD

Foreword by
Peter Gay

THE GUILFORD PRESS
New York   London

© 1992 The Guilford Press
A Division of Guilford Publications, Inc.
72 Spring Street, New York, N. Y. 10012

Printed in the United States of America

This book is printed on acid-free paper.

Last digit is print number: 9   8   7   6   5   4   3   2   1

Library of Congress Cataloging-in-Publication Data

Hanly, Charles Mervyn Taylor, 1930–
    The problem of truth in applied psychoanalysis /
    Charles Hanly.
    236 p.   cm. — (The Guilford psychoanalysis series)
    Includes bibliographical references and index.
    ISBN 0-89862-329-4
    1. Psychanalysis and philosophy.   2. Truth.
    I. Title.
    II. Series.
    BF175.4.P45H36   1992
    150.19'5—dc20   91-23001
                                                              CIP

Foreword

Let me perform a thought experiment. Suppose this book had been published in Freud's lifetime; it is a good bet that he would not have liked it. But suppose that Freud were alive now; then, I want to argue, it is highly likely that he would have welcomed it as a necessary corrective. We know that after flirting with philosophy during his student years, he radically turned against it as shallow and unrevealing. Did it not limit its researches to the conscious mind alone? Whatever the merits of this rejection of philosophy—and it is nothing less than unfair—what matters is that he kept his distance from it to pursue his work as a scientist of the mind. As an empiricist he was alert above all to the pressures of the psychic facts of life he was discovering from his analysands on the couch. He did offer occasional epistemological comments, but they, as Charles Hanly shows, were far from consistent. For the most part, in any event, he preferred to think, talk, and write psychology. The acceptance on Freud's part of Charles Hanly's thoughtful essays on applied psychoanalysis that I am inviting the reader to imagine would stem not from his mounting appreciation of current philosophic discourse. Quite the contrary: philosophers and, for that matter, psychoanalysts considering the great issues impinging on psychoanalytic science have not reformed. Instead, they are selling us nostrums with their notions of double truth, the presumed damage that overdetermination does to prospects of certainty, the primacy of language over substance, a peculiar tolerance of two competing theories as possessing equal claims to correctness, and other fashionable subjectivities.

It is against this modern antiscientific nihilism—and this is what in the end it all comes down to—that Charles Hanly has launched his connected essays. I shall not spoil the reader's pleasure by anticipating his argumentation as he moves deftly from metaphysics to Hobbes, Kant to aesthetics, Shakespeare to autobiography and Plato. Writing as a historian trained in psychoanalysis, engaged every working day in doing a special kind of applied analysis—I call it history informed by psychoanalysis—I want rather to follow out some of the thoughts that these pages have stimulated in me. What Hanly's essays have in common is a serious concern with meaning and truth, and I will illustrate them both from a historian's perspective.

Consider the question, What is the meaning of Rousseau's *Contrat social*? Historians of ideas face a question of this sort with any text from the past. Rousseau's thought, it is worth noting at the outset, has remained controversial for more than two centuries. To be sure, the thought of all major thinkers from Plato to Machiavelli, Hegel to Dewey, has remained contested terrain; in itself there is nothing unusual about the battles over the meaning, and the legacy, of Rousseau. But it is fair to say that the disputes he has aroused are as intense as, perhaps more intense than, any other debates among interpreters of significant philosophical texts. He has been categorized as an individualist or as a collectivist, as moving from individualism to collectivism, or, for that matter, as so incoherent that he defies any classification whatever. He has been called the father of nationalism, of democracy, of fascism—or of all together.

It is in the face of such irreconcilable views that the historian approaches the question I have posed: What is the meaning of Rousseau's *Contrat social*? It will turn out that no single answer is wholly satisfactory, and that several answers are necessary. First, the book was a chapter in Rousseau's mature thought; it should be principally read therefore in conjunction with other texts he produced around the same time, notably his bulky tract on education, *Emile*, and his famous epistolary novel, *La nouvelle Héloise*. This approach proves fruitful since the Utopian elements in his novel, and the pedagogic principles underlying his tract, illuminate his view of human nature in his masterpiece in political theory. The participatory democratic society Rousseau envisions in the *Contrat social* would be possible only to humans formed to become Emiles. Secondly, the book was an integral part of Rousseau's life history; hence it is necessary to read it in conjunction with all his earlier work, notably the discourses that gave him such dubious celebrity a decade before he turned to the *Contrat social*. This, too, is a useful exercise, since Rousseau elaborated and significantly revised the politics largely implicit (and partly explicit) in the *Discours sur les arts et les sciences* and, even more, the *Discours sur l'origine de l'inégalité*. Thirdly, the *Contrat social* was a contribution to contemporary Genevan politics. This, too, is a fertile reading. Not only did Rousseau intervene in the venomous political and constitutional disputes that were tearing his native republic apart around 1760; beyond that, his critique of large states and his insistence on face-to-face contact among citizens as the general will is discovered make sense as a fantasy transferring certain Genevan realities into ostensibly universal validity. Fourthly, as a classic in political philosophy, the *Contrat social* stands out as a position taken by a fully qualified participant in a centuries-long controversy among political theorists. The *Contrat social*, on this showing, must be read with Plato's *Republic*, Machiavelli's *Prince*, Hobbes's *Leviathan*, and Locke's *Second Treatise on Civil Government* in mind. And, as before, this is a useful approach to the meaning of the book: Rousseau was demonstrably no stranger to these giants of political philosophy and was in fact explicitly arguing with his predecessors as an equal partner in a great debate. Fifth, the *Contrat social* is a clue to Rousseau's psyche, documenting the strength of his *ressentiment*, his explosive desire to be liberated from all shackles combined with an almost tragic need to control ("forcing people to be free"). And again, the psychoanalytic approach, reading not only this text but others—including Rousseau's letters and drafts, and his openly autobiographical writings—provides access to the meaning—we should rather say, meanings—of the book.

There are no doubt other dimensions to Rousseau's classic in political thought, but the five just mentioned are the principal ones. Each of the readings I have instanced is productive; each contributes to an understanding of a complex, sometimes baffling text. The interpreter who takes all of them into account is no doubt obliged to take one more step, and a difficult one: to assign relative importance to each and to arrange them in a hierarchy of explanatory power. Controversy over the *Contrat social*, in short, does not end once one has established its multiple facets. But the recognition of this difficulty, any more than the acceptance of the wealth inherent in Rousseau's text, is no argument against the doctrine of a single truth, and against the possibility of an interpretation that, apart from marginal differences, will come to convince reasonable students of Rousseau.

It is essential to distinguish between conflicting and complementary interpretations. The reader who holds that the *Contrat social* is an intervention in Genevan politics and nothing more must inevitably clash with the reader who holds that the *Contrat social* is exclusively part of a debate stretching back to Plato. These incompatible readings cannot both be true, though they may, of course, both be false. But— and this elementary point has been lost on such psychoanalytic theorists as Arnold Goldberg—there is a more modest way of assigning meanings, and that is to see each as part of a larger configuration. Certainly with a thinker as multifarious as Rousseau, in whom divergent intellectual and emotional tributaries met and merged, multiple meanings seem almost inescapable. In short, meanings can be complementary rather than conflicting, and then their coexistence should offer no difficulty to the philosopher willing to contain multitudes, yet insisting at the same time that the *Contrat social* was only one book, a book written in the past, and not some invention, or construction, of a 20th-century reader. The commonplace that every generation must rewrite history in its own way has done great damage.

To be sure, an account of meanings is on principle always incomplete, for events—and a book is an event—cast their shadows into the future, and that future is unpredictable. Readers of Rousseau, even careful readers not seduced by his gift for telling and misleading *bon mots*, will study the *Contrat social* with their own needs, and their own times, weighing on them. It is a curious tribute to the varieties concealed in the *Contrat social*, for example, that during the French Revolution it served the leaders of rival factions, served Robespierre and Madame Roland, equally. And a future may revive an old event to bestow on it a significance it had never had before. The stubborn resistance of the Jewish Zealots to the Roman legions at Masada from 66 to 73 A.D. was largely forgotten for centuries, until in our time it became a subject of interest to archeologists and, later, to Jews everywhere as a symbol of heroic self-assertion. This was a meaning of Masada that the fighters around 70 A.D. could not have anticipated. Of course, not all the meanings that historians assign to the past event they are studying will withstand critical examination. In recent years, after the horrific disclosures of the Nazis' efforts at genocide, some historians have chosen to interpret the French Revolution as the first act in an obscene drama of which the Holocaust was the climax and inescapable conclusion. These interpreters see not just certain fortuitous similarities but a causal thread leading from the 18th to the 20th century. I am persuaded that this is an unfortunate present-minded misreading which will not endure. But, then, it *will* endure, if in a different way: as a symptom—in short, one of the meanings—of a certain mood widespread in the 1980s.

Take another instance. When, on July 14, 1789, rebellious Parisians invaded the hated Bastille, killed its commander, and freed the prisoners confined in it, they were making history. But what is the "real" meaning of this historic event? Does the small number of prisoners—there were only seven of them—make July 14 into a mockery of popular indignation, a mere outburst by an idle mob looking for trouble and enjoyment? And who were the "liberators" of the Bastille? As historians of the French Revolution know, for almost a century two conflicting theories held sway: writers hostile to the French Revolution like Hippolyte Taine insisted that the crowd taking the Bastille were prostitutes and drifters and idle apprentices; writers sympathetic to the

Revolution like Jules Michelet argued on the contrary that they were the French people rising in righteous wrath. Then, some 50 years ago, an English historian named George Rudé decided to examine the surviving documentation with some care and found that the conquerors of the Bastille were neither the one nor the other, but mainly residents of the neighborhood around the Bastille, many of them quite respectable. This discovery, undisputed and indisputable, has not silenced the debate over the "ultimate" meaning of July 14, but it has discredited the two extreme views that had before then held the field.

What this episode makes plain is that new information can serve to drive out slapdash historical interpretations based on hunches and prejudices, and thus narrow the range of acceptable interpretations of events. And this raises a related criticism of subjectivity: as we all know, it is an only too familiar notion that researchers find what they are looking for, that their preconceptions color their findings, their passions their results. They see what they seek. There is ample evidence that this holds true often, not in the writing of history alone but in anthropology or, for that matter, in psychoanalysis. Taine wanted to disparage the Revolution; hence he discovered the most discreditable rabble attacking the Bastille. Michelet wanted to rescue the Revolution; hence he discovered the most impressive patriots destroying the appalling symbol of despotism. And there are innumerable other instances of theories compromising results.

But what these instances do not prove is that it has to be so. Rudé, a political radical, no doubt wanted to find favorable things to say about the conquerors of the Bastille, but that did not compromise his findings in any way. The most savage critic of the French Revolution can read his pages on July 14, if he can bring himself to read them, without dissent. There are, after all, safeguards that professional researchers build into their work, safeguards that the best among them internalize to serve as a scholarly superego. Whether a psychoanalyst finds that an analysand puts him to sleep or a historian that the more he reads about Bismarck, the more he detests the man, both have ways of dealing with this artifact—the analyst by analyzing his countertransference or by consulting a colleague on his momentary disability; the historian by learning a salutary fear of his colleagues and reviewers. The fact remains that the taking of the Bastille happened, and happened once, and happened in only one way, and that most meanings of the event, if not all, can be established to the satisfaction of all reasonable students of the past.

Skeptics, though they do not like to admit, can be made to admit that historians are in agreement most of the time, perhaps 99 percent of the time—when facts are involved. It is interpretations that lead to disputes. Yet this distinction is in danger these days: every fact, we are told, is already an interpretation, every presumably objective assertion is fatally infected by the researcher's mental set. But this is a subjectivism stronger in assertion than in proof. Moreover, the investigator's political bias or emotional stance may be enlisted not to establish distorted conclusions but hitherto neglected truths. In 1974, I published a little book, *Style in History*, on Gibbon, Ranke, Macaulay, and Burckhardt, in which I tried to demonstrate this point in some detail. It was (to mention but one instance), precisely Gibbon's feline pleasure in scabrous anecdotes and in attributing wicked motives to statesmen professing noble aims, a taste with deep roots in his unconscious, that gave him access to the deviousness of Roman politics. Of course, that he was a deeply learned scholar, with access to all the printed documentation then available, helped him to write his witty, wicked, and eminently scholarly *Decline and Fall of the Roman Empire*. But it was his particular personal style that made him see Roman politics more clearly than it had ever been seen before. Another instance from a more recent period: in the late 1890s, the German Social Democrat Eduard Bernstein, then in political exile in England, was commissioned to write a volume on 17th-century political thought that would demonstrate the existence of popular ideologies which modern socialists could take as worthy precursors. He sat down in the British Museum and studied documents that other historians of the Cromwellian period had studied just before him. But he found a small, if interesting, communist sect called the Diggers, that his predecessors, such authorities as S. R. Gardiner and Charles Firth, had quite simply overlooked. Bernstein found what he had sought, and if he had not been animated by his commitment to socialism, he would, like Gardiner and Firth, have overlooked those interesting seventeenth-century communist pamphleteers. In short, the psychological origins of scientific inquiry may be murky indeed; their results must never be judged by them alone. It is against these common heresies that Hanly has uttered his sober protest, and it would indeed be most desirable if his critique should help to loosen their grip.

I want to make one more point before I release the reader to the main text. As a historian, I find it particularly gratifying to have a psychoanalyst devote time and energy to what is called, often a little derisively, applied psychoanalysis. In general, applied psychoanalysis— the analytic study of children's books, or a film, or a historic event— rides in the back of the bus. There are signs of better things in the air: occasional plenary sessions at the meetings of the American Psychoanalytic Association devoted to issues neither of psychoanalytic theory nor of clinical practice, study groups formed to foster the psychoanalytic reading of novels. But many analysts remain uneasy: they prefer their discipline as hermetic as possible, sealed in a nondescript consulting room with neutral decorations on the wall and a conspicuous couch. As for historians—the less said about the willingness of my profession to grant applied psychoanalysis access to its sacred domains, the better. But that is another story.

—Peter Gay
Yale University

Contents

The Problem
of Truth
in Applied Psychoanalysis

chapter one

The Concept
of Truth in
Psychoanalysis

Why begin a study of method in applied psychoanalysis with reflections on the concept of truth? The concept of
truth is the cornerstone upon which method in applied or clinical
psychoanalysis must rest. It is the assumption that lies behind all other
assumptions about psychoanalytic observation and theorizing. An inquiry into truth is itself, in part, an applied psychoanalytic study.

Psychoanalysis is passing through a difficult period in its history
(Wallerstein, 1988): It is still unclear whether there will emerge further splintering, dilution, or a gradual reunification and reintegration
(Rangell, 1988). A core issue in our current differences is the concept
of truth in psychoanalysis. What at first appears most abstract and
remote has become most germane.

I shall begin with a philosophical clarification.

Two Philosophical Ideas of Truth

Philosophers have advocated two different theories of truth: correspondence and coherence. The correspondence theory is that truth
consists of the correspondence between an object and its description. It
is assumed that under normal conditions the human mind is able to
gain knowledge of objects by means of observation and its experimen-
tal refinement, and that this observational knowledge can then be used
to test beliefs and theories. The correspondence theory is intrinsic to
natural science. It is implied with oblique eloquence in Galileo's
"eppur si muove" (see Drake, 1978, pp. 356–357). Neither his official

1

recantation of his astronomical discoveries nor the majestic coherence of Ptolemaic astronomy nor its obvious agreement with experience nor the consensus of generations of scholars could alter the fact that Galileo's observations of the moon, planets, and sun had enabled him to describe much more accurately what was actually happening in nature. This same view of truth and of science has been held by the great seminal scientists: Harvey, Newton, Darwin, and Einstein. Whether Freud should be included in this list the analysis below will seek to decide. That Freud was a great seminal scientist there can be no doubt. For the moment let us suspend judgment concerning the concept of truth that informs his work. The school of thought in philosophy with which the correspondence concept of truth is associated is realism.

The coherence theory of truth allows the question:

> *What objects does the world consist of?* to make sense only *within* a theory or description. . . . Truth . . . is some sort of (idealized) rational acceptability—some sort of ideal coherence of beliefs with each other and with our experiences *as those experiences are themselves represented in our belief system*—and not correspondence with mind-independent or discourse-independent "states of affairs." (Putnam, 1981, pp. 47–49).

The coherence theory of truth is compatible with the view that there is more than one true description of the world. The correspondence theory is not. In effect the coherence theory abandons *objects as they actually are* as the ground of truth for *objects as they are constructed or constituted* by the belief and theory investments that govern their observation and the way in which they are experienced by observers. Although the connection of the coherence theory with idealism is not unambiguous—Berkeley (1710) is usually regarded as an idealist because of his denial of matter, but he espoused the correspondence view of truth—Bradley (1897), who gave the coherence theory its first formal statement, was an idealist. And although realism is the dominant school of thought in philosophy, there are many variants of the coherence theory in Merleau-Ponty's (1945) phenomenology, in Sartre's (1943) existentialism, in Habermas's (1971) hermeneutics, and among the philosophers of science such as Putnam (1981), Kuhn (1970), and Feyerabend (1965). Putnam (1981) characterized this view of truth in philosophy as "the *internalist* perspective," appropriately enough, for what they all have in common is the assertion that the ground of truth is to be found in the human mind itself—because the mind must, as a matter of psychological and epistemological inevitability, subject the objects that it seeks to know to the conditions under which it is able to know them. This idea is ultimately traceable to Kant (1781). The school of thought, in philosophy, to which the coherence theory belongs is idealism.

Two further ideas tend to accompany the correspondence idea of truth, one epistemological, the other ontological. The epistemological premise is that objects are able to cause our senses to form more or less correct observations of them as they actually are. These observations can be, or can be made to be, sufficiently independent of theories held by observers concerning their objects that theories can be objectively tested. The ontological premise is that anyone's thoughts, and actions of any kind, are caused. Minds are part of nature.

Similarly, two further ideas tend to be associated with the coherence idea of truth. Epistemologically, it is assumed that our ways of thinking and perceiving unavoidably condition what we observe. Objects are unable to exert an independent influence upon our senses such as would enable us and oblige us to correct our theory-laden ideas of them. Facts are theory bound, never theory independent. Objects are amorphous and unintelligible in themselves. They have no means by which to define themselves. They must wait upon the definitions inherent in the theories we invent to try to understand them. The ontological idea is that human beings are unique in nature on account of a consciousness that supports the capacity for voluntary actions of a special kind—actions that are motivated by reasons rather than by causes. Minds give nature meaning.

The ideas of truth as coherence, of the intrinsic indefiniteness of persons as objects of knowledge, and of voluntarism are logically interconnected in the following way: If a person's actions are motivated by reasons that are neither causes nor caused, if a person freely chooses his motives, then his actions become at once both immunized against the influence of his past and unpredictable.[1] Voluntarism is a source of an intrinsic indefiniteness of the human mind that allows it to always slip away from any description that would seek to correspond with some fixed and determinate nature.

The link between voluntarism and the indeterminacy of psychic life has been nicely stated as follows:

> It has often been said that one's past determines one's present and future. Let it be underlined that one's present and future—how he commits himself to existence at the moment—also determines his past. (May, 1958, p. 88)

---

1. The masculine pronoun is used throughout to refer to both sexes on account of linguistic felicity only.

Present choice determines the meaning of the past and the motives of actions. Psychic life ceases to be sufficiently determinate to be a suitable object for descriptions whose truth resides in their correspondence with an objective state of affairs.

Bound to this view is the hermeneutic, phenomenological, existential, and idealist idea that self-consciousness involves the capacity for self-transcendence. Self-transcendence allows for the abrogation of causality, the transformation of motives as causes into *sui generis* reasons at the disposal of consciousness. Thus, Habermas (1971) has claimed that, when a neurotic conflict is resolved, self-reflection has actually "dissolved" or "overcome" the causal connection between the symptom or inhibition and the repressed drive demands. Where psychic determinism was, the uncaused choice shall be.

This controversy in philosophy, unless it is merely verbal, poses the problem of objectivity. Realism assumes a world and a human psyche that have natures in their own right: The task of perception and thought is to approximate our observations and ideas more and more closely to them. Idealism, broadly defined, assumes that objects are "mute," unable to communicate themselves through human languages and the systems of belief inherent in these languages: Any true description is an interpretation that coheres with the beliefs and theories of the observer and with his "belief- and theory-invested" experience of the object described. A description is true as a result of the way in which it fits in with other descriptions.

By contrast, the correspondence theory shifts the requirement of truth to the "fit" between the description and the object described. To know which was true, the Aristotelian/Ptolemaic description of celestial bodies as completely actualized substances or Galileo's description of them as physical bodies similar to the earth, it was only necessary to study the moon and planets telescopically to see which description fitted, without considering whether or how this description cohered with other beliefs or experiences. Isolated bits of information can be true and be known to be true. The correspondence theory is the viewpoint of common sense and natural science.

Truth as Coherence in Psychoanalysis

The coherence theory of truth and its attendant ideas have found their way to contemporary psychoanalytic theorists, who have used them in a number of ways.

Sometimes there is an appeal to the coherence theory of truth as a means of defending a theory against criticism. Goldberg (1976, 1988) has used the coherence theory to defend self-psychology against its critics. The philosophical idea that observations are theory bound is used to explain differences in clinical observation:

> . . . when two individuals with roughly similar neurophysiological equipment view the same thing or event and each see it differently, it is not necessarily true that one is incompetent or even wrong; rather it may be that they each observe with a different theory. (1976, p. 67)

This agrees with Putnam (1981) that there may be more than one true theory about the same thing because the observations that confirm theories are contaminated by the very theoretical concepts they confirm. As Putnam stated it, "the very (experiential) inputs upon which our knowledge is based are conceptually contaminated. . ." (p. 54).

For purposes of illustration in psychoanalytic terms, let us consider an example: Brenner (1982) did not include narcissistic insults (severely frustrated merging, mirroring, or idealizing needs) among pathogenic infantile calamities. Yet Brenner insisted, and Goldberg would not deny, that his theory of pathogenesis is based on observation of the process of free association under appropriate clinical conditions. Nor would Goldberg question Brenner's clinical competence or objectivity. Nevertheless, self-psychologists routinely observe the pathogenicity of narcissistic injuries consequent upon parental inadequacy or neglect in relation to which the calamities identified by Brenner are secondary. Goldberg proposed to account for these observational discrepancies as the result of the way in which Brenner's theory influences his observations and the way in which the self-psychologist's theory influences his observations. Both sets of observations are as objective as any observations can be. Classical psychoanalysis and self-psychology, it is claimed, are two coherent theories each of which interprets clinical phenomena in its own way.

However, three difficulties arise when the coherence theory is used in this way. First, the argument is a double-edged sword. The observations of classical analysts cannot falsify self-psychology, but neither can the observations of self-psychology falsify classical—or any other—theory (Hanly, 1983). Second, one and the same patient can have a neurosis caused by a failure to resolve oedipal conflicts when he is treated by a classical analyst, and a failure to find a suitable object for idealization when he is treated by a self psychologist. The Oedipus complex is both a cause and not a cause—only a symptom. This consequence defies the principle of identity, an elementary principle of logic which states that nothing can be both what it is and what it is not. Third, a scientific theory must be falsifiable in principle. Goldberg's use of coherence implies that neither self-psychology nor classical theory is scientific, because neither has a domain of observations that could ever falsify it. This use of the coherence theory results in theoretical solipsism: knowledge of truth as conversion to a point of view.

Goldberg (1988) has implicitly addressed these difficulties by considering the conditions for theory testing in psychoanalysis. Goldberg has suggested a pragmatic test, although unlike scientific pragmatic testing, this form of testing requires "commitment" over time to the theory being tested (p. 27). This requirement opens the door to the claim by adherents of a theory that falsifying observations are the result of a lack of such "commitment." It is of interest for our argument, however, that in the end Goldberg indirectly appeals to correspondence. If, for example, we are to be able to carry out the injunction to "remain alert to the effects of our observations" (p. 110), we must be able to make observations of objects that are not subject to these effects. This critical issue is further considered below.

At first glance Spence (1982a, 1982b) appears to be presenting an intermediate position between realism and idealism; but there is an ambiguity. It is not clear whether Spence is asserting that objective clinical observations in psychoanalysis are, in principle, unavailable or that they are available but so difficult to obtain that, thus far, none has been established. It is not always clear whether his critique of objectivity in psychoanalysis is heuristic or epistemological. Spence seems to think that objectivity could be achieved both in clinical descriptions and in theoretical formulations as long as these descriptions are limited to the here and now and theory is limited to generalizations from them. If strictly adhered to, such a limitation would imply that there is no such thing as historical truth, because a historical truth concerns a past event. This in turn would suggest that Spence's view, wittingly or unwittingly, is that objective knowledge of past events is not possible, that is, that his view is epistemological. Moreover, Spence (1982b) has argued that "the analyst functions more as a pattern-maker than a pattern-finder" (p. 60) and goes on to refer to analyses as "artistic masterpiece(s) . . ." (p. 60). And although Spence has insisted that what "makes a particular formulation persuasive and compelling is precisely the fact that it is carefully tailored to the patient's life," in his terms, for a formulation to be tailored to a patient's life it must be coherent with the pattern made largely by the analyst for the patient. Thus, we have here, in full or in statu nascendi, an idealistic, hermeneutic epistemology. It is a view that is in basic agreement with Habermas's (1971) idea that human psychology, and with it psychoanalysis, "escapes" or "transcends" the ordinary world of other animate and inanimate things. The adoption of a hermeneutical epistemology of pattern making requires a denial of psychic determinism and the assumption that individuals are able to create themselves. This idea has implications for our understanding of the clinical process and our therapeutic orientation.

In the analytic process, for example, when a man, previously so crippled by a depressing self-doubt that he could only act with the authorization of others, finds his own competence in the course of the analysis, Habermas would say that he not only freed himself from the causalities that brought about his depression and passivity but that he also entered into a new condition in which decisions transcend causalities and provide for an uncaused self-direction.

The nature of the analytic relationship is also at issue. Within a hermeneutic epistemology of pattern making, interpretations do not exert a causal influence upon the patient; they offer him a new self-understanding. Interpretations act in the intersubjective domain of meaning and comprehension. The interpretation of resistance does not alter the balance of the play of forces between repressing and repressed thoughts by reducing the anxiety driving the repression. Interpretation enables a patient to comprehend a meaning in the form of a motive for his oppositional attitudes and actions, and interpretation does its work *only* by means of this comprehension. The interpretation of transference does not simply describe the attitudes, thoughts, and feelings of a patient toward the analyst caused by repetitions of earlier conflicted relationships. The description is already an interpretation that is informed by the analyst's view of the nature of transference. The patient's life is reconstituted into a more cohesive and more adaptive form out of the conjoint pattern-making activities of analyst and analysand. The interpreted past comes to cohere with what the patient remembers of it and how these memories motivate his "new" life—the life brought about by the reconstruction of his past. And thus it is that there are as many true reconstructions of a person's past as there are interpretations that could bring about the resolution of his neurosis.

Spence's account agrees with the existentialist notion (Sartre, 1943), repeated by May (1958), that a present intention or perception interprets the past—that there is no discrete, specific, particular past that continues to be what it was; there are only the diverse perspectives on the past brought about by the intentions inherent in current projects, moods, affects, attitudes, and beliefs. The idea that the meaning of a person's past, as well as its influence upon his current life, is determined by present choices is very different from the idea that contemporary affective experiences activate chains of associated memories leading back to infantile precursors. The latter idea assumes that memories thus reactivated have inherent meaning that remains the same even if their conscious recall does not; the former idea assumes that memories are a kind of opaque mass that can be redesigned and informed with meaning by present intentions and investments: that is, by volitions conceived as uncaused causes.

These ideas belong with those of Habermas (1971) and Ricoeur (1974, 1981). Habermas (1971) advanced the view that psychoanalytic "self-reflection" is able to suspend or transcend psychic causality.

Although some self-psychologists may not agree with his position, Kohut (1959) rested his theorizing on the coherence theory premise of indeterminacy:

> What we experience as freedom of choice, as decision and the like, is an expression of the fact that the I-experience and a core of activity emanating from it cannot at present be divided into further components. . . . They are, therefore, beyond the law of motivation i.e. beyond the law of psychic determinism. (p. 252)

Psychic causation becomes a product of self-disintegration along with the Oedipus complex. The cohesive self rises above the bounds of causality. Kohut (1977) in explicit agreement with Habermas (1971) introduced the idea of the mutuality of observer and observed in order to claim on behalf of self-psychology a more fundamental knowledge of human nature than that of psychoanalysis. Kohut's concept of empathy disallows the degree of epistemological independence of subject and object required by correspondence. Goldberg (1988) has extensively elaborated the epistemological implications of this self-psychological version of empathy. Ricoeur (1974) asserted, in line with Habermas, that "there are no 'facts' nor any observation of 'facts' in psychoanalysis but rather the interpretation of a narrated history" (p. 186). And although Ricoeur (1981) intended to abandon his earlier (1970) view that reasons and motives are *sui generis*, he failed to do so insofar as he continued to conceive of the relation between unconscious wishes and dreams, neurotic symptoms, or parapraxes as one of referring, denoting, signifying: that is, as an acausal, semantic relation. Ricoeur (1981) appealed to coherence in a particularly naïve and unsatisfactory form: "a good psychoanalytic explanation must be coherent with the theory or, if one prefers, it must conform to Freud's psychoanalytic system" (p. 271). Such a dictum makes nonsense of the clinical testing of his ideas, which Freud advocated.

The relationship of the concept of causality to the problem of truth in psychoanalysis is also raised by Schafer (1976, 1978) and Klein (1976). Schafer (1978) asserted that "thinking historically, we do not say an agent is causally motivated to perform some action . . . we say that *this* agent did *that* and perhaps gave or could have given *these* reasons for doing so" (p. 56). Like Klein, Schafer wants to deny that reasons, intentions, purposes, wishes, motives in general, are causes. Grunbaum (1984) has argued that Schafer has erroneously identified causality with necessary and sufficient causes and has thus constructed a specious argument against causal thinking in psychoanalysis (pp. 73–74). In effect, Schafer and Klein identify causality with fatalism as did Sartre (1943). (For a further discussion of this issue see Hanly, 1979, and Wallace, 1985.) Schafer and Klein are also committed to a coherence theory of truth. As Schafer (1978) reiterated: "There are more ways than one to understand reality" (p. 66). "Reality is not, as Freud usually assumed, a definite thing to be arrived at or a fixed and known criterion of objectivity" (p. 66). Once motives become reasons rather than causes, they acquire a wonderfully amorphous, open-textured nature that allows them to be "correctly" construed in a variety of ways. Interpretation is an expansion and complication of the context of an action. Different theories expand and complicate the context differently. Narrative coherence becomes the operative criterion of truth. There are as many true understandings as there are coherent, comprehensive, unified narratives about the motivating reasons.

Schafer stated the ontological basis for this relativism: "the concept of action requires us to regard each action as inherently spontaneous, as starting from itself" (pp. 48–49). This assertion provides the basis for a "free" construal of the reasons for an action; but if actions are not the outcome of past and present events, if they really are free creations, as Kant (1785) believed of willed actions—actions that have consequences but no antecedents—then they do not have a history at all. Schafer's position is shown by this comparison to be much more radical than Kant's dualistic view of human nature, which allowed for the causation of a wide range of human behavior, indeed, all save moral actions. It is closer to the existentialist view of Sartre (1943) despite Schafer's (1976) disavowal, and it is fundamentally at odds with the view of Ryle (1949), upon whose ideas Schafer otherwise has relied for his critique of Freud's metapsychology. Schafer's concept of action undermines the very historicist, hermeneutical approach with which he wants to replace psychic determinism. It provides no justification for widening the context of an action to earlier events and actions (conscious or unconscious); it provides a justification for a life history that is an existential, phenomenological chronology. Anything more, if indeed every action, as Schafer claims, spontaneously starts from itself, would be sheer invention: an invention for which the only possible criterion of truth would be coherence. Here we have unlimited opportunity for Spence's pattern making.

Some Considerations on Behalf of Coherence

However, a number of considerations lend credence to the coherence criterion of truth for psychoanalysis. Freud appears to have espoused coherence. Freud (e.g., 1895b, pp. 194–195; 1909c, pp. 165–169) often testified to his awareness of the complex, seemingly arbitrary, fragmentary, subtle, evasive mass of material produced by associations. Is not this material typically so ambiguous, so rife with uncertainties, that the best we can achieve is a coherent account with the possibility of other no less coherent accounts being constructed? In apparent support of Goldberg, Freud (1915) pointed out that even at the earliest stages of description a new science already applies concepts that are not drawn altogether from the field of observation to which the descriptions apply. Freud pointed out that, although science begins with descriptions, "even at the stage of description it is not possible to avoid applying certain abstract ideas to the material in hand, ideas derived from somewhere or other but certainly not from the new observations alone" (p. 117). One is reminded of Heisenberg's autobiographical assertion that his concept of indeterminacy owed its origin to the notion of matter in Plato's *Timaeus*. And, of course, similar points are made by philosophers on behalf of the coherence theory (cf. Putnam, 1981, p. 54). When Freud (1927) remarked that "a number of very remarkable, disconnected facts are brought together . . . into a consistent whole" (p. 23) by his *Totem and Taboo* hypothesis, he was appealing to a coherence criterion.

Certain aspects of clinical experience itself seem to be especially congenial to the coherence concept of truth. Often early childhood memories remain fragmentary. Crucial childhood events, whether subjective or objective, can only be reconstructed on the basis of the indirect indications of derivatives. These derivatives have to be themselves interpreted in order to connect them to the hypothetical pathogenic events. The same can be said of the routinely incomplete association to dreams, associations that seldom enough terminate in the unequivocal recovery of even the contemporary dream wish let alone its infantile precursors. Transference shifts take place in the course of an analysis that signal themselves in subtle ways and are often difficult to identify clearly or describe. Or, again, there is the constant problem of sorting out what a patient has brought upon himself through neurotic provocation and what he has suffered at the hands of others. Given these inevitable sources of uncertainty is it not justified, or at least heuristically judicious, to adopt a concept of truth that refuses to lay claim to an objectivity that is not attainable? These facts of normal clinical working conditions seem to offer at least a pragmatic justification for a coherence concept of truth in psychoanalysis.

Moreover, does not an analysis bring about changes in the meaning that events in the patients' pasts have for them in the present and future? Take, for example, the case of a woman who was unable adequately to enter into, let alone resolve, the conflicts of the oedipal stage but who manages to do so in the transference neurosis. She comes, in the course of this experience, to remember her father as a sexually exciting object when, during childhood, she had experienced him only as an indifferent, zombielike figure who was silent and remote. Is not this routine clinical experience evidence for Spence's "pattern making," for Ricoeur's "narrated history," for Schafer's action language, for Habermas's "self-reflection," for the determination of the past by investments in the present and the concept of truth in psychoanalysis as coherent narration? And why should there not be more than one path to this result; why should there not be as many narratives (interpretations) that in part describe but that also really create the path in collaboration with the patient as there are different possible paths? Is not such an attitude to psychoanalytic truth necessary to a genuine respect for the individuality of each patient? Is it not simply a reflection of the fundamental working condition of the analyst, which constantly confronts him with conundrums, puzzlements, and unintelligible conjunctions to which he is called upon to offer solutions and to give intelligible shape, while all the while facilitating the full participation of the patient in the construction of the narrative—a narrative whose chapters have unknown endings even as they are being written, a narrative that is never finally complete?

Moreover, the current state of psychoanalytic theory lends plausibility to the idea of coherence. There is no unified theory. There are only divergent, often mutually inconsistent, theories supported by clinical observations. Does not this state of affairs cohere rather well with the coherence theory? Perhaps there are as many true-life histories as there are theories that can give a consistent account of them?

These questions lead to others. What role did coherence and correspondence play in Freud's work? Was he an exception among seminal scientists in espousing the idea of truth as coherence? Which theory about the nature of truth is true? Which should be the foundation upon which psychoanalysis is built and controversies in psychoanalysis are resolved?

Coherence and Correspondence in Freud

Freud (1900, 1923b) was certainly aware of the complexity of dreams and the extent to which they are representative of all mental phenomena; however, Freud (1905a) also believed that the obscurities of a dream can be cleared up, that each manifest element can be traced along the paths of displacement and condensation from whence it came, and that the meaning of the dream is to be found in the unconscious wishes of the dreamer. We are not always able to find the meaning, but it is there to be found, independently of any pattern-making activity on the part of the analyst. The task of interpretation as Freud conceived it is to make the interpretation correspond with the operative unconscious wishes of the dreamer—wishes that have a definite nature of their own. (For an opposing view see Viderman, 1970, 1972.)

It is also true that Freud appreciated the extent to which any inquiry has to be guided by preliminary ideas. In this respect Freud's grasp of epistemology was more realistic and empirical than was that of Bacon (1620), the great founder of modern empiricism. But Freud also thought that these preliminary ideas can and must be continually criticized and made to reflect the facts of observation more accurately. Having made the statement cited above, Freud (1915) went on to argue:

> it is only after more thorough investigation of the field of observation that we are able to formulate its basic scientific concepts with increased precision, and progressively so to modify them that they become serviceable and consistent over a wide area. (p. 117)

In the context of a discussion of the doubts about objectivity in psychoanalysis aroused by "obliging" dreams, Freud (1923b) had recourse to an analogy in order to outline the conditions under which one can be assured of objectivity:

> What makes him certain in the end is precisely the complication of the problems before him, which is like the solution of a jig-saw puzzle. . . . If one succeeds in arranging the confused heap of fragments, each of which bears upon it an unintelligible piece of drawing, so that the picture acquires a meaning, so that there is no gap anywhere in the design and so that the whole fits into the frame—if all these conditions are fulfilled, then one knows that one has solved the puzzle and that there is no alternative solution. (p. 116)

In one respect this analogy with a jigsaw puzzle suggests a coherence point of view. By taking the individually meaningless pieces and fitting them together so that they form a coherent, unified picture one can be sure that one has found the true meaning of each of the intrinsically meaningless bits through finding their correct fit with every other bit. Only in this way does each piece find its correct meaning by finding its place in the ensemble. However, in addition to the picture to which each piece contributes, there is the fact of the spatial position it must assume because of its shape. Here we also have a question of "fit" but there is no possibility of a variety of "fits" according to the requirements of different possible pictures. The puzzle has a unique solution. Thus, the overall thrust of Freud's analogy is that the objects of psychoanalytic investigation have determinate natures that can be given unequivocal, intersubjective descriptions that provide the basis for inferences to no less determinate causes. It is only by remaining ignorant of or disregarding some of the evidence that a plurality of explanations can be made to appear plausible. In this Freud may have been in error. The puzzle analogy in itself proves nothing. But it does reveal Freud's notion of truth.

Freud (1918) inadvertently provided a test of his view in his discussion of the Wolf Man case. The more general theoretical hypothesis he was testing is whether infantile developments and impressions are factors in the occurrence of neurosis in adults, or whether the place of infantile memories in neurosis can be explained as a consequence of a regressive flight from the tasks of adult life, as Jung asserted. The more specific clinical hypothesis at issue is whether, in the case of the Wolf Man, the primal scene (the *coitus a tergo, more ferarum* of his parents) was an impression or a fantasy. Was Freud's inquiry guided by a realist or an idealist point of view?

There is one point in Freud's discussion that supports coherence. Whichever theoretical hypothesis one adopts makes no technical difference. Even if one assumes that the repressed infantile material has been in part created by and entirely activated by a regressive flight from current life tasks, the analyst will have to treat it clinically in the same way that he would if he were working on the basis of the hypothesis that the infantile material had an etiological as well as a symptomatic significance. (This statement holds as a generality even though technically one would have to couch specific interpretations differently depending on whether the pathogenic experience was a real experience or a fantasy; (Hanly, 1986.) Further, Freud was at pains to point out that the Wolf Man's primal scene was not remembered in the course of the analysis; it was reconstructed by the analyst. If this were the whole of the matter, Freud's account would be evidence for the coherence thesis because two different hypotheses would equally well explain the clinical observations and would have equivalent practical consequences. The question of the precise nature of a crucial pathogenic event, the primal scene, would be decided by a theoretical preference.

But this is not the whole of the matter. Freud was able to show that certain facts of the case were inconsistent with the regression hypothesis. (Freud, of course, did not discount regression. His opposition was to Jung's unilateral notion of regression.) The unilateral regression hypothesis does not explain why certain current life tasks become too difficult and have to be escaped—something that the hypothesis of infantile factors can explain. In the case of the Wolf Man his adult neurosis was preceded by an infantile neurosis, that is, by pathogenic events and consequent conflicts that had actually happened. His infantile neurosis had not been "invented," by a regression. It is upon this fact of the Wolf Man's history that the unilateral regression hypothesis foundered.

Nevertheless, Freud raised a further objection to his thesis that the Wolf Man had actually observed the coitus of his parents at age 1-1/2 by offering an alternative explanation, itself consistent with at least some of the facts of the case. The material of the analysis indicated that during the period prior to the dream of the wolves, the boy had been taken on repeated visits to flocks of cholera-infected sheep on the estate. On these occasions he had ample opportunity to see large, white sheepdogs, which he associated to the wolves in the dream, and which the dream wolves/dogs resembled in their color and in the shape of their ears. It is perfectly possible that he saw these dogs copulating. Freud supposed, on the basis of his analysis of the dream, that he had made three such observations. Could it not then very well be, Freud reasoned, that the child imagined intercourse between his parents on the model of these observations and, using the memory of having been in his parents' bedroom during his illness at age 1-1/2, formed the impression (really a fantasy) of having observed his parents in the act of making love *more ferarum*? His later curiosity about sexual differences would enhance the scene with imagined opportunities to observe the parental genitals in operation. This assumption would better account for the "details" of the child's "observations." A real experience would not likely have allowed him, confined as he was to his bed, an opportunity for a clear view of both his parents' genitals and the sight of his father's penis first disappearing into his mother and then reappearing as it was withdrawn. In any case, Freud at this stage of the argument declared that no decision is possible.

Freud then introduced the Grusha scene, which he did think was decisive. Late in his analysis the Wolf Man recalled that he had had a nursemaid before his much-loved and abused Nanya. He recalled a

scene with this young peasant woman, whose name he initially confused with his mother's and who was quite unexpectedly associated
with his fear of butterflies with yellow stripes, itself a derivative of his
castration anxiety. He had come upon this Grusha while she was on
her knees scrubbing the floor with her bum in the air, a pail and a
broom made of twigs by her side. At the sight of her he had taken out
his penis and had urinated on the floor, an action that had called
forth a scolding from Grusha and a castration threat. This action,
while made possible by a well-supplied bladder, had been motivated by
feelings of sexual excitement. How could it come about that this 2-1/2-
year-old boy was already susceptible to having feelings of sexual excitement aroused in him by the display of a woman's posterior? How later,
in adulthood, could it come about that he would routinely fall passion-
ately in love with any woman he chanced upon in this posture (for
instance, the young peasant woman from whom he had at 18 con-
tracted gonorrhea)? How could it come about that when, as an adult
patient, the Wolf Man in recalling the incident first thought that
Grusha had had the same name as his mother, and then realized that
the name was the same as the word for a species of pear that had
yellow stripes on its skin and that had later on become associated with
butterflies? It could come about if he had identified Grusha with his
mother and if he had already observed his mother having sex with his
father in this same posture. These pieces of the jigsaw puzzle fit together in this direction and in others as well (e.g., in relation to his
castration anxiety and his anal eroticism).

However, although Freud withdrew his *non liquet* of the earlier
discussion of the evidence, he did so with a skeptical reservation. No
final decision can be made because it remains *possible* that the child's
urinating was only accidental at the time of its occurrence and that it
acquired a sexual significance for him only retroactively. Freud concluded:

> Nevertheless, I cannot deny that the scene with Grusha, the part it
> played in the analysis, and the effects that followed from it in the pa-
> tient's life can be most naturally and completely explained if we consider
> that the primal scene, which may in other cases be a phantasy, was a
> reality in the present one. (1918, p. 96.)

However, Freud's doubt is justified on another score that he does not
explicitly mention. The Wolf Man did not recall having urinated at
the sight of Grusha. This part of the picture is added by Freud. Freud
referred to "the fact that the boy micturated" (p. 96), but it is an
inferred and not a remembered fact. Is not this just the very sort of

theory-laden amplification to which Spence and others have called our critical attention? Earlier (pp. 91ff.) Freud elaborated the basis for inferring that the urination occurred and that it expressed sexual excitement—the connection in the patient's associations between the twigs that formed Grusha's broom and the bundles of twigs that were used to burn John Huss at the stake. The reliability of this inferred fact, then, depends upon the reliability of the theoretical connection established between a fascination with fire and urination. The corroboration for the inference to a sexual significance is to be found in the Wolf Man's adult sexual behavior, which had every appearance of being modeled in its essential intimate details (choice of object and choice of mode of gratification) upon the Grusha scene with its primal scene precursor. Yet these crucial considerations are based upon an interpretation that, although theoretically justified by the associations, still lacks the certainty of a memory released from repression, hence Freud's final tentativeness and skepticism. Thus, implicit in Freud's thinking is the idea that coherence is not enough even though it is the best that is available under the circumstances. The skepticism and criticism with which Freud greeted his own conclusions and theories were motivated by his adherence to the correspondence view of truth.

Freud employed the coherence criterion as a necessary, but not a sufficient, criterion of truth. He used coherence as a logical, methodological tool for discriminating among competing hypotheses. Freud claimed that his *Totem and Taboo* theory was more plausible and convincing than other existing theories because of the consistency with which it explained an array of facts; but he did not claim that it was true for this reason, or that such coherence constituted a limit beyond which knowledge could not reach. He allowed that further anthropological findings would corroborate, qualify, or falsify his theory. Freud's implicit adherence to the correspondence theory is evident in his assumption that further investigation into the decisive anthropological facts could be conducted in such a way as to make them independent of his or any other theory. A theory, if it is true, has to be able to predict what should be found; but it does not follow that the theory need dictate what is found or what will be required to explain it. Freud assumed that the truth of a statement depends upon whether or not it describes what actually exists: for example, the truth of the statement that the Wolf Man, in early childhood, observed a primal scene depends upon whether he did, in fact, observe rather than imagine his parents having intercourse. An explanation is true only if it correctly describes the causes and the mechanisms by which they bring about specific, identifiable states, activities, and so forth: for example, the Wolf Man's bowel malfunction or his sexual compulsion.

Freud (1927) defended the ability of science to gain objective knowledge against those who claim that "being bound to the conditions of our own organization, it [science] can yield nothing else than subjective results, whilst the real nature of things outside ourselves remains inaccessible" (p. 55). Freud offered the following defence of science:

> In the first place, our organization—that is, our mental apparatus—has been developed precisely in the attempt to explore the external world, and it must therefore have realized in its structure some degree of expediency; in the second place, it is itself a constituent part of the world which we set out to investigate, and it readily admits of such an investigation; thirdly, the task of science is fully covered if we limit it to showing how the world must appear to us in consequence of the particular character of our organization; fourthly, the ultimate findings of science, precisely because of the way in which they are acquired, are determined not only by our organization but by the things which have affected that organization; finally, the problem of the nature of the world without regard to our percipient mental apparatus is an empty abstraction, devoid of practical interest. (1927, pp. 55–56)

Some of Freud's statements could have been made by some philosophers who espouse the coherence theory. His third and fourth arguments agree, for example, with Putnam's "internalist" view that knowledge is only and always knowledge of things as they are experienced by human observers and that a God's ideal view of objects as having an intrinsic nature independently of any observer is meaningless. Moreover, Putnam, as against other coherence theorists such as Kuhn (1970) and van Frassen (1984), agrees with the implication of Freud's first argument, that the fact of the survival of the species is evidence that our sensory apparatus has undergone an adaptation that allows it, when functioning normally, to pick up indications of what things are actually like. Our senses normally have to function, in this respect, at a level of expediency well above trial and error in order to account for the history of the adaptation of human beings to their environment. However, the thrust is on behalf of correspondence and scientific realism. Freud (1933) stated his realist view in an unequivocal way in reverting to the biological imperative that sanctions the search for objectivity:

> The relation to the external world has become the decisive factor for the ego; it has taken on the task of representing the real world to the id—fortunately for the id, which could not escape destruction if, in its blind efforts for the satisfaction of its instincts, it disregarded that su-

preme external power. In accomplishing this function, the ego must observe the external world, must lay down an accurate picture of it in the memory-traces of its perceptions, and by the exercise of the function of "reality-testing" must put aside whatever in this picture of the external world is an addition derived from internal sources of excitation. (p. 75)

Freud offered three arguments on behalf of scientific realism: biological, methodological, and epistemological. Mental activities have developed because they have facilitated an exploration of the world that has survival value; it is likely that they have acquired a structure that facilitates that exploration (the biological argument). These mental activities are a part of the world; they can, themselves, be investigated in order to discover their degree of facility, its causes, and methods of improvement (the methodological argument). Scientific knowledge, because of the methods of investigation upon which it is based, is determined not only by our mental activities and their structures but, primarily, by the objects observed (the epistemological argument). Freud used coherence as a formal, logical criterion; he used correspondence as a material, epistemological criterion. Freud takes his place along with other seminal scientists whose thinking was premised upon the correspondence view of truth and empiricist realism.

Concluding Psychoanalytical and Philosophical Considerations

Yet Freud may have been in error. And, in any case, it would be to argue fallaciously from authority to treat as evidence what Freud believed rather than to weigh the force of the arguments on which his view was based.

One can adduce supporting evidence for each of Freud's arguments. I have elsewhere (Hanly, 1967, 1983) set out supporting evidence from cultural history for Freud's biological argument. In Chapter Nine, on the transition from animism to rationalism, further evidence is offered. Freud's methodological and epistemological arguments are supported by evidence from the history of science. Science has been able to identify and to take into account the influence of our sensory apparatus upon our experience of nature. Copernicus and Galileo discovered the influence of the earth's daily rotation upon our observation of stars and planets and, by correcting for it, they were able to construct a genuinely objective description of the solar system. Einstein's relativity theory enabled the human mind to realize that the apparently self-evident rectilinearity of space is only a consequence of the organization of our sensory apparatus. Psychoanalysis has made its own contribution to this process of observational "correction" for the field of human phenomena. These examples indicate that the expediency of the adaptation of the human sensory apparatus and thought activity to reality brought about by environmental pressure has been sufficient to allow it to proceed beyond the requirements of survival.

The idea of correspondence is intrinsic to the psychogenesis of the reality principle in the infant's first encounter with the distinction between fantasy and reality in the hallucinatory breast that comforts for a time but does not satisfy and the real breast that may not be present but that comforts by satisfying when it is (Freud, 1895a). From these precarious beginnings, utterly dedicated to the most immediate and forceful demands for survival, there have developed, out of centuries of human endeavor, the conceptual and technical instruments of modern science for testing reality. Among these instruments is Freud's contribution of free association as a method for observing the human mind itself.

In addition, there are philosophical arguments that need to be taken into account. Euclidean geometry is a mathematical system that is complete and completely coherent. For this reason it escapes Gödel's theorem. Yet it turns out that it does not describe the space of the universe. Physics has been able to identify facts that show this to be the case. The axioms of Euclidean geometry were believed to be self-evidently true. Plato, Descartes, and Leibniz considered them to be innate to the mind. Kant considered them to be *a priori* conditions of experience. Yet despite this self-evidence and coherence, and despite the fact that we actually do observe the world in a Euclidean fashion, these axioms have been shown by relativity physics to be approximations suitable only to regions of space smaller than the solar system.

Psychoanalytic findings should also alert psychoanalysts to the limitations of coherence as a criterion for empirical knowledge and reality testing. Psychoanalysis is familiar, in the psychoses, with systems of belief, observation, and behavior that are remarkable both for their coherence and for their detachment from reality. The following bit of case history is representative: A student suffering an acoustical psychosis experienced growing agitation in a university seminar when certain topics were under discussion while the sound of shuffling feet was accompanied by the sound of a passing streetcar; this agitation cohered perfectly with his belief that such conjunctions of sounds signaled the approach of evil forces at work in his Manichaean cosmos, and with the ritual precautions he undertook to oppose the advance of those forces. Nowhere are the shortcomings of coherence as a sufficient criterion of truth more forcefully demonstrated than in the clinical investigation of delusions and illusions. Just as an argument may be valid and yet have a false conclusion, so a system of beliefs or a narrative may be coherent but false. The concept of coherence is not sufficient to bridge the gap between ideas and objects.

The human mind as an object of knowledge requires a special concept of truth no more than does psychoanalysis as a method for investigating and treating that mind. The description above of the uncertainty of associations is tendentious and incomplete. Even when a patient is filling the hour with reports of manifest dream contents to the exclusion of associations, the details of the material are clear and determinate. There is nothing indefinite or illusive about it. Of course, it is unintelligible and uninterpretable in the absence of associations, but this fact has itself an obvious interpretation. The patient is anxiously clinging to the manifest dream content. This interpretation, properly timed and expressed and linked to the transference, will begin a process of change that will enable the patient to begin associating to his dreams. These associations will then also be determinate and discrete. If they are incomplete—as they are likely to be—it will be because further resistances are at work. If they become vague and uncertain, it is for the same reason. Vagueness and uncertainty are themselves determinate states of affairs that have an explanation. They are not characteristic qualities of mental contents and states as such. The same is true of fantasies, memories, character traits, and so forth. Pattern making by the analyst is not required so long as resistances and defenses are interpreted in such a way as to allow the intrinsic forces at work in the psychic life of the patient to make themselves known. These forces will determine the pattern as they will determine the transference (see also Kris, 1982; Merendino, 1985). The forces in question are the drives, their vicissitudes, and their derivatives. The ideas of pattern making, of theory-bound observation, and the like may serve as rationalizations for countertransferential resistance to the threats posed by the drives, that is, by the instinctual unconscious. Psychoanalytic theories that repudiate the drives tend to employ coherence as a concept of truth.

It is of course true that in order to make effective, systematic observations of anything it is necessary to have some preliminary ideas; but from the need to have a theory that will enable us to make predictions about what we will observe in order to make systematic observations, it does not follow that these predictions must govern what we will find. The preliminary ideas Harvey had concerning the circulation of the blood did not add or subtract anything from his crucial measurement of the amount of blood ejected by the heart in a single pulse. Hawking's (1988) mathematical derivation, which proves on current thermodynamic and quantum assumptions that black holes emit particles, does not affect the observations that will now have to be made on cosmic radiation to test the empirical truth of this derivation. Freud's estimation of the incidence of infantile seduction required by his seduction theory did not in some subtle way influence the number of such occurrences or Freud's ability to estimate them. Adequately formulated scientific theories or common-sense beliefs yield predictions and give rise to expectations that can be tested by observing what actually happens. These observations have meaning in their own right, independently of the theories or beliefs we have about their objects.

It is true that creative changes in the life of the patient are brought about by any successful analysis. These commonly include as a part of the process such things as a transference recurrence of an important developmental stage, which brings about a change in a patient's experience of his past as it releases needs and affects in the present. A young woman had lived through her oedipal stage in an incomplete and unsatisfactory way because her father was an exceptionally inadequate object for her incestuous romance. He took no interest in her. He largely isolated himself from his wife and children. My patient's memories of him were of a silent, shadowy figure dominated by her mother, who openly derogated him. She could recall being disappointed in him and dismissive of him, but never admiring or loving him. Her incest feelings found their place in her experience only in a fear of falling asleep at night lest an intruder make his way to her room and murderously attack her with a knife in the dark. Unknown to her were tender, receptive, seductive feelings toward her father, as were feelings of excited pleasure in being physically close to him. An edition of these feelings emerged, in due course, in the transference. The patient was able to recall anger at her mother because she had failed to provide her with a father who loved her. Of this meaning she had always been aware, but she could now appreciate that her anger was also fueled by a furtive and confusing rivalry with a mother who disparaged her father by day and slept with him at night. The patient was now able to recall the excited, fearful pleasure and disgust she experienced at the prospect of eating certain foods when her father was present at the table. In the present, she began to be able to trust her own spontaneous affects and to take satisfaction in sexual intimacy.

But the positive transference did not alter her past or supply to it a meaning it did not have before; rather, it enabled her to uncover, first in dreams and screen memories and then in memories removed from repression, her fixed/regressed oral longings and the sexual fantasies in which they found expression: a painful but necessary and salutary advance in self-knowledge. It was her fear of these longings, and the sadistic, incorporative want bound up with them, that caused her to collude with her mother's derogation of her father. She did not re-create this sad past with her father and make it into a happy transition to mature womanhood. It would have been a falsification of the past, a symptom of denial, had she done so. Her only recourse was to mourn the barrenness of her first romance and to use its later rendition in the transference to work through both the sadness and the conflict. Creativity in psychoanalysis does not involve remaking or repatterning the past or investing it with new meanings made possible by self-transcendence. It does not involve "sculpting" a new form out of the potential interconnections of the associative material of the analytic process. Creativity in psychoanalysis is like that of the midwife who helps nature in mother and infant to accomplish its work—who helps what is there to come out. The mourning of patients for what they have irretrievably lost, have never known, or have suffered, testifies to a past that is what it is.

Psychoanalysis does not need any concept of freedom in the form of self-creativity in order to understand the processes of change involved in the analytic cure. To say that the change of an infantile sexual organization into a mature genital organization is an instance of self-transcendence adds nothing to our knowledge of the processes through which maturity comes about or of the analyst's capacity to release those processes therapeutically. Moreover, the concept of freedom in its ordinary sense—in the sense in which we talk about "freeing up" a wheel by removing rust from it and oiling its moving parts so that it can function properly, or "freeing up" a brook by removing debris that has blocked its course—is, as numerous philosophers have pointed out, compatible with psychic determinism (Hanly, 1979).

Psychoanalytic findings offer a defense against one of the philosophical criticisms of the correspondence theory. Putnam (1981) has argued that realism requires, in addition to the observer and the observed, a third party to whom reference can be made in order to compare the observer's perception with the object independently of the observer. How else could we form a judgment about its correspondence? Because the human observer is not in a position to form this judgment, realism is flawed with the hidden theological assumption of a God whose perception of objects is the ideal against which human perceptions can be measured.

But psychoanalysis has shown that this third-party observer is none other than the human observer himself. During the period of the pre-oedipal anaclitic bond, children, while having their own perceptions of things, use their idealized parents to carry out the very function assigned to God by Putnam's argument. Parental perceptions are taken to be authoritative—the standard against which children are able to measure their own experience. Certain ego-regressed patients continue to have to establish a relation with an idealized figure because they cannot trust the evidence of their own eyes unless vouched for and authenticated by an authority. Even Harvey had to attribute his discovery of the truth about the circulatory system to Galen, in whose works no such idea is to be found. Psychoanalysis (Freud, 1923a; Waelder, 1934; Hanly, 1979; Weinshel, 1986) has shown that the identifications involved in the resolution of the Oedipus complex normally bring into play a capacity for critical self-awareness that includes the perception of objects. An individual acquires the ability to objectify his own perceptions and beliefs sufficiently to enable him to consider how adequately they correspond with the object and to what extent they do not. This capacity forms the psychological ground for critical common sense and for scientific realism. The reality principle requires neither the alleged olympianism of correspondence nor the demiurge of coherence.

In psychoanalysis, through sympathetic identification clarified by countertransference awareness, this same self-critical capacity can facilitate the analyst's search for an understanding of patients in their terms rather than his own. The complement of this self-critical receptive observation on the part of the analyst is the struggle for self-honesty in the analysand. The view that an analysis consists of a mutual construction by analyst and analysand of the analysand's life fails to do justice to this struggle. There are analysands who have been able to use the analytic process to discover more about themselves, to recover more of their past and find ways to reconcile themselves with it, than their analysts could comprehend. Fortunately for psychoanalysis and for patients, the process that the analyst facilitates can yield for the analysand a degree of resolving self-knowledge and improved function exceeding those of the analyst. There is a common human nature, although to be sure not in the form of an Aristotelian essence, that awaits our better understanding. It is embodied in the lives lived by individuals. These individual lives are part of nature. They are there to be known, however difficult that may be. The self-honesty of an analysand in his realization that he feared his father because he wanted to murder him, or of an analysand in her realization that her frigidity and the pleasure she took in rape fantasies were caused by her wish to use intercourse to castrate the man, implies that these realizations correspond with real wishes that continue to influence the individual's life. Neither the pain of those realizations nor their beneficial effects can be accounted for by any other assumption. In the end, each person has only his own life to live, however shared with others. At the core of the being of each person there is a solitude in which he is related to himself. Truth about oneself resides in subjectivity to the extent that one can remember one's own past as it actually was. The ground of genuine analytic work is respect for this solitude.

This concluding comment poses a question that will arise from time to time in various contexts: that of the relationship between fact and value in psychoanalytic knowledge and epistemology. It is a metapsychological question that poses itself as soon as one considers the psychological basis for objectivity. I have said that an attitude of respect for the subjective individuality of persons is the psychological ground of the objectivity that realizes correspondence or renders it operational. Truth is already a value. It is something that we *should* seek, acknowledge, accept, and act upon. An attitude of respect appears, at least, to include some reference to moral values. A consideration of this question will have to be deferred until the final chapter.

chapter two

Method in Applied Psychoanalysis

The correspondence theory of truth implies a basic principle for method in applied psychoanalysis: No argument in applied psychoanalysis is acceptable except insofar as its hypothesis is epistemologically independent of the evidence cited in support of it and insofar as the evidence that could refute it can be specified. The correspondence theory also implies that there are correct interpretations, however difficult they may be to reach.

Overdetermination and Interpretation

There is, however, a complication that cannot be avoided. It concerns the psychoanalytic concept of overdetermination. Many mental activities have more than one significance. In addition to the multiple social, cultural, and historical determinants of human actions, there is also a plurality of psychological determinants. Would not such phenomena amply justify a retreat from correspondence to coherence? Would not a principle of interpretive permissiveness, subject only to the criteria of coherence, be both more expedient and more correct? Nevertheless, psychological overdetermination does not imply an indeterminacy of mental activity. Overdetermination arises in two ways: as a consequence of the nature of the dream work and as a consequence of the structure of psychic processes generally. Displacement and condensation may each involve overdetermination. For example, a building in a dream may both be a day residue—an impression formed during the previous day and utilized in the dream as a substitute for a frustrating experience with someone in front of that building—and function symbolically in the dream to represent certain sensual aspects of the frustrating person or of an associated person. Such an example occurs in a dream in which a train journey is both a day residue and a symbol of the patient's anxiety about death. Similarly, condensation brings together, in a novel synthetic dream image, elements from the dreamer's experiences of different persons toward whom he has felt a similar important emotion. The meaning of such a dream element may include the complete series of antecedent experiences from different epochs of the dreamer's life. However difficult it may be in any given instance to completely unravel all of these meanings, the meanings themselves are both determinate and intrinsic to the dreamer.

The same is true of the overdetermination that results from the structure of psychic processes. Waelder (1930, 1965) rendered this implication of Freud's (1923a) structural theory explicit theoretically and clinically, and for applied psychoanalysis in his elaboration of multiple function. Nevertheless, from the fact that the thought activities and actions of persons are a composite of unconscious instinctual motives (id), unconscious moral and aesthetic motives in opposition to them (superego), along with efforts to find the best available satisfactions for these conflicting demands compatible with reality (ego), it does not follow that the interpreter is at liberty to form his own construction of the nature of the forces (motives) at work. These are determinate processes that give evidence of themselves in specific, definable ways. Of course, any particular investigation may encounter obstacles that give rise to uncertainties and that, therefore, allow only conjectures of varying degrees of probability.

One may consider overdetermination from yet another point of view. A novel, a historical event, a biography, or the like may be considered to be interpretable in several different ways according to different theories: Freudian, Kleinian, Winnicottian, Kohutian, Jungian, Adlerian, Sartrian, and so on (see Renik, 1978). The question of ideological interpretation within and without psychoanalysis will be further considered below.

The notion that several explanations of anything are equally possible has a venerable history. The ancient Epicureans held that it is possible to construct several hypotheses to account for any natural phenomenon, and that it is advantageous to do so as long as the hypotheses conform to a certain general type: that is, that they postulate only physical (natural) events and forces. Thus, the Epicureans hypothesized that the moon shines because it is itself a kind of fire that emits light, or because it is composed of a surface that is able to reflect the light of the sun. Given the state of knowledge at that time, it was reasonable for them to think that a further choice between these hypotheses could not be made. We now know that they were wrong. Improvements in observation have enabled us to discover which hypothesis is true. The advantage they saw in their multihypotheses was a dual aspect of the quietude that they considered to be of highest worth in life. Insofar as the explanations of phenomena were naturalistic, they provided a bulwark against the anxiety caused by the superstitious beliefs in the supernatural which subjected their contemporaries to irrational, futile anxieties; the Epicureans considered it to be the task of philosophy and science to deanthropomorphize nature, to construct an intellectual bulwark against the narcissistic projections onto nature that still troubled the ancient Greeks. Insofar as there were several hypotheses of this naturalistic type, knowledge was complete in being incomplete and indecisive. No further work could be done, they believed, to gain more determinate knowledge that would allow humans to intervene in nature in order to influence the outcome of events. The Epicureans' philosophy, in this respect, was a noble experiment that failed. That failure is itself a strong historical argument for the correspondence idea of truth.

The confusion of overdetermination with indeterminacy finds its way into applied psychoanalysis in two ways: as the justification for ideological interpretation and as special pleading for the correctness of psychoanalytic interpretation. Each involves a material fallacy. Ideological interpretation involves a kind of explanatory permissiveness cloaked in pseudoliberalism. It owes its appeal to the fact that human phenomena are, in fact, often multidetermined. A historical event such as the passage in the British Parliament of the reform bill of 1832 can be legitimately studied from different vantage points: the psychology of those who were its advocates, the economic and social circumstances of the period, the political struggle between the parties contending for power, and so forth. It is a different matter to claim that there is a Marxist and a capitalist interpretation of the passage of the first Reform Bill, and that both are correct because the meaning of the event is determined by the assumptions about the nature of history that the historian brings to the interpretation of its meaning. Of course, it must be acknowledged that such histories are written. But it is one thing to say that economic factors contributed to the occurrence of the event, to its nature (who was enfranchised and who was not), and to its consequences, and quite another to say that one has a right to interpret these factors according to assumptions of one's own choosing, whether these assumptions be Marxist or capitalist. The question is what reconstruction of the economic factors influencing political actions during this period of British history is the correct one. Either the ascertainable facts can make a decisive contribution to the choice of an interpretive frame of reference, or we cannot reconstruct their significance at all: We can only make more or less arbitrary conjectures. We can either engage in ideological thinking—deriving reality from *a priori* principles—or we can admit that we do not know, that the best that can be done is to speculate or make more or less well formed conjectures.

This generalization about humanistic thought applies to psychoanalysis as well. Conjectures can be highly useful, but they also involve risks. Freud (1920) justified his exploration of the hypothesis of a death instinct on the sensible ground that "it is surely possible to throw oneself into a line of thought and to follow it wherever it leads out of simple scientific curiosity" (p. 59). He acknowledged the lack of decisive evidence in favor of his hypothesis; yet 3 years later, in the absence of any further confirming evidence, Freud (1923a) introduced the death instinct into the general theory as though it had been established.

Applied psychoanalysis can be done ideologically. A text, an event, a life, or an artifact can always be interpreted along psychoanalytic lines; but such an approach omits two essential steps: identification of the evidence in the object that warrants a psychoanalytic approach, and identification of the evidence in the object that warrants the particular interpretation made. A specialized form of ideological thinking in applied psychoanalysis is the interpretation of, say, a novel, from a classical, self-psychological, object-relational, Kleinian, or some such point of view without consideration of what evidence there is in the text that justifies the application of one theory rather than another. Legislating reality is a poor substitute for discovering it. Legislating human reality is not justified by psychic overdetermination.

No more can overdetermination be appropriately used as a defense of a psychoanalytic interpretation against its critics. The only legitimate defense a psychoanalytic or any other interpretation can have is the evidence for it. Gedo (1987) has defended his interpretations of Cézanne against criticisms by the art historian Reff by appealing to psychic overdetermination:

> psychoanalytic interpretations cannot be falsified by proposing competing interpretations, be they psychological or not, for one of the basic tenets of psychoanalytic psychology is that all behaviour is overdetermined, that is, every act and every artifact will simultaneously encompass several meanings. (p. 232)

This use of the notion of psychic overdetermination immunizes psychoanalytic interpretations against falsification, and in doing so, it makes psychoanalytic interpretations unverifiable (see Hanly, 1983, p.

395). Overdetermination is not a tenet. It is an empirical generalization based upon evidence. That an act or artifact encompasses several meanings must be established in each case, even though the evidence for its being overdetermined will be the same as the evidence for the interpretations that articulate its meaning. One interpretation may falsify another in whole or in part. The concept of overdetermination cannot save us from differences, controversies, and the difficult work of trying to find where the truth lies. In practice one establishes that a particular text or other artifact is overdetermined through setting out the evidence for its psychological explanation. But this explanation will depend upon the findings of clinical analysis. What, then, is the relation between applied psychoanalysis and clinical psychoanalysis?

Applied Psychoanalysis, Clinical Observation, and Theory

Applied psychoanalysis relies upon the findings of clinical psychoanalysis in a special way because it does not have available to it the observational resources of clinical psychoanalysis. When a patient in analysis imagines seducing a woman he has recently seen, we are able to observe what preceded these images of seduction in his thoughts and the associations that follow on after them, as well as concomitant transference manifestations. These data, and the associations linked to them, are what enable the clinical analyst and the patient to discern the meanings that the imaginings have for the patient beyond those of which he is already aware. The applied analyst does not have the resources of free associations, transference, and the analytic process available to him (Eissler, 1965). Plato is no longer available to tell us through his associations the identity for him of the shepherd he imagined in his tale of Gyges in the *Republic*, or the meaning of Gyges' remarkable discovery of the magical ring, or the import of the crimes of seduction and murder he committed with its help.

The interpretation of Plato's story nevertheless relies upon clinical findings, in this instance the finding that kings and queens in dreams represent fathers and mothers, and that shepherds or other figures of low estate represent the sons or daughters of royalty according to the logic of the family romance (Freud, 1909b; Rank, 1909). The fact that the "Oedipus" of Plato's legend is not detected or punished for his crime, unlike the Oedipus of the tragedians, allows one to interpret the legend as an oedipal triumph. Clinical findings that show the connection between the son who has achieved an oedipal triumph, severe castration anxiety, the turning away from women and development of homosexuality, then allow one to conceive of the story as a homosexual variant of the Oedipus legend. Thus, the probability that the interpretation is true depends upon the probability of the clinical findings on which it is based. The probability that the clinical findings are true is based on the clinical evidence for them.

However, there is yet another assumption that has to be made. The associations that confirm the clinical findings essential to the interpretation of the legend are those of modern persons. The interpretation assumes that similar associations would have occurred to Plato had he analytically investigated the meaning of his imaginative creation. These associations can never be recovered; they died with Plato. Thus, a supplementary hypothesis is required: that the psychic developmental processes of ancient Greeks of the fourth century are in these respects fundamentally similar to those of moderns. In addition, there is an indirect access to Plato's associations to his tale of the ancestor of Gyges the Lydian in the themes and imagery of the *Republic*. Thus, the probability of the interpretation of Plato's Gyges story can be increased by calculating what else, if it is true, one should find in the work in which it appears. Among the things one should find are a dread of the instincts, evidence of homosexuality, a fear and mistrust of women, a dread of parricide. One thus uses the interpretation to make a series of predictions, which the text can either confirm or falsify.

Textual Predictions as a Means of Interpretation Testing

"Textual" predictions have one advantage over clinical predictions. The evidence for or against them is open to public scrutiny as the data of analytic sessions are not: The text of Plato's *Republic* is accessible to anyone, who can discover for himself whether Plato said what has been attributed to him. The extent to which these textual predictions can be made depends upon the extent to which the text in question is rich in revelations of the personality, beliefs, imagination, and emotional investments of the author. In this respect the early and middle dialogues of Plato are more suitable for this sort of applied psychoanalytic investigation than, say, most of the works of Aristotle. Greenacre (1955) has stated that certain artistic works provide "material as usable for psychoanalytic investigation as the dreams and free associations of the patient" (p. 13). With this assertion one need not quarrel; but, as Eissler (1965) put it, one "is dealing with a petrified record. The material at his [the applied psychoanalyst's] disposal is in its final form" (p. 165).

The advantage that this state of affairs seems to offer to the complacent and the doctrinaire—that a given interpretation cannot be falsified by new developments—is in reality no advantage at all. On the contrary, the extent to which an interpretation cannot be falsified is the extent to which it is unsatisfactory, either because of its own vagueness or because the text or art object may be enigmatic and inaccessible on account of its psychological poverty. Not all human creations reveal whatever unconscious origins they may have had. Euclid's geometry is surely one that does not, despite the subjectivity of its postulate concerning parallel lines. Thus, if an interpretation in applied psychoanalysis is to be formally adequate, it must be possible to specify not only what it is in the object examined that requires it, but also under what conditions it would be false or inapplicable. The strength of clinical analysis is that the object can change (the symptoms may be cleared up) as a result of interpretations, and hence provide evidence of their truth; or the object may not change, or change only temporarily, and oblige us to question their truth or the timing with which they were made. It was for this reason, among others, that Freud abandoned the general form of the seduction theory. It is for this reason that interpretations in applied psychoanalysis have to depend largely on clinical findings and upon theories established by clinical findings.

Thus, constructions in applied psychoanalysis are limited to the status of more or less probable hypotheses. Their degree of probability depends on the richness of the material available and the extent to which the theoretical concepts required to make the constructions can be clinically validated.

Contributions of Applied Psychoanalysis to Psychoanalytic Theory

Despite this limitation, the findings of applied psychoanalysis have made some significant contributions to psychoanalytic theory. Freud's deep familiarity with Oedipus Rex, Hamlet, and other literature (e.g., the novels of Dostoyevski) must have contributed to his discovery of the Oedipus complex and its place in psychosexual development, which is one of the foundation stones of psychoanalysis (Freud, 1897, Letter 71, pp. 263–266; 1900, pp. 260–266). Moreover, these plays were used by Freud as evidence for the generalization of the Oedipus complex from neurotic to normal development. How else could one account for the fascination these plays have had for generations? Applied psychoanalysis has an important role to play in linking the psychology of the neurosis to general psychology. Further, creative writers have often an exceptional intuitive grasp of human relations and their predicaments. Literature and other art forms can be a useful source of ideas for clinical psychoanalysis. Calef and Weinshel (1981) used the concept of "gaslighting," drawn from a classic film, to clarify certain aspects of introjection and its influence upon transference and counter-transference. Applied psychoanalysis can enrich clinical understanding through the use of the evocative descriptions of, for example, perverse character and behavior as imagined by creative writers. These descriptions can offer a more lively, vivid, detailed, and precise elaboration of clinical concepts than one could derive from clinical observation because of the greater freedom of the creative imagination, noted long ago by Aristotle. Shengold (1988) has used Proust's brilliant evocations of anal homosexual sadomasochism and of the narcissism associated with fetishistic defenses to give illustrative definition to these clinical concepts. Just as the scientific experiment is able to avoid the "clutter" of nature, so too the creative imagination can avoid what is accidental in psychological situations, in individual character, and in relationships, and throw into heightened relief what is essential. In this sense, to state it paradoxically, the imaginary may more closely approximate the real than do descriptions of what is real. Applied psychoanalysis can exploit these resources of psychological truth in works of art in order to clarify, enrich, and explore the scope of clinical and theoretical concepts. Despite its methodological limitations, applied psychoanalysis thus amply repays the debt that it owes to clinical psychoanalysis.

The Problem of Reductionism

Psychoanalysis in general and applied psychoanalysis in particular have been criticized for reductionism. In one respect this criticism is merited, although it is not the fault that the critics of psychoanalysis have thought it to be. Psychoanalysis provides a natural psychological explanation of, for example, the categorical imperatives of morality on account of which some philosophers, especially Kant, have attributed an ontological status to the human psyche that raises it above and locates it outside nature. By showing how moral imperatives develop out of the resolution of the Oedipus complex, psychoanalysis does reduce morality to a natural phenomenon. Similarly, if applied psychoanalysis can show that critics have idealized King Lear out of masculine narcissism and filial dread, it has only reduced Lear to the stature of a man who exercises the power of an absolute monarch and a father as portrayed by Shakespeare. Lear certainly does not then become an ordinary man, but neither does he transcend human nature, or its laws, its frailties, and its fatalities. This reductionism is no different from the inclusion of the moon, sun, planets, and stars in nature brought about by Galileo's telescopic observations, which revealed them to be of the same physical nature as the earth. Nor is it any different from the inclusion of man among the animal species that was brought about by Darwin's discovery of the process of evolution. These reductions reverse the narcissistic projections that took the place of adequately discriminate observation and accurate knowledge and thereby softened and obscured the reality of human animality and mortality.

It is true that there are applied psychoanalytic studies that fail to do justice to the complexity of art or history and to the complexity of the human reality to which they give expression. In these instances psychoanalysis is used to make an unwarranted reduction, but it would be a mistake to think that psychoanalytic theory justifies such oversimplifications. The crux of the problem concerns the nature of psychic defenses, among which sublimation has particular importance. It is one thing for a writer to write a story about a husband-and-wife murder-suicide and quite another for a person to be compelled to take scopophilic pleasure in dead bodies, even though both activities may owe their origin to an unconscious, violent primal-scene fantasy.

In the writing and the reading of such a story some approximation to the scene of sexual carnage is not sought out in reality; it is imagined. Instead of acting on an impulse, the writer displaces the impulse onto a character who is able by chance to satisfy the scopophilic wish in a disguised form. Contemplation is substituted for action. The gratification is to that extent modified in itself, and it is accompanied by a demand for a different activity—that of understanding. The original wish is veiled; the writer in this case (I expect this is a characteristic of good story writing generally) designs the story in such a way as to raise the question of the meaning of the experience of the scene in the life of the character and, in the course of the telling, provides the reader with clues to that meaning. As a result the writer, in the same way as the reader even though the writer has created the character and the story, is able through identification with the character in the story to explore a truth of human nature in himself at a safe distance from action. We are thus given an opportunity to reexperience in an acceptable form and from the vantage point of adult life a scene or the fantasy of a scene that once aroused intense sexual curiosity, excitement, and fear. We are able to remember, sometimes only affectively (emotional repetition), sometimes also verbally (intellectual insight), and sometimes also literally, without reenacting. In this there is a rudimentary form of neutralization. The cathected memory does not generate an impulse that requires discharge in action. Instead, the demand for gratification is satisfied within the bounds of an aesthetic, imagined experience that, at its best, cultivates the self by reducing the ego's need to maintain defenses against the memories of the experiences out of which it was itself formed. The advance in human psychological functioning that is made possible by these artifacts of sublimation is comparable to the advance achieved by the ancient Greeks when, in supplicating the gods for a prophetic dream, the sacrifice of a ring was substituted for the sacrifice of a finger (Dodds, 1963).

Sublimation involves three factors: object substitution, alteration in the mode of gratification, and neutralization. Plato's *Symposium* contains the first detailed philosophical description of sublimation. Plato described a process that begins with homosexual love for handsome youths and proceeds to the love of the beauty of their character rather than of their bodies, to the love of the moral ideals on which beauty of character is based, to the "vast sea of beauty," which seems to have meant to Plato approximately the source of beauty of whatever kind wherever found. One aspect of this process involves object substitution. The physical person of a young man is replaced by an invisible "reality" beyond nature. Physical sexual activity and sensual pleasure are replaced by contemplative activity and intellectual pleasure. The energy that drives the search for the love object has lost its original sexual and aggressive character. The love (libido) has become neutralized.

There is no more a justification in psychoanalytic theory for the assertion that metaphysical contemplation is nothing but homoeroticism than there is for such an assertion in Plato's account. The only differences are that Plato's account was genetic/moral and based on a preference for homosexuality, whereas the psychoanalytic account is genetic/descriptive and neutral. (Plato seems to have thought that heterosexuals have little need for sublimation or ability to sublimate, concerned as they are with physical procreation. Freud rested the most crucial step in emotional maturation on the ability of the child to replace the oedipal sexual wishes for the parent of the opposite sex with aim-inhibited—sublimated—affection.) But to trace a certain form of thinking to an origin in a sexual activity does not amount to treating it as the same thing. In this respect, psychoanalysis does not involve reduction; it describes development.

There is another respect in which psychoanalysis is not reductionistic. Psychoanalysis, as we have argued above, takes the test of the truth of an idea to be whether it tallies with an objective state of affairs. Even if it can be shown that an idea is the result of wishful thinking, even if it is, psychologically, an illusion, it does not follow that the idea is false. Even though an individual believes x only because he wants x to be true, and not because he has objective evidence for his belief, it still may be the case that x does happen to be true. Freud (1927) made it clear that to prove that the belief in God is an illusion is not to prove that the belief is false.

Applied Psychoanalysis and the Sphinx of Interpretation

Applied psychoanalytic studies may profitably take as their point of departure some problem of interpretation that other methods of scholarship have failed to solve. Two such problems motivated Freud's (1910b) study of Leonardo da Vinci: the enigma of the Madonna's smile and its ubiquity in his three great late paintings, and the difficulty Leonardo had both in finishing his paintings and in devoting himself wholeheartedly to the art for which he had such genius. Freud's study, with its erroneous translation of *nibio* as "vulture" rather than "kite," reminds us of the reliance of psychoanalytic interpretations upon traditional methods of scholarship for such things as textual reliability. In this instance, Freud compounded the error by supposing that Leonardo had read the analogy drawn in the writings of the church fathers between the Virgin Birth and the hermaphroditic vultures who impregnated themselves by opening their cloacae to the wind and had formed the "vulture fantasy" when his reading had stimulated memories of his own fatherless early childhood. Given the initial mistranslation, Freud's extensive knowledge of ancient Egyptian, Greek, and medieval lore only managed to make the compounding of the error ingenious and highly interesting, but nonetheless clearly wrong.

No one has been bold enough to attempt a different reconstruction of Leonardo's kite fantasy. Yet fantasy it is, rather than memory as Leonardo described it. It is no more likely that a kite would have landed on his cradle and struck him "many times with its tail against . . . [his] lips" (Freud, 1910b, p. 82) than that a vulture would have done so. This is no ordinary bird. It is a fabulous bird, the representative of memories and thoughts that have been subjected to repression. It is a derivative of unconscious processes that must have made a significant contribution to Leonardo's life—as Leonardo himself asserted on the basis of the limited familiarity he had with this aspect of his destiny. The core of Freud's argument can be summarized as follows: When a mental content, such as the "memory" Leonardo recorded in his notebooks, could not have been an actual memory, it must have been a fantasy symbolizing life-significant events. On the basis of clinical observation of dream symbolism the bird fantasy is the derivative of an unconscious homosexual fellatio fantasy that has its roots in an arrested libidinal attachment to the mother's breast and an identification with her as a means of preserving the attachment. Freud's error in translation did not affect his interpretation—a kite (which is a bird of the same order as the vulture, in any case) can bear this symbolic significance as easily as can a vulture.

But the crucial question, given the methodological principles enunciated above, is whether Freud was able to confirm his interpretation of the bird fantasy with evidence of the influence of such a libidinal fixation and maternal identification in the life and work of Leonardo. If as an adult Leonardo took an exceptional pleasure in the physical care of young men, it would mean that he was adopting a maternal attitude toward them and was seeking to provide for them, in a sublimated form, the libidinal pleasure that could be provided by a mother, for whom he himself still longed. That is to say, he would have been forming a narcissistic relation with them in which he identified himself with his mother and the young men in his care with himself as a child. The roots of this narcissistic relation would be found in the pregenital fixation of libido and an identification with the mother as a means of retaining her (If I cannot have her, I will be her). Freud found evidence of such a maternal preoccupation in Leonardo's treatment of his apprentices, chosen for their youthfulness and physical beauty rather than for their talent (Freud, 1910b, pp. 101ff.).

Apart from other biographical evidence there is also, perhaps most importantly, the internal, thematic evidence of Leonardo's last great paintings. However one may interpret the meaning of the enigmatic smile of the Mona Lisa, the fact that Leonardo used this same facial expression bisexually is an observable fact that is independent of the interpretation of its more subtle ramifications. The smile appears on St. Anne, Mary, and Leda, but also on John the Baptist and Bacchus, with the result that these male figures acquire an androgynous quality that would make them peculiarly alluring to a certain kind of homosexual:

> They are beautiful youths of feminine delicacy and with effeminate forms; they do not cast their eyes down, but gaze in mysterious triumph, as if they knew of a great achievement of happiness. (Freud, 1910b, p. 117)

This sentence is a description of the figures in the paintings rather than an interpretation of them, but any interpretation must take the description into account. Freud's interpretation is firmly based on the description, and it connects Leonardo's last paintings to his life without disconnecting it from his art or from the cultural and social influences that also shaped it. For the correctness of this interpretation Freud claimed only possibility, by no means certainty:

> It is possible that in these figures Leonardo has denied the unhappiness of his erotic life and has triumphed over it in his art, by representing the wishes of the boy, infatuated with his mother, as fulfilled in this blissful union of the male and female natures. (pp. 117–118)

Gay (1988) has rightly connected Freud's personal struggle with homosexual feelings toward his erstwhile friend Wilhelm Fliess to his interest in the lives of Leonardo and Schreber, and has no less correctly pointed out that this connection does not "compromise the scientific value of his findings" (p. 277). One might however add that, although they may not have done so in the case of Freud, such factors can disturb both descriptions and interpretations when they are working unconsciously. What is decisive, whatever the motives for research might be, is the quality of the evidence for any interpretation; but it must also be acknowledged that the psychology of the researcher or scholar is an important factor in the search for objectivity in this field of inquiry. Freud's capacity for objective perception, imagination, and thought about Leonardo's life and work depended upon his acquired ability to comprehend his own homosexuality without fear, disdain, pity, or exaggeration. Only such an inner relation to one's own instinct life, and the memories of the experiences owed to it, can both open up this field of observation and thought and keep it as free as possible of distorting projections, denials, and idealizations. In applied psychoanalysis to know depends upon being able to remember, but to demonstrate requires objective evidence.

Concerning the Egyptian and Christian Medieval Lore about Vultures

Freud's flawed argument from the mistranslation of *nibio* offers an example of the inadequacy of coherence as a criterion of truth. Freud's error allowed him to elaborate a complex, internally coherent scholarly argument that linked many elements of Leonardo's life to contemporary and ancient cultural influences. This account has great explanatory power. It is altogether a brilliantly coherent explanatory edifice, but it is nonetheless in error for that. Its coherence, its apparent explanatory power, the details that it is able to render intelligible, do not advance the cause of Freud's argument one whit, for the simple reason that *nibio* continues with supreme indifference to all these efforts to refer to a kite and not to a vulture. It is an example of how a great thinker can construct a brilliant edifice upon the sand of a false premise. It is a reminder of the implacability of a factual error, however small. I, therefore, agree with Gay's (1988) assessment of this part of Freud's argument. I do not, however, agree with Kohut's (1960) view:

> [Freud's study of Leonardo is] not primarily a contribution to the comprehension of Leonardo's personality and the vicissitudes of his creativity; it was a medium for the presentation of a particular form of homosexuality. (p. 572)

This view assumes that Freud imposed an interpretation, for which there was no evidence, because he wanted to elaborate his view of a certain form of homosexuality and used the life of Leonardo as a convenient means of doing so. Among other evidence for his reconstruction are the kite fantasy, the details of Leonardo's domestic relations with his apprentices, and the bisexual ubiquity of the Mona Lisa's enigmatic smile. Anyone who is able to come up with a reconstruction that better explains, or explains more of the facts of, Leonardo's life and work, and that contradicts Freud's reconstruction, will have shown Freud to be wrong. But it is a fallacy of *pars pro toto* to treat an error that affects only part of an argument as though it affected the whole. To be sure, the facts of Leonardo's life and work have to be interpreted in order to support the reconstruction, but that is true of any reconstruction, of any study of Leonardo that goes beyond treating the details of his life as objects in a museum and attempts an understanding of them.

Subjectivity, Objectivity, and the Unconscious

There can be no doubt that perceptions can be subjectively determined. There need be no less doubt that we can often separate what is subjective from what is objective. A range of situations exists, from the easy through the difficult to the impossible; but I shall argue that the impossibility, when it occurs, is an empirical, physical, or psychological impossibility rather than an *a priori*, logical, or epistemological impossibility. We have no difficulty in identifying as hallucination the perception of a youth who on a visit to Ottawa saw a large number of Soviet amphibious troops gathering upstream on the shores of the Ottawa River to launch an attack on the capital. Although his account of what he saw had certain realistic elements—the river and its relation to the city, its banks, and so on—the central content of his perception had a subjective source.

The perception of the affective qualities of others is more complex. A woman who had perceived her mother prior to and during part of her analysis to be an aloof, withholding, authoritarian person, came at the end of her analysis to wonder how she could have perceived her in this way. The mother now appeared to her to be caring and interested. She now considered her new perceptions to be objective; before, she had been convinced that her earlier perceptions were objective. Were both perceptions correct? Were neither? It is likely that the daughter's earlier perceptions had been in part objective. A divorce had left the mother solely responsible for her daughter's upbringing from the age of 11. There was evidence of her having become an anxious, severe, rather accusing disciplinarian. One method of discipline was to refuse to speak to the child, despite her tearful pleading, for several days on end.

At the same time, it became evident from the analysis that the daughter had reasons of her own (for instance, phallic wishes that caused her to believe that her father would not have deserted them had she been a boy) that caused her to perceive her mother to be withholding and uncaring to a greater extent than she actually was and in ways that she was not. At the end of a successful analysis that resolved the patient's hysterical frigidity and enabled her to blossom sexually, she found it difficult to believe that she had once seen her mother as meriting so much ill will.

It must be acknowledged that this account is itself a reconstruction: The analyst is unable to make direct observations of the significant figures in a patient's life as they are in themselves, but only as they appear through the eyes of the patient. This, however, is a technical limitation; it is not an epistemological barrier. Forming the most objective impression one can of the important persons in the life of a patient is an inevitable part of the continuing discrimination by the analyst of what is conflicted from what is not conflicted in the patient. An essential part of this discrimination is the estimation of what is objective and what is subjective in the experience of the patient.

One of Freud's (1912c) clinical recommendations was that the analyst should maintain an attitude of "evenly suspended attention" (p. 111). This recommendation parallels the one to the patient (Freud, 1900), which encourages uncritical self-observation. The aim of evenly suspended attention is to allow the patient's associations to speak for themselves by restraining the analyst's interests, ideas, and purposes from imposing their own selection and emphasis upon them. It is a passive form of observation only in the sense that the links among the associations (the text of the analysis) and their significance are to be formed by the associations themselves and not by the analyst's preconceptions. Intuitions, hunches, and trial identifications with the object are involved, but their results must be impartially tested by the evidence (Arlow & Beres, 1974; Brenner, 1976).

Nevertheless, Freud (1912c) appears to have claimed a unique cognitive capacity on behalf of the unconscious. His initial statement is unexceptionable:

> Just as the patient must relate everything that his self-observation can detect, and keep back all the logical and affective objections that seek to induce him to make a selection from among them, so the doctor must put himself in a position to make use of everything he is told for the purposes of interpretation and of recognizing the concealed unconscious material without substituting a censorship of his own for the selection that the patient had forgone. (p. 115)

But Freud proceeded, metaphorically,

> to put it in a formula: he must turn his own unconscious like a receptive organ towards the transmitting unconscious of the patient. He must adjust himself to the patient as a telephone receiver is adjusted to the transmitting microphone. Just as the receiver converts back into soundwaves the electric oscillations in the telephone line which were set up by sound waves, so the doctor's unconscious is able, from the derivatives of the unconscious which are communicated to him, to reconstruct that unconscious, which has determined the patient's free associations. (pp. 115–116)

This metaphor appears to assert (or can be taken to assert) that primary process thought activity has a cognitive capacity akin to the perceptual and thought activities of the ego. It would appear to lend itself to the view that countertransference registers transference (Heimann, 1950; Little, 1953; Racker, 1953; for a historical overview see Abend, 1989). It would also appear to suggest that there is an ineradicable subjectivity in psychoanalytic interpretations.

This rendering of Freud's use of the term "unconscious" is, however, inconsistent with what he elsewhere has to say about its nature: for example, that it has no indication of reality available to it, that it cannot differentiate fantasy from reality, and that its activities are not subject to the reality principle. The activities of the unconscious are driven by the pleasure principle, which seeks the most direct possible discharge of the drive demands that arise within it. In the absence of the discipline of the perception of reality, the analyst's unconscious would simply create a fantasy of the patient. Moreover, the materials available to the unconscious for forming such a fantasy are the repressed memories of the analyst. The product of these factors would be a fantasy of the patient that would be congenial to the satisfaction of whatever repressed drive demands happened to be at work in the life of the analyst at the time. Far from being a means of gaining an objective understanding of another person, such an image would interfere with this effort by thrusting upon the ego a convincing chimera. It would be an example of the countertransference about which Freud (1912b) cautioned psychoanalysts. Freud never subscribed to the view that the countertransference reveals the hidden motives of the patient's transference or, in any of his works, that countertransference is a function of the ego as Heimann (1977) has asserted. Did Freud's telephone metaphor get the better of his thought, or is there some way of reconciling this statement with Freud's theory?

Freud (1912a) identified an ambiguity in the use of the term "unconscious": It could refer either to the descriptive or to the dynamic unconscious. The former consists of all those memories to which we are not attending but that are available for recall without resistance. The dynamic unconscious consists of all the memories that have been subjected to repression; cannot be recalled on account of resistance; and, apart from the removal of the repression, can only be known by means of their derivatives, which are always subject to distortion. It is to the work of the descriptive unconscious, which is stored with the impressions of the patient's free associations impartially received by evenly suspended attention, that Freud referred in the telephone metaphor. It is the countertransference, which interferes with this process, that is the handiwork of the dynamic or repressed unconscious. The descriptive unconscious is part of the ego: It is subject to the reality principle, and it is connected with the cognitive processes of the ego (Freud, 1923a).

However, the matter is not so simple. There is a respect in which the dynamic unconscious plays a part. Perhaps Freud left the term ambiguous for this reason. The descriptive or latent unconscious was identified by Freud (1923a) with the preconscious, which links the conscious to the dynamic unconscious. Typically when we discover that we have forgotten the name of someone or something, we cannot recall either ever having tried to forget it or having a motive for forgetting it. The name, having become latently unconscious as a consequence of attention having been directed elsewhere, has become associatively connected with a group of repressed memories with which it has something or other in common.

Although that commonality may consist of a variety of elements, some of which may be accidental, the presence of a common affective significance is essential. For example, a patient had turned off the valve of the hot water radiator in his room, had forgotten having done so, and had for several days complained bitterly about (but not to) his landlady as cruel, avaricious, and negligent in failing to provide his room with adequate heat in winter. He felt victimized by her. The memory of turning off the radiator had become associatively connected with being rejected by his common-law wife so that he had to leave the house they had previously shared. He was feeling victimized by her as well. The need to feel victimized by a woman was a reaction formation against his attempts to victimize his common-law wife by making threats of physical abuse, which he no longer remembered having done. When she had insisted upon a separation, it was he who had offered to leave, partly out of guilt at his attempts at intimidation and partly out of the hope that his leaving might make her feel guilty, so that she would have him back on his terms.

This example of unconsciously motivated forgetting shows that its results include more than a gap in cognition. Through the small rent in reality testing caused by the amnesia there pour the derivatives of the fantasy of being victimized by a woman. The fantasy, which denies its unconscious opposite (the wish to victimize a woman), serves as a meaning-assigning template or a distorting lens through which the innocent landlady is seen to be the epitome of penny-pinching cruelty. Freud (1924b) has pointed to the loss of reality in neurosis. In this example of a neurotic parapraxis, for the real landlady is substituted a fantasy that is preserved by avoidance. The patient did not make his complaints to the landlady; he reserved them for the ears of his analyst, whose sympathy and indignation at these outrages he wanted. Had he complained to his landlady he could easily have discovered the cause of his external predicament, although he might well not have recovered the memory that would have enabled him to own his action. If he did not, some secondary suspicion (e.g., that the landlady had herself turned off the heat and now only made a show of solicitude to cover her culpability) would probably have been formed to protect the original fantasy. As it was, the analysis enabled him to remember that he had himself turned off the radiator on the night of his arrival because the room was too hot.

This example illustrates but one of the many ways in which conflicts generated by unwanted drive demands can interfere with the way in which reality is experienced, imagined, remembered, and thought. The preconscious allows the transfer of memories from the latent unconscious to the repressed unconscious, and it allows drive-dominated ideas to gain access to the ego in the form of wishes and desires. Given infantile sexuality, aggression, and narcissism, given the conservative nature of the instincts, and given that repression cannot extinguish a drive demand but only render it unconscious and force upon it a substitute satisfaction, there must always be in everyone an ample supply of unwanted drive demands clamoring for access to the ego along the frontier between the unconscious and the preconscious. Now it is also the case that the ego depends upon a preconscious synthesis of ideas in order to carry out its functions. Without such a synthesis it would be impossible to speak, write, or think, but how are we to know whether this synthesis has been determined by unmodified perceptions of objects or by the demands of unconscious fantasies? We have returned by a different path to the same problem: Are we not confronted here with an impasse that justifies the view that in psychoanalytic observation and interpretation what is subjective and what is objective cannot finally be differentiated with any reasonable degree of certainty? If so, are not coherence criteria the most appropriate for psychoanalysis?

It is not difficult to state the ideal epistemological conditions for analytic work. The analyst should have preconscious and, if necessary, conscious access to the important memories of his childhood: for example, memories of his oedipal love for his mother and his rivalry with his father, as well as of what happened to these motives. He will be able to recall the excitement of the onset of the phallic phase and the newly intensified genital sensations to which it gives rise. He will be able to recall his mother's seductiveness, if seductive she was; his growing fear of his father; the punishments for misdemeanors he may have received at his father's or mother's hands, and what they meant to him at the time; and because these memories are available to the adult ego they will become subject to criticism for their accuracy and tested for their reliability like any other memory, probably even more than other memories. Because this self-knowledge is at his disposal the analyst is able to observe the traces of the patient's Oedipus complex in the associations and transference of the patient, to reconstruct its history and sequel, and to make interpretations without a predisposition to assume that what happened to himself must have happened to everyone else. It is in this way that the dynamic unconscious makes an indispensable contribution to the evenly suspended attention of the analyst.

However, because amnesia is the mechanism of repression and the dynamic unconscious is the repressed unconscious, can we any longer speak of a dynamic unconscious when its contents (memories) have become subject to recall? What has become of the conservatism of the instincts? Do well analyzed people cease to dream because they cease to have repressed infantile wants? Obviously not: Dreaming changes but it still occurs. It is a question of the play of mental forces. A successful analysis substantially reduces the amounts of energy invested in infantile organizations, but there is no evidence that they can be reduced to zero. Nevertheless, the pathogenic infantile organizations have to be sufficiently reduced to allow for a specific kind of plasticity of repression.

Plasticity of repression is analogous to, but different from, what Freud (1917a) called "laxity in the repressions" of creative artists or what Kris (1953) referred to as "flexibility of repression." Laxity of repression, as Freud described it, does not depend on a reduction of the investments in infantile fixations but rather on a talent for expressing their derivatives (Freud mentioned daydreams specifically) in a form that makes them pleasurably available to others. Whereas it is possible for a successful artist to be neurotic, it is not possible for a successful analyst to be neurotic. Just as analysts, in their quest for an objective empathic grasp of the life situations of their patients, need to be able to make trial identifications with them (Arlow & Beres, 1974), so too analysts must be able to allow temporary suspensions of repressions in themselves in order to recall what some aspect of their own infantile lives was actually like so that they can differentiate memories of events in their own lives from similar events in the lives of their patients.

This view is in agreement with Brenner's (1985) account of countertransference as compromise formation. Although acknowledging the ubiquity of countertransference, Brenner denies that it is a form of intuition or empathy: Countertransference may support or interfere with the cognitive tasks of analysis, but it cannot substitute for them. To this I would add that the compromise formations need to be flexible enough to allow the defenses involved to be suspended under the influence of the associations of a patient. To use one of Brenner's examples (p. 160): The analyst, whose wish to help persons resolve neurotic conflicts is partly motivated by a reaction formation against a wish to see people suffer, should be able to abandon the reaction formation sufficiently to be able to recall such childhood memories as having tortured insects, having teased and bullied other weaker children, having fantasies of killing a younger sibling, and so on, when derivatives of the patient's latent sadism appear in the associations. At other times the reaction formation can continue quietly in place. It is the capacity for such flexibility of repression that allows the ego to use the dynamic unconscious as a receiving instrument attuned to the inflexibly repressed unconscious of the patient. It is on the basis of this basic differentiation of self from other that the preconscious of the ego is able to become stored with impressions of the other out of which integrating imaginings and thoughts of what happened in the life of the other can be formed. It must, however, be emphasized that these imaginings and thoughts are not guaranteed to be objective. The differentiation of self from other that is involved does not guarantee objectivity: It only makes objectivity possible. It provides a basis for reaching objectivity, if there is sufficient evidence.

A personal analysis, preserved and extended by self-analysis, can generate self-knowledge and liberate the capacity to increase it as life proceeds. This self-knowledge is not merely abstract. It involves a continuing potential awareness of the memories that shape one's motives and of the identifications that form one's character. It enables one to use one's ego (in the sense of the unity of all three structural agencies, or self) to gain empathic access to the life of another as it is and was in itself rather than after the image of one's own ego. Clinical experience and study enriches this self-knowledge with knowledge of the lives of others. This clinical knowledge is the bedrock of psychoanalysis as a science. Upon this foundation psychoanalytic hypotheses are built up, tested, and either are abandoned or take their place in the evolving theory.

To the task of interpretation psychoanalysis adds the precept that the exploration of the meaning of the behavior, motives, and creations of others requires self-exploration. The study of the object requires a preconscious and sometimes conscious dialogue with the self. This dialogue is not the same as the deliberate effort to be fair, to search for evidence that contradicts one's own ideas, perceptions, and beliefs, important and indeed necessary as that effort is. It is involuntary. When it fails, the best efforts at fairness and conscious self-critical objectivity may fail too. When it fails, the analyst should be able to identify the failure and take steps to correct it before proceeding, or else leave the undertaking to another who may be better equipped psychologically to tackle the problems of understanding involved. This dialogue goes on in everyone practicing the arts of interpretation. It is not the exclusive province of psychoanalysis. Every good scholar has experienced the sense that some understanding of a text, a painting, a life, an event, beckons but eludes because of some internal obstacle; but then, after some scarcely identifiable inner changes have occurred, the material becomes accessible to understanding. Psychoanalysis is the only method we have to cultivate and to give eyes to this otherwise blind struggle. The coherence advocates are correct in saying that the ego (self) cannot be eliminated from knowledge. After all, it is the observing instrument, and special difficulties arise when it comes to observing and understanding ourselves, our actions, and our creations. The question is a practical one. Can psychoanalysis sufficiently refine the observing instrument to permit it to be objective enough to separate what belongs to itself from what is in the object? Ariadne's thread was fragile and slight, but it enabled Theseus to find his way out of the labyrinth. Where psychoanalysis is concerned the test will have to be the value of the contributions it can make to the better understanding of man, his history, and his condition. The interpretive studies that follow are intended as small contributions to this end.

Applied Psychoanalysis as an Interdisciplinary Discipline

Applied psychoanalysis is inescapably an interdisciplinary field. It requires that the expertise of the scholar be yoked to the expertise of the analyst. Whether or not the analyst is an expert in the field of application, he must be prepared to find his explanations, or aspects of them, overturned by new scholarly findings that invalidate the evidence upon which he has based his conclusions: Freud's Leonardo study offers us a good example. Thus, applied psychoanalysis is built upon two dependencies, the one on clinical psychoanalysis, the other on scholarship and research in the humanities and social sciences.

Studies in applied psychoanalysis can take several forms. The study of the relation of the life of the creator to his creation is essentially psychoanalytically informed biography, although the emphasis may be placed primarily upon the work (e.g., Bonaparte, 1933; Gay, 1988) or upon the life (e.g., Greenacre, 1955), or it may be equally distributed (e.g., Freud 1910b; Jones 1953–1957; Eissler 1961, 1963). However, while agreeing with the defenses of biographically oriented studies offered by Bonaparte (1939), Reed (1982), and Gay (1985), there is the problem, also alluded to by Reed (1982), of the intentional fallacy—that of basing the interpretation of a text on what its author intended its meaning to be. The problem with the intentional fallacy is that it assumes that the author must always have a conscious meaning that he is seeking to express in the work; but writers may be surprised by what they write just as painters may be surprised by what they paint; or they may not have an interpretation of what they have written— they may not be any surer about its meaning than another reader or viewer. It does not follow that there was no intention at work: The intention that finds expression in the work of art may be an unconscious one that requires interpretation. A knowledge of the life of the artist may be useful in shedding light upon these unconscious intentions, which form the deepest source of the artist's inspiration. Leonardo may not have fathomed his own fascination with the Mona Lisa smile, and Freud may not have done so either: But the kind of biographical study of Leonardo that Freud undertook is one that may well shed light on its meaning.

Psychoanalysis can also study a work of art in its own right, independently of the life of its creator. Freud (1905a) made the point, in a clinical context, that people constantly and unwittingly give expression to their unconscious thoughts and wishes, "if his lips are silent, he chatters with his finger-tips; betrayal oozes out of him at every pore" (p. 78). Even if the work of deciphering may not always be so simple as this statement suggests, it can be assumed that any great work of art will have an unconscious dimension that may be deciphered from the indications that are to be found within the work itself. Accordingly, applied psychoanalysis can construct interpretations of works of art from the works themselves. An excellent example of such a procedure is Freud's (1907) study of the novel *Gradiva* using dream psychology; another is Jones's (1949) study of *Hamlet*, which, drawing on Freud's (1900) comments, relied for its interpretation upon the content of the play itself rather than upon a study of Shakespeare's life. Reed (1985) has suggested one means of doing so that exploits the universality of unconscious fantasies. Waelder (1965) has shown how the structural model lends itself to such an undertaking once the work of art is viewed as a compromise formation.

Applied psychoanalysis may also employ a comparative method. This method is particularly useful when considering the psychological aspects of theories in philosophy, the social sciences, or biology—any theory that makes assumptions or assertions about human nature. One can also study the understanding of human nature implicit in the works of a writer or artist in this way, or the beliefs about human nature that inform an epoch. When there is agreement, one has discovered additional grounds for the reliability of the psychoanalytic theory in question. Aristotle's aesthetics, for example, offer a confirmation of the centrality of the Oedipus complex. This kind of confirmation is particularly important when the theory from the cognate field is based on the use of different methods of observation and a different field of investigation: if it were shown in genetics, for example, that the stages of infantile sexuality were genetically determined. Freud (1920) attempted to ground his death instinct theory in clinical evidence, infant observation, and upon evidence drawn from biology. When there is disagreement and there is strong evidence for the contradictory or contrary theory in another field, psychoanalysis must either abandon its theory or show that although the two theories appear to be in contradiction they actually are not. Given the special pleasure all kinds of otherwise impartial people take in proving Freud wrong, psychoanalysis must find a path between dismissing genuine contrary evidence by complacently analyzing it away and treating weak criticisms with more seriousness than they deserve. Freud's (1939) reliance on the inheritance of acquired characteristics, which psychoanalytic theory does not logically require and for which there is still no scientific evidence, is an example of something else—Freud's misinterpretation of the clinical and cultural evidence that appeared to support the existence of "archaic residues," and his failure, because of his underestimation of the power of cultural inheritance through identification, to realize that psychoanalytic theory did not require the inheritance of acquired characteristics. One important undertaking of applied psychoanalysis is to maintain links with cognate humanistic and scientific disciplines.

Comparative studies obviously involve the examination and conceptual analysis of theories, and they can lead to and be combined with psychological interpretation, independently of the author of the theory and his life history. For example, one can show that in Hobbes's political theory concerning the genesis of the state there is an implicit theory of drive mastery. When this theory is formulated and compared with psychoanalytic findings, one discovers that Hobbes had failed to take into account the effects of the resolution of the Oedipus complex upon the acquisition of drive mastery. He implicitly assumed that human beings do not have a capacity for autonomous self-control, and consequently had to assign this function to an absolute external authority, the state, with absolute power to coerce obedience. Hobbes's implicit psychological model is that of the pre-oedipal child in relation to his parents. I have referred to this procedure as translating theories into the psychologically concrete (Hanly, 1979). By means of it, I was able to show that the central tenets of existentialism, as formulated by Sartre, are descriptions of experiences that have been structured by narcissistic defenses that betray the very psychological determinants that Sartre was at pains to repudiate in his philosophy. This approach to the study of theories is comparable to the interpretation of works of literature and art that treats the text or painting as being interpretively self-sufficient.

There is a view that would repudiate as a distorting vulgarization any interpretive approach that relates art to life and society. Frye (1957) has put this view in its most persuasive form by claiming that works of literature and art can be correctly interpreted only in relation to other works of literature and art. Words in a poem refer to words in other poems and not to individual or social reality or to nature. Works of creation exist in a universe of their own beyond nature. This view has several problems. It has to rely on a *deus ex machina* to get the universe of the arts started. It does not itself have very substantial support from the study of works of art. References to other works of art and quotations from them occur in music, painting, and poetry: T. S. Eliot's *Wasteland* for example, not only exploits allusion and direct quotation but explores the implications and limitations of this poetic method. There is as well the more general influence of tradition; but, even allowing fully for these factors, it would be arbitrary to disregard the personality of the creator, his culture, society, and time, and his responses to them (cf. Eliot, 1919). Works of imagination and thought vary in the extent to which those influences contribute to their formation and hence to their interpretation. To remove art from life and locate it in a universe of its own beyond nature is an idealization of art that scarcely disguises the aggression that also does violence to it.

If psychoanalysis can be applied to philosophy, philosophy can in return be applied to psychoanalysis. Freud's work is laced with arguments defending the concept of the dynamic unconscious from philosophical criticism. A tradition continues in the philosophical literature that is committed to the task of showing that psychoanalysis is not a science, and there is another tradition that tries to modify psychoanalysis so that it can be incorporated into a philosophical system such as ordinary language philosophy (MacIntyre, 1958; Schafer, 1976) or hermeneutics (Ricoeur, 1970; Habermas, 1971), despite the fact that Freud (1933) took pains to show that psychoanalysis is not a philosophy. Another possibility is for philosophy to draw on psychoanalysis by incorporating its findings and concepts into philosophical arguments (Hospers, 1952; Lazerowitz, 1955, 1964). I have used the example of philosophy, but similar observations could be made concerning political theory (Laswell, 1930), international relations (Steinberg, 1991), sociology (Hartmann, 1950; Parsons, 1950), anthropology (Roheim, 1947, 1950; Devereux, 1967, 1972), and history (Langer, 1958; Gay, 1985). Similarly psychoanalysis can draw on philosophy in order to seek to shore up its theories, to clarify concepts, or to indicate their precursors. Freud, for example, drew on philosophy in this way when he cited (dubiously, in my opinion) Empedocles' cosmological principles of love and strife as a precedent for his theory of Eros and Thanatos and Kant's categorical imperative as a precedent for the superego. The introductory chapter to this book is an examination of this sort of use of philosophy in psychoanalysis with reference to the nature of truth.

The studies that follow are not in the least exhaustive of these possibilities or in any way comprehensive. They are further probes into a field already rich with many excellent studies undertaken against the background of the methodological issues explored above. They are tests of the methodological ideas presented. They are limited to those areas of applied psychoanalysis into which the author dares to enter even if with trepidation.

chapter three

Metaphysics
and Innateness

There are particular advantages in choosing as a point of departure for an applied psychoanalytic study some problem that has arisen in the field of application. It demonstrates the utility of applied psychoanalysis when it is able to solve, or at least to shed light on, a problem that has proven intractable before the traditional methods of the discipline(s) involved, even when this assistance is neither welcomed nor accepted by the practitioners of the discipline(s). The problem tackled by the study that follows is the difficulties in which some philosophers have found themselves as a result of exaggerating the reliability of introspection. This approach parallels that of clinical psychoanalysis: Every clinical investigation begins with a problem in the life of another human being. One should not take this parallel too far, however, even though each of the studies that follow does take a problem as its starting point. Applied psychoanalysis has a right to identify problems where none has been perceived from the typical perspectives of the discipline. In the field of practical ethics, psychoanalysis has demonstrated the problems inherent in treating homosexuality as a crime. In the administration of justice it has shown the futility of believing that certain forms of criminality can be reformed by imprisonment. In philosophy it has demonstrated that, contrary to the views of some philosophers who have continued to adhere to outmoded concepts, neither consciousness nor preconsciousness can be defining characteristics of the mental. Philosophers no more appreciated the difficulty they had in espousing this apparently self-evident idea than creationists understood the difficulties inherent in their ideas until Darwin's discoveries made them glaringly evident or than Ptolemaic cosmologists could appreciate the radical nature of their misconceptions until the work of Copernicus and Galileo had made these apparent.

In addition, although it is appropriate that clinical psychoanalysis be restricted to the investigation of psychopathology, there is no similar need for such a restriction of applied psychoanalysis. The observation of infant development includes the study of the seeds of psychopathology, but is by no means restricted to it. Psychoanalysis is also a general psychology that can be used to explore the origins of characterological strengths as well as weaknesses, of creativity as well as inhibition and conformity, of happiness as well as misery. It would be an unnecessary and distracting restriction of the resources of applied psychoanalysis to limit it to various forms of pathology.

This examination of ideas of the innate in philosophy employs methods of argument that combine theoretical analysis with empirical (observational testing) and psychological explanation. The psychological explanations, however, are at the level of common human nature rather than individual biography.

Philosophical Notions of Innate Ideas

Metaphysical systems, however otherwise diverse, are commonly based on two assumptions: the ontological assumption that there is a reality beyond the world of physical objects, physical forces, and animal kinds; and the epistemological assumption that the human mind is able to apprehend something of this mysterious transcendence or hidden immanence by gaining access to special ideas inherent in the mind or by engaging in special operations of thought. This chapter is a psychoanalytic reflection upon the epistemological assumption.

The belief that there are ideas innate to the mind that contain the secrets of the universe has had a distinguished history among metaphysicians. Plato (*Republic, VII*) thought that progress toward a true grasp of reality depended upon a dialectical uncovering of ideational replicas of the forms within the mind. (The forms were, of course, the archetypes according to which Plato believed the cosmos was constructed.) These ideas lie obscured within the mind by its carnal and sensuous preoccupations with appetite (instincts) and matter. Descartes (1641) believed that ideas of God, mind, matter, and the elementary notions of logic, mathematics, and physics are innate. For Descartes the idea of God was like the signature of the creator upon his creation after the fashion of the Renaissance masters who signed their large canvases by painting a self-portrait into them, as did Michelangelo, for example, in his Sistine Chapel frescoes (although Michelangelo's self-image is by no means idealized or exalted).

The intensive sifting of mental contents involved in psychoanalysis has not uncovered any such innate ideas. Thus, the question that is posed for a psychoanalyst is, How could philosophers of the psychological genius of Plato or the mathematical and scientific genius of Descartes find the doctrine of innate ideas to be self-evident? It is true that Plato (Meno) attempted to demonstrate this aspect of his epistemology. But the demonstration consisted of such leading questions as would move a judge in a court of law to caution Socrates against leading the slave boy witness. Neither does the fact that an idea is clear and distinct (Descartes) prove that it is innate to the mind let alone that it is true. The idea that the shortest distance between two points is a straight line is clear and distinct and appears to the mind to be self-evidently true. But this idea actually owes its appearance of truth to the fact that our senses allow us only a circumscribed experience of objects and their motions in space. Perhaps we are entitled to wonder whether the belief that some metaphysicians have had in the innateness of ideas has a subjective origin.

A Psychogenetic Account of Innate Ideas

The subjective experience from which the doctrine takes its origin must be the impression that the ideas in question spring forth from the interior of the mind fully formed—that, in some sense, they have always been there—that they do not owe their origin to sense experience. The conviction of truth must arise from the vividness and intensity of this impression and the inevitable sense of mystery that attends it, a sense that parallels an attitude that people commonly have toward their dreams and that artists may experience in relation to their creative ideas. Psychoanalysis is able to offer us a natural history of the genesis of this experience and of the conviction of insight that accompanies it.

It is true that the human mind can, by means of its own operations, give rise to the idea of God during an early period of its development. Indeed, the first flowering of metaphysical speculation occurs approximately between the ages of 2 and 5 among normal, intelligent children, before formal education or serious religious indoctrination is begun. There is a natural religion that antedates institutional religion. Conversations with preschool children reveal their wonderfully constructed cosmological ideas, which regularly reinvent those of ancient cultures as, for example, in the question of a 3-year-old, "Daddy, if you built a big, big ladder could you fasten it to the sky with Scotch tape?" This question is premised on the idea that the sky is a solid crystalline sphere—an idea commonly found in ancient cultures. The most common image of God, spontaneously produced in the psyche of small children, is to be found in the family romance.

The family romance (Freud, 1909b) is born of the disappointments a child must encounter at the hands of his own parents. The romance is founded on the image of a perfectly caring and all-powerful father who, unlike the real father, will gladly satisfy all of the child's longings. In this image there is the seed of the idea of the *ens realisimus* who incorporates in his being every perfection that a child can conceive of. The real father, after all, is already magnified very far beyond his true proportions: He is invested, by means of a projective identification, with the narcissistic grandeur and overestimation of the child's own self during the earliest stage of his development. But the child painfully discovers that this demigod of a father not only fails him and disappoints him in many ways but also, greatest indignity of all, punishes his misdoings. These painful disappointments and fears give rise to the image of an alternative father who is more perfect than the real father and who becomes for the child, during this period of his life, his "true" father. This father is the father beyond the father—the prototypical image that contains the kernel of the idea of "being beyond being" and of qualitative "infinity." So convincing to the child is this image of the "true" father (and the "true" mother) that he will come to believe in them, and to fear that he has only been adopted by his real parents. It is not difficult to observe this anxiety in healthy children as they enter into the oedipal phase expressed in worried questions about whether or not their parents are really their parents.

This archaic image of an all-powerful being is the subjective precursor of the culturally sanctioned idea of God that the child is taught. This culturally sanctioned idea will usually have transferred into it the narcissistic investment of the spontaneously created image of the perfect father. This displacement is part of the process of repression, which brings about the dissolution of the Oedipus complex and its fateful psychological consequences: the mortification of the oedipal drive organization, the formation of the superego, and childhood amnesia. Henceforth, the archaic image of God and the experiences associated with it usually remain unconscious, but they also remain associatively linked to the conscious idea of God formed spontaneously by children by means of their own thought activity and shaped by culture through education. Religious instruction in the idea of God teaches children what they already "know."

This linkage is not a logical or cognitive one; but by means of it, unconscious primary process thought activities are able to influence conscious thought activity. For example, an obsessional individual becomes subject to uncertainty about having locked the doors to his house before going to bed, and soon he feels obliged to check the doors again despite his realistic thoughts to the contrary. What he knows to be real and true is rendered uncertain and ineffective by a nameless, unconsciously determined fear. Similarly the idea of God, in all of its variations, will acquire an influence upon conscious metaphysical speculations according to the force of the unconscious archaic images and memories in which it is psychologically rooted. In this way the later "metaphysical" stages of mental development in adolescence and old age are bound to and are influenced by the earliest one in childhood. The adult belief that one ultimately owes one's origin and allegiance to God, for example, is a repetition in modified form of its childhood precursor. The intensity of the "family romance" and the extent to which the resolution of the Oedipus complex has been achieved will subjectively decide the metaphysical attitude of the individual along a spectrum from skepticism to otherworldly piety. There are as many different systems of philosophy as there are types of human character.

I have focused on the father in the family romance in order to simplify the linkages between its central images and the idea of god. The expression "the 'true' mother" above is placed in parentheses for this reason only. The ancient Greeks paid homage to the place of their mothers in the formation of their idea of divinity in the originating role they assigned to Gaia, the earth mother in Hesiod's creation myth (*Theogony*). Modern children pay no less respect to their mothers through the enhancement of the object upon which their well-being and survival depend with transferred omnipotence. This "respect" finds its expression, for example, in the regressive, fusional, elational experience of being one with nature as a defense against oedipal conflicts. However, ancient Greek theogony (Hesiod, *Theogony*) also recognized the primary influence of the Oedipus complex in the lives of men and women and hence the eventual preeminence of the father. For although Uranus, the god of the sky, owed his origin to Gaia, his power over her grew until out of his sexual domination of her the gods and demons were created. Incited by his earth mother's complaints against Uranus, and armed by her with a scythe, the Titan Cronus castrated his father and established himself as king of the gods, only to be replaced by his son Zeus according to Uranus's curse. The influence of the earth mother is preserved in this dark genealogy unfolding in the depths of the cosmos, but it is the phallic father Zeus who dominates in the end. The genealogy of ancient Greek gods corresponds to the libidinal development of moderns. Girls switch their primary investment from their mothers to their fathers in the course of normal development. Boys normally form only a secondary homosexual submissive attachment to their fathers, but their castration anxiety and their feelings of phallic inferiority invest the object of this attachment with awe.

Family romances of patients provide evidence for this gender-differentiated phallocentrism of the Oedipus complex. A patient who had been cruelly abandoned by her father during childhood and who had suffered a severe enhancement of her infantile feelings of narcissistic injury had a family romance in which such enormous wealth had been bestowed upon her by her "true" doting father that she would never have to need anything or anybody but everybody would need her (Hanly, 1982). The shadow of the mother with whom she was abandoned by the father was to be found as well in the theme of bountifulness, but the endowment was to come from the father. Another female patient, at a crucial juncture of her analysis, had a family romance dream in which the theme emerged of a father who would have a libidinal interest in her, prefer her to the ideal mother (who in the dream was dispatched to the kitchen to prepare food), and who would exercise an exalting moral refinement. Her real father was a debauched and crude alcoholic. She could experience her sensual feelings for him only as disgust, her respect for him as fear, and her love for him as hate. The reawakening and repetition of her family romance in the transference eventually allowed her to begin to experience sexual fulfillment with her husband. The morality of the idealized "true" father was not dreamed in order to prohibit the oedipal wish but both to permit and to limit it.

A male patient in childhood believed himself to be the son of a great foreign military family who would surpass his ancestors in heroism and success in war. Waiting in a cloister for his return from battle was his virginal sweetheart (mother). His neurosis consisted largely of a latent homosexual defense against anxiety enhanced by a real mother whose complaints about the father and expectations of the son encouraged him to believe that his fantasy could and had to be made true. Where genuine courage and strength of character might have been, there was a faltering, presumptuous, timid bravado. Another patient formed a family romance out of stories told him by his mother. His "true" father had been a powerful and wealthy aristocrat altogether "above" his real tradesman father. Evidently it was the *droit du seigneur* that had made this variant of the family romance so personally appealing to this young aspirant, no less than the way in which the aristocrat is entitled to order tradesmen about. As an adult he had to revive some version of the fantasy while having sexual intercourse in order that its narcissistic gratifications could compensate for the loss of pleasure imposed by a psychical impotence caused by guilt and fear (Hanly, 1984). In these male versions of the family romance the mother appears as the object of libidinal interest, but the father has to be vanquished in order to consummate it. The phallus and he who bears it thus come to acquire a position of equal but different importance in the fantasy life of girls and boys.

However, the picture is not even as simple as this account would make it. It not uncommonly happens that monotheistic deities (who united what Greek polytheism had kept separate) are bisexual and have both male and female characteristics (Hanly, 1970b). We may speculate that, at the phallic stage of development, the positive and negative forms of the Oedipus complex, which provide for an ambiguous experience of sexual identity, may also give rise to the idea that what is divine (most perfect in every respect) unites maternity and paternity. This idea could then be the precursor of more rationalized and abstracted philosophical ideas of deity as self-generative (*causa sui*). If it seems absurd to treat the idea, in the example above, of a powerful aristocrat (who is, after all, quite finite and mortal) as a precursor of the idea of God, we should remind ourselves for a moment of the cognitive life of preschool children. It is easy to observe small children who can use the numbers "one" and "two" correctly, who know that "three" follows "two" and can use "three" correctly to identify classes of three, but who also use the number to express any greater number of things, exactly as the ancient Greeks used "myriad" (literally, 10,000). There are "three!" cookies in a large tin full of them. The night sky has "three!" stars. These uses of "three!" or its equivalent are expressed with a solemnity and awe befitting the immeasurable or infinite. If fathers within the ken of a small boy are responsible for cars, houses, buildings, bridges, crops, and so forth, then a father whom he believes to be responsible for these fathers must seem to him more powerful and perfect than he can comprehend, and thus becomes a fitting object in which to invest the residues of omnipotence carried over from the earlier stages of his life. And further factors may also exercise their influence.

The "family romance" may itself undergo a significant variation. If, as a result of trauma, disappointment in a child should be intensified into violent, helpless rage when his ego is still very imperfectly developed, his psyche may be forced to submit him to powerful hallucinatory experiences of divine and demonic beings. These projected beings acquire the status of a vision of omnipotent agencies of good and evil beyond the world revealed to the child by his normal perceptions.

It must be fully appreciated that these fantasies and hallucinatory objects come to have a special reality for the developing mind in the period of their occurrence. The typical mode of perceptual experience during this early period of life is animistic and magical. Children of this age are subject to omnipotence of thought. Even in the absence of trauma, children often have imaginary friends. These factors limit the capacity of children for reality testing. The fantasies and hallucinatory experiences are powerfully charged with wishful ideas, affects, and fears. They represent either the gratifications of these dangerous impulses, and hatred (the demonic), or defenses against them, and love (the divine). The force of their investment gives to these ideas their special meaning, reality, and truth in the mind of the child. They acquire the quality of a visual revelation because the mind is not aware of their subjective origin, the issue of unconscious thought processes. The fantasy or hallucinatory experience will have enabled the ego of the child to survive a period of real psychological peril, and its psychic usefulness in the life of the child will give to it a position of importance in subsequent development. If, later, the ego is endangered sufficiently to cause regression, the unconscious constellation of ideas made up of these memories will recapture its influence upon conscious thought activity (Hanly, 1984).

We may, then, ask ourselves whether the metaphysical doctrine of innate ideas owes its origin to a partial "return of the repressed." The original memories of the family romance and of religious hallucinations, as well as the experiences bound up with them, do not become conscious. But the cathexis of these memories is increased by the regression. This cathexis is then distributed forward, as it were, onto the conscious metaphysical ideas, causing them to appear as though they had arisen from the mind itself. It dawns upon the conscious ego, under such circumstances, that these ideas have a mysterious origin within the mind itself. And this impression contains a kernel of truth: The archaic originals were in reality created by the mind. The ego is left at the mercy of an impression it cannot correctly comprehend and may easily idealize into an ontology. The ontological argument (which seeks to derive the existence of God from the idea of God) is an attempt of reason to rationalize the conviction of ontological truth that has its origin in this vicissitude of man's psychic development (see also Feuer, 1968).

Language, Animism, and the Belief in the Innate

The account I have given of the psychogenesis of the doctrine of innate ideas has an evident inadequacy. It accounts for only one of a great variety of ideas that have been accorded this status by metaphysicians. The idea of God may be thought to be the most important candidate: But what of the ideas of natural kinds, the elements of mathematics and logic, moral and aesthetic ideals, ideas of substances, all of which have also been elevated to this special epistemological status? An additional hypothesis of greater generality is evidently required.

It is seems certain that when language was first developed by our ancient ancestors they experienced words as being magically conatural with the objects to which they referred. This experience of the meaning of language was part of the animism that globally invested primitive man's perceptions and thoughts no less than his imaginings. Although this experience of language had been culturally transcended by the time of Plato, it still recurred then, as it does today in the earliest stage of the mental development of each person. This attitude to language represents the most primitive idea of knowing—to be identified with something and thus to partake of the nature of that thing. The child first learns who he is and who his parents are by identifying with them. According to this rudimentary model, words are identified with the things they name; and to use the name for a thing correctly is to know that thing. For the same reason, words were thought to describe things. A thing was either properly or not properly named, as though a question of truth or falsehood were at stake. The ancient Greeks, for example, believed that Helen of Troy, wife of Menelaus, was properly so named because she was "Hell-on" men, "Hell-on" ships and "Hell-on" cities (Woodbury, 1958). Had she not been named Helen, her parents would have made a mistake; they would have falsely named her. Small children still take narcissistic pleasure in learning that their names connote some desirable quality, as "Richard" connotes "bravery." This belief about language is one aspect of the omnipotence of thought in which the animism of ancient people and of contemporary children are alike grounded.

This way of experiencing language is the source of its magical use. Word magic, in turn, is linked with the belief that all objects are, like human beings, endowed with an animate psychic life that governs their behavior. The following anecdote illustrates this facet of the life of children. One of my children, when she was 2, picked up my watch to play with it, only to have it slip from her grasp and fall onto a tile floor. I chided her for this, whereupon without hesitation she turned again to the watch where I had placed it on a low shelf and, wagging her finger admonishingly at it, she told it to be good and not to fall on the floor again. The premise of the child's behavior is that the being of the object is conatural with her own. Animism in all of its essentials repeats itself in the psychic life of modern children.

However, animistic forms of thought are never completely extinguished. They recur in the dreams and parapraxes of everyday psychic life of normal adults and in the symptoms of neurosis. In dreams the body of the dreamer appears as though it were magically responsive to the volitions derived from the dream wishes: Thus, in dreams one is able to perform actions that defy gravity. Dreaming is influenced by the nocturnal regression (formal regression) to an omnipotence of thought, which is never extinguished but only kept in abeyance by the mature, rational forms of thought and experience of daily adult life (Freud, 1900). Similarly, when we commit a parapraxis, for example, a temporary amnesia such as forgetting the name of an individual, we are engaging in a magical attempt to harm him by treating his name with contempt. Or again, the ritualized behavior of the obsessional neurotic is aimed at altering a painful reality. Lady Macbeth compulsively washed her hands, trying magically to cleanse her soul of the murder she had persuaded her husband to commit by washing the guilt (blood) from them. Omnipotence of thought can and too often does also intrude upon the conscious, rational thought activities of adults.

Innate Ideas and the Omnipotence of Thought

The doctrine of innate ideas in metaphysics in all of its forms owes its plausibility to the omnipotence of thought. The doctrine is a significant advance in thought insofar as it is no longer the word that is thought to be conatural with the object it names, but the idea of the object; nevertheless, the narcissistic exaggeration of the scope and power of the psyche is evident enough in the belief that there are subjective mental contents that are complete and perfect instruments for knowing the objects of nature because they are conatural with the natures (laws of being, forms, essences) that give existence to and fix the nature of the objects that make up the world. In order to know the nature of things, it is only necessary to intuit certain epistemologically privileged mental contents: The secrets of the universe lie locked up in the human mind itself. In this way the basic concepts of a philosopher's system of ideas such as Plato's ideas of forms or Descartes's ideas of substance (*res extensa* and *res cogitans*) can acquire the privileged status of innateness. The innateness of moral and aesthetic ideals can, similarly, be shown to be an illusion of consciousness caused by the archaic identifications that form the nucleus of the superego and that remain unconsciously influential. These narcissistically invested images will be seen to have an additional relevance below.

Thought and the Thinker

It must be acknowledged that, although the psychological process through which this transformation of the subjective force and significance of ideas come about may be comprehended in a general way, the specifics of these processes in the development of the thought of great individual metaphysicians such as Plato and Descartes is not and cannot be thoroughly understood. One can surmise that some personal intensification of anxiety precipitated a regression that withdrew drive energy from objects resulting in an intensification of narcissism that constructed intellectual defenses against painful realities (Freud, 1914, 1915, 1923a; Hanly, 1982). The generalized and depersonalized nature of these anxieties is evident enough in the thought of Plato and Descartes. In Plato's thought the dread of animality, of the material and the instinctual, is pervasive (see Chapter Eight). In Descartes's thought the fear of the loss of reality—of depersonalization and derealization—at the hands of the Malignant Deceiver underlies the *Meditations*. It is the narcissistic overestimation of the power and status of ideas that generates the conviction of their unique, intrinsic epistemological worth. On Plato's "line" and in the allegory of the cave the ideas of objects are more real than the objects themselves (Plato, *Republic, VII*). For Descartes (1641), only the clarity and distinctness of ideas can dispel the shadows of skepticism cast everywhere by the thought of the Malignant Deceiver. We are presented here, not so much with the return *of* the repressed, but with a formal return *to* the repressed via a regression to omnipotence of thought. This regression does not remove repressions of the memories of childhood. It involves, however, a narcissistic intensification of ideas associated with these memories, which causes them to appear to the ego as though they were its innate possessions rather than its hard-won acquisitions.

This conjecture is strengthened by the fact that the empiricist tradition in philosophy, from Democritus and Epicurus to Locke, has been premised upon the recognition of the ontological priority of things over ideas. Locke (1690), for example, had this to say about the ontological argument:

> For the having the idea of anything in our mind, no more proves the existence of that thing, than the picture of a man evidences his being in the world, or the visions of a dream make thereby a true history. (p.365)

The empiricist tradition in philosophy and science has a more secure footing in the distinction between fantasy and reality, and is accordingly more rational, than rationalism or idealism, which exaggerates the ontological status of ideas or other mental contents and processes.

Two Modern Philosophical Versions of Innatism

The metaphysics of innateness is by no means exhausted by Platonism and Cartesianism. Although Kant rejected the Cartesian doctrine of innate ideas, he substituted for it the proposal that certain rules of understanding, such as causality and the attribution of properties to substances, are both innate to the mind and also apply necessarily to the natural world because they are preconditions for knowing it. Although these categories of understanding do not have any content (in the sense that they already connote the nature of the events that are causally related or the nature of the substances that have properties), Kant (1781) believed that they nevertheless impose upon experience and thought structures without which knowledge of objects would be impossible. Accordingly, in Kant's view, it is the mind that lays down the general condition for objectivity, and in that sense, the mind is the ground of the objectivity of nature. The mind is the ultimate lawgiver, if only of nature insofar as it is able to make an impression of itself upon the human mind, that is, as it appears to us to be.

Although Kant's *Critique of Pure Reason* is an attack on metaphysics, the weapons Kant chose for his attack constitute, as Paton (1936) has noted in the title of his study of Kant, a *Metaphysic of Experience*. It is not enough for our concept of causality to develop gradually via infantile animism to the empirically tested principles of science and common sense. It must owe its origin to something more elevated than the merely pragmatic commerce of the senses and thought with the natural world. The "synthetic unity of apperception" must insist upon its prerogative of imposing conditions upon an otherwise potentially errant nature in order to vouchsafe its lawfulness, order, objectivity and intelligibility.

In Kant, omnipotence of thought has abandoned the Platonic and Cartesian positions, which lay claim to innate ideas and intrinsic knowledge of reality. But the retreat is only partial: The Kantian mind still retains a form of juridical omnipotence over knowledge and nature. What is abandoned is the claim to an inherent knowledge of things as they are in themselves. What is retained is the belief that the natural world as we can know it is ruled by laws imposed by the human mind.

Kant's categories of the understanding (as well as space and time, his pure forms of intuition) have two faces. Like the face of Michelangelo's famous statue of David, which regarded from one side presents the aspect of a serene, courageous, idealized youth, and from the other a troubled, angry, depressed man, Kant's categories present themselves as purely epistemological rules for the formation of cognitive judgments on the one side, and on the other as dynamic organizing principles of experience, and, via experience, of nature. In fact, it is on account of their dynamic, regulatory function that they acquire their epistemological status as synthetic *a priori* principles.

What is the source of the belief that the idea of causality has this legislative, juridical character? Logical rules have a constraining influence upon the thought of individuals for whom rationality and consistency are ideals. Persons react with anxiety and painful feelings of inadequacy to infractions of the rule of consistency in their thought. It was not always so. The capacity of logic to regulate thinking is not an intrinsic property of logical ideas or of the logical operations of the mind. To a certain extent the logical organization of conscious thought activity is sanctioned by the reality principle and survival. To think logically is to keep in touch with reality and to be safe, but these sanctions are not sufficient in themselves. Logic guarantees truth only if the premises to which logical reasoning is applied are true. Logic leads a deceived person only further into deception. Psychotic thought can be masterful in its logical consistency and remain all the more fantastic. Logical rules also acquire their regulatory capacity as a result of the formation of the superego along with the related capacities for self-observation, self-evaluation, and self-motivation (Freud, 1923a; Waelder, 1934). This capacity depends, originally, upon the idealized parental images and the capacity of these cathected images to act as internal agencies that proscribe and prescribe thought and conduct, including perceptual conduct. Examples are the parental injunctions "Be kind to others" and "Do not tell lies," which, with the development of the superego, the child is able to apply to himself. Thus, the ego, having developed this capacity, acquires the sense of itself as a lawgiving agency: an agency that prescribes and proscribes what may and may not be experienced and how it may be experienced; what may and may not be thought and how thought should proceed; what may and may not be done and in what way. This inner awareness of self, by the ego, is no illusion. What is an illusion is the belief that this agency can extend beyond the self to the objects of nature. In Kant's thought a return to the repressed omnipotence of thought converts a kernel of psychological truth into the grandiose structure of a metaphysic of experience. All illusions, including this illusion of Kant's, have psychological functions to perform. Kant's pure forms of intuition and his categories of understanding offer the reassuring idea that nature is regulated by the laws that regulate the mind itself (Feuer, 1970). Kant, like Cézanne in a very different medium of expression, felt obliged to "join the erring hands of nature."

Ironically, this narcissistic factor in metaphysical thought (the projection of self into nature) is present even in the underlying assumptions of linguistic analysis, a philosophy that was explicitly aimed at the destruction of metaphysics. Linguistic philosophy seeks to trace philosophical ideas, such as Descartes's idea that the mind is a thinking substance, to a confusion caused by language. In language, nouns such as proper names have the function of naming objects. The noun "Freud" in the sentence "Freud was the founder of psychoanalysis" refers to the person who founded psychoanalysis. A word such as "mind" can also function as a noun in diverse sentences—for example, "The mind is able to perceive objects." Would it not, then, be all too easily supposed that the word "mind" names a thing just as the noun "Freud" names a person? And is it not, also, just as easily supposed that the mind is a thing akin to a person or other natural object—a mental substance? Thus, linguistic analysis presupposes that certain ambiguities in the logical grammar of language (e.g., the fact that abstract nouns may be the subjects of sentences as readily as may proper nouns) can exercise an insidious influence upon philosophical and theoretical thinking.

Linguistic philosophy conceived of itself as a therapy for thought misguided by language. In psychoanalysis one does not cure a patient's paranoid fear of being attacked by trying to show him that his fears are objectively groundless. Similarly, linguistic philosophers do not seek to refute directly the Cartesian notion of independent mental substance by, for example, assembling facts from neurology or elsewhere that point to the dependency of all mental activities upon the brain. Instead, just as analysts will try to make a paranoid patient aware of the source of his fear in repressed homosexual desires, the linguistic philosopher will try to make metaphysically confused philosophers aware of the linguistic origins of their leading ideas. The choice of this clarifying metaphor is historically justified by the fact that the Oxford linguistic school derived its view of philosophy as a therapy for our use of language from Wittgenstein, who in turn derived it from psychoanalysis (Hanly, 1972).

The basic unacknowledged assumption of linguistic analysis, the acknowledgment of which led to its demise, was that the structure of things could be found in the logical grammar of the languages we use to describe them. Inherent in this idea there is a belief in a special congruence between language and objects such that our thoughts will always be reality bound as long as we use the correct logical grammar. But language is a social and cultural artifact. It owes its existence to human behavior and thought activity. Thus, we come again upon the omnipotence of thought. Just as Helen was properly so named, so language is properly used only when, for example, dispositional expressions are substituted for expressions employing abstract substantives. The philosophers who make these substitutions can be vouchsafed an understanding of things as they are; others, who do not, become lost in darkness and confusion. In this conviction one finds not the invidious influence of language but the insidious influence of narcissism.

Linguistic philosophy has a second historical connection with psychoanalysis. Although philosophers no longer take Ryle and ordinary language philosophy seriously, it is of interest to note that certain psychoanalysts, prominent among them Schafer (1976, 1978), have used these philosophical ideas (the dispositional nature of mental terms) and arguments (translation into adverbial expressions) as weapons against metapsychology. This enterprise appears to be motivated, in part, by two beliefs: first, that the use of abstract substantive terms such as "the instinctual unconscious" or "the superego" has a detrimental effect upon clinical interpretive work with patients; second, that the use of abstract substantive terms in theory building involves a distorting reification of persons and their psychic lives. It is as though these psychoanalysts believe that the use of these terms will theoretically cause psychoanalysts who do so to make such interpretations as "Your id is making you want to offer yourself to me sexually because it makes you afraid that it wants to attack me," instead of "Your wish to offer yourself to me sexually covers over a wish to attack me." But if there are psychoanalysts who make interpretations in this fashion, no amount of translating terms such as "the id" into adverbial qualifications of dispositional terms would help. The real problem would be a psychological one—a defensive countertransference reaction to the patients' conflict that causes them to dehumanize and distance both the patient and corresponding conflicts in themselves. It is a form of magical thinking to suppose that one can solve countertransference problems by taking special care when theorizing never to use an abstract, substantive term. Similarly, it is an overestimation, and misunderstanding, of the power of words to suppose that an abstract substantive must have the function of naming a thing. And it is equally an overestimation of the power of words to suppose that by adopting a particular grammatical style one can avoid misunderstanding whatever it is one is seeking to describe and explain. Avoiding the use of the terms "id", "ego", and "superego" in theoretical discourse adds nothing to one's grasp of the nature of the psychic processes in individuals that they denote. Freud's use of theoretical terms was always highly sophisticated logically and epistemologically. Freud (1900) cautioned his readers to treat the topographical model as nothing more than a scaffolding upon which one could climb up to get a better view of the building (the mind) and never to confuse it with the building itself. Freud (1900, 1917a) was perfectly well aware and unequivocally stated his awareness that his spatial models were devices for clarifying the nature of temporal relationships among intrapsychic processes. Freud (1915), in discussing the role of instinct theory in psychoanalysis, demonstrated his exceptional grasp of the place of hypothetical thinking in theory construction. The philosophical attack on Freud's metapsychology is launched against one of its most impregnable positions. Freud made it perfectly clear that the terms "id," "ego," and "superego" do not refer to any objects at all, let alone Platonic forms or Cartesian substances; they refer rather to groups of psychic processes, activities, and contents that form parts of the total psychic lives of individuals and that can be relatively, significantly, and usefully differentiated in terms of their development, functions, and interrelations.

Objections Considered

There are two obvious objections to the line of argument of this chapter. It does not explore the reasons these philosophers (Plato, Descartes, Kant, and the Oxford philosophers) had for adopting their various forms of the doctrine of innate ideas. Moreover, to claim that the doctrine has psychological roots in the unconscious does not tell us anything about the truth or falsity of the doctrine itself. Certain psychoanalytic findings have a direct bearing on these issues.

Plato understood the failure of the many to recover the innate ideas with which their souls were stored to be the result of an amnesia caused by the trauma of incarnation. Psychoanalysis involves the removal of the common amnesia of early childhood because amnesia is the mechanism of one of the major defenses—repression. Among the many mental contents that are recovered as a result of psychoanalytic work, ideas of forms are never found. Descartes blamed the failure to recover innate ideas on willful inattention. Psychic avoidance or "inattention" is also something that psychoanalysis is at pains to undo. Of all the painful wishes and memories uncovered by the analysis of defensive avoidance, never has it occurred that what an individual has striven to overlook in himself is a Cartesian innate idea. Similarly, splitting of the ego does occur, and it results in perceptual and intellectual confusion. But it is never found that it is Kantian categories of the understanding that restore unity and harmony to the functioning of the ego or clarity and realism to a person's perceptual life. Neither has the reality-testing capacity of an individual ever been improved by his learning to abandon "reifying" substantive usages in favor of adjectival or adverbial expressions. Many thousands of psychoanalytic hours of minute observation of psychic life have failed to uncover data that could lend credence to the doctrine of innateness in any of its forms.

Psychoanalytic findings support the idea that all of our concepts are empirical. Einstein (1921), on behalf of the physical sciences, has set out a compelling pragmatic argument against the elevation of ideas to *a priori* status:

> I am [wrote Einstein] convinced that the philosophers have had a harmful effect upon the progress of scientific thinking in removing certain fundamental concepts from the domain of empiricism where they are under our control to the intangible heights of the *a priori*. (p. 2)

There is some reason to think that the various forms of the doctrine of innateness cannot be substantiated and, therefore, that the intense conviction that they are true has primarily a psychological origin that then motivates the search for supporting rationalizations. If this is true, then the meaning of the doctrine must be interpreted psychologically and its truth must be similarly understood.

The human mind is fundamentally conservative in the sense that a pleasure once known is not relinquished except by finding a substitute (Freud, 1915). The various forms of the idea that the secrets of life and the universe lie locked away in the recesses of the human mind provide a substitute compatible with mature forms of thought for the child's narcissistic, triumphant ecstasy at thinking himself able to master the world by means of thoughts and words alone. Omnipotence of thought is adaptive in childhood because the child is in reality quite helpless, and omnipotence reduces the anxiety to which he would otherwise be subject. The derivatives of the omnipotence of thought remain psychologically adaptive for the same reason for adults. They are the ideational expression of the unconscious thought "I need not fear life or the world for they are my constructions." (I have not touched upon the doctrines of existentialism and phenomenology here. It is obvious that a similar analysis would apply to this same element in these philosophies; Hanly, 1979, 1985.) The problem with the doctrine of innate ideas, as Einstein's statement suggests, is that, like all denials, it interferes with reality testing, which is the only method we have for gaining knowledge that will allow us to reduce our helplessness.

Psychologically, the doctrine of innateness is, then, a residue of the stage of omnipotence of thought through which each person must pass in the course of his psychic development. It is a repetition in a circumscribed area of thought of a belief that was once an inevitable and psychologically correct, although illusory, impression of the global nature of all thought. Two psychological truths find expression in distorted form in the doctrine of innate ideas. Everyone must pass through a stage of omnipotence of thought in the course of his development. The events of that period are fateful for, and, in part, hold the key to the mystery of, our own individual destiny in life. But the mind does not innately possess the secrets either of life or of the universe. In the end, the psychoanalytic point of view is Socratic.

Innate Ideas in Freud's Theory

Yet it must be acknowledged that Freud felt compelled to find a place for innateness in psychoanalytic theory itself. The innate possessions of the mind, referred to by Freud as its archaic heritage, do not include memories of the soul's preexistence (Plato), ideas of God and substance (Descartes), or even the collective unconscious (Jung, 1936–1954), stored as that is supposed to be with abstract and spiritual remnants of ancestral religious experience (Glover, 1950). But Freud did at various times store it with instinctual ambivalence (Freud, 1915), the Oedipus complex (Freud, 1919a, 1923a, 1939), castration anxiety (Freud, 1939, 1940), dream symbols (Freud, 1939, 1940), primal scene fantasies (Freud, 1918, 1939), and defence preference (Freud, 1937). Freud did not increase the credibility of these speculations by his adherence to a Lamarckian explanation of their occurrence as inheritances of acquired characteristics. These residues of experience were supposed to be transferred to the genetic material as a consequence of trauma or repetition (Freud, 1923a). Because morality is, according to Freud's primal horde theory, a male acquisition, women are supposed to acquire the psychic potentials necessary for its development through cross-inheritance. None of these ideas—inheritance of traumatic or repetitive experiences, or cross-inheritance of morality—are scientifically tenable. Freud (1939) believed that one should give to individual life experience (ontogeny) its full due in explaining psychic phenomena; but, having done so, he believed that psychoanalytic clinical investigations of dreams and neurosis come upon residuals (universal dream symbols, the Oedipus complex, and castration anxiety) that can only be accounted for by genetic inheritance (phylogeny). Freud also believed that these assumptions were necessary to the link between individual and group psychology.

There are several issues here. Freud continued to rely upon the idea of the inheritance of acquired characteristics even though he was aware that it had been scientifically discredited and he had been long familiar (since his teens) with the powerful role played by natural selection in evolution (Jones, 1957). Freud believed that his theory required the inheritance of ancestral memories, but it does not.

Freud's theory, as he formulated it, does not require that the ancestral experience of wishing to kill the father out of love for the mother be inherited in the form of a memory that acts as a template for organizing the male child's experience of the phallic stage. All that is required is that there should occur in childhood, in about the fourth year, a preconscious intensification of phallic libido. The dominant tendency of the experiences arising out of the child's earlier anaclitic attachment to the mother are sufficient to account for the investment of this libido in her. What person, other than his beloved mother who has always cared for his needs, could merit this increased sensual erotic excitement with its ill-defined promise of new pleasures? Rivalry with the father and the wish to get rid of him follow from the libidinal demand for the mother that dominates the son. The fear of castration does not require the awakening of an inherited memory; it is the natural consequence of the child's phallic ambition joined to the advent of intensified phallic pleasurable sensitivity. The child comes to fear the loss of what he has come to value next to life itself and that he knows to be the source of his wish to remove his father. In the imagination of the son, where else would the father's retaliation for the son's dark purposes be aimed? It is the need to mitigate this fear that then sets in motion the processes out of which the superego is formed. Nothing here requires the postulate of a phylogenetic inheritance of the Oedipus complex, castration anxiety, or the superego insofar as choice of defense is concerned. The exigencies of the oedipal situation sufficiently mandate the identifications, repressions, reaction formations, and sublimations. The identifications themselves select the details of the choices of sublimation. Everything here is compatible with Locke's cornerstone of empiricism, the tabula rasa hypothesis, which he forged as a weapon with which to attack Cartesian innate ideas. A different account but with the same import can be given of the parallel development in girls.

The generality of dream symbols and the occurrence of primal-scene fantasies in one form or another in many people do not require their explanation in terms of the inheritance of unconscious ancestral memories. Symbolic representation is expedient for thinking about anything the contemplation of which arouses anxiety. Infantile sexuality, combined with the common, inevitable exigencies of the human infant's situation, can account for the commonality one finds in the unconscious symbols and fantasies in adults—a commonality that is circumscribed by culture and the accidents of individual life.

The disproportion that may exist between the impact of a pathogenic experience in the life of a child and the external circumstances that gave rise to it can also be accounted for by psychoanalysis without recourse to phylogenetic inheritance. In the case of Little Hans, for example, Freud (1909a), unlike the boy's father, did not attribute the intensification of the child's fear of his father to an increase in his libidinal attachment to his mother resulting from her allowing the little boy into bed with her while on holiday, but to a spontaneous intensification of Hans's libido. The spontaneous intensification of libido that accompanies the onset of the phallic phase in humans is no doubt genetically programmed, but it no more requires the guidance of an inherited memory than the sucking reflex, which is spontaneously activated in the womb, requires an inherited memory of the breast. In general, spontaneous shifts of libido, earlier traumatic life events, object failures, fixations, regressions, and the common exigencies of the human situation are sufficient to account for the disproportion that appears between the immediate stimulus and the response to it.

Why did Freud advocate a concept that he knew to be at odds with his knowledge of the mechanisms of evolution? If ancestral experience can be transmitted, one's own mind shares directly in itself in the heritage of the past and has the potential to contribute something of itself as an inheritance to future generations. In this there is a kind of impersonal immortality. If the mind is, as Freud supposed, unable to altogether renounce a gratification once known, perhaps the stubbornness with which he clung to the inheritance of acquired characteristics derived from an unconscious retention of some infantile omnipotence (Jones, 1957). The link is suggested in Freud's (1917b) letter to Karl Abraham, about a project with Ferenczi:

> The idea is to put Lamarck entirely on our ground and to show that the "necessity" that according to him creates and transforms organs is nothing but the power of unconscious ideas over one's own body, of which we see remnants in hysteria, in short the "omnipotence of thoughts."

There is an undercurrent of magical thinking in this idea. Thought, driven by narcissism, can create the illusion of transformed organs but not the reality. Schur (1972) considered this idea to be a return of a belief in the omnipotence of thought in Freud as distinct from an analysis of it, that is, a causal explanation of it. Gay (1988) links Freud's Lamarckianism with his sense of racial identity as a Jew, a link that Freud (1939) made in general terms when he sought to explain national character by means of the inheritance of ancestral memories.

If some such explanation is correct, it only exemplifies the truth of Freud's (1927) psychology of religion. The anxieties to which human beings are inevitably subject cause them to devote some part of their original narcissism to the task of defying reality, if only by means of an illusion. Freud refused the traditional consolation of religion. He may have clung unwittingly to his own version of immortality.

Ethical Theories
Kant, Hobbes, and Mill

This attempt to use psychoanalysis to construct a unified moral theory employs a method of theoretical analysis and comparison. The moral theories explored in this way are those of Hobbes (1651), Mill (1863), and Kant (1785). Although there is no psychoanalytic study of the life and thought of Hobbes, there are such studies of Mill (Mazlish, 1975) and of Kant (Feuer, 1970). The argument of this chapter does not draw upon them, however, because its emphasis is thrown upon the ideas themselves rather than upon their origins in the life experiences and characters of their creators. It does not even attempt the psychogenic accounts of certain types of philosophical ideas of the kind found in Chapter Three.

One could reasonably suppose that there were certain libidinal determinants involved in the different forms of submission to authority found in the moral philosophies of Hobbes, Mill, and Kant. It is plausible that masochism would be needed to underwrite with secret pleasure the extent of this submission thought necessary by Hobbes for social existence. Psychoanalysts are familiar with the excited pleasure homosexual feelings engender in men at the prospect of a forced submission to an overpowering male. Kant's categorical imperative seems to be rooted in a moral masochism, which takes a hidden pleasure in the pain of self-imposed resignation. These possibilities raise questions that the following analysis does not seek to answer.

Even so there is an objection sometimes raised by philosophers to even the limited objectives of a comparative study at a theoretical level. These philosophers claim that philosophical discourse has nothing in common with psychoanalytic discourse: They are logically and conceptually distinct domains of inquiry. This objection implies that there are no psychoanalytic propositions that, if true, would falsify a proposition of moral philosophy. Contradiction is a logical relationship and thus implies at least some common domain of discourse. Hobbes's postulate that there is no capacity for self-restraint in human nature is false if the psychoanalytic theory of the normal resolution of the Oedipus complex is true. Kant's postulate of an uncaused will with an unlimited capacity to cause behavior is false if the psychoanalytic postulate of psychic determinism is true. Mill's concept of the work of the pleasure principle is at odds with the psychoanalytic concept. The immunity thesis, which seeks to protect philosophy from contact with empirical sciences such as psychoanalysis, is unsound. If it were sound, it would have the effect of isolating philosophy from science and life, thus rendering it pure, abstract, irrefutable, and irrelevant. The counterpart in the study of literature is the idea, examined in Chapter Two, that works of literature form a self-contained universe of discourse that is independent of life.

The premise of this study is that philosophical theories of morality (and other branches of philosophy that take human nature as their subject matter) contain explicit or implicit psychological ideas. It is these ideas that provide the basis for a comparative study with psychoanalysis.

The specific point of departure for this inquiry is the far-reaching disparities among philosophical ethical theories. Hobbes, Mill, and Kant have been chosen for this reason, and because they are modern without being contemporary; the ideas of other classical philosophers are considered elsewhere in this work.

I shall argue that psychoanalytic findings concerning the genesis and nature of morality provide a basis for constructing a unified moral theory that can integrate the partial, and often opposed, insights of three classical moral theories: the contractualism of Hobbes, the utilitarianism of Mill, and the duty morality (deontology) of Kant. I shall also argue that psychoanalysis provides a naturalistic understanding of the role of duty in moral behavior. Finally, I shall elaborate briefly, from a psychoanalytic point of view, the fallibility of moral judgment—what one might call the psychopathology of conscience.

Moral philosophy no less than other branches of philosophy is governed by contradictions and dichotomies that result in endless disputes. Lazerowitz (1964, 1968) has put forward a hypothesis to explain the undecidability of philosophical questions: that philosophical theories involve altered uses of language that apparently tell us something about obscure aspects of reality but that, in fact, originate in and find their meaning in unconscious wishes. One is left with the impression that moral experience must be highly individualized: How otherwise could philosophers of roughly equal (if unusual) intellectual gifts come to such disparate conclusions when they reflect upon it?

The problem is more than an intellectual one. The worth of human existence, even human existence itself, depends upon the moral values and imperatives by which people live. A coherent, realistic understanding of morality is a perennially urgent need that, thus far at least, philosophy has not been able to meet. I propose to explore the extent to which the understanding of the psychology of morals developed by psychoanalysis could lead toward a more adequate understanding of morality.

Disagreements among Three Philosophers Concerning the Foundations of Morality

These conflicting differences in moral philosophy become evident when one compares the moral philosophies of Hobbes (1651), Mill (1863), and Kant (1785). Hobbes based morality on a fundamentally egoistic attitude modified by the anxious realization that a life of unqualified self-interest would be "solitary, poor, nasty, brutish, and short." Hobbes tells us, in effect, that, constitutionally, man is an amoral, self-seeking, aggressive animal who is prepared to steal from others what he cannot make for himself. As Freud (1930) stated it:

> men are not gentle creatures who want to be loved, and who at the most can defend themselves if they are attacked; they are, on the contrary, creatures among whose instinctual endowments is to be reckoned a powerful share of aggressiveness. As a result, their neighbour is for them not only a potential helper or sexual object, but also someone who tempts them to satisfy their aggressiveness on him, to exploit his capacity to work without compensation, to use him sexually without his consent, to seize his possessions, to humiliate him, to cause him pain, to torture and to kill him. *Homo homini lupus.* (p. 111)

Moreover, according to Hobbes, man's only subjective means of controlling his acquisitive drives are his attempts to gratify them directly. Human survival has, consequently, depended upon man's reason—his capacity to calculate the consequences of his actions and to react with appropriate anxiety to the calamity this calculation predicts. It is this realistically anxious perception of the consequences of the unmodified pursuit of egoistical aims that brings into force what Hobbes conceived as the second and third laws of nature: the willingness to forgo actions against others that one would not want to have perpetrated against oneself and, to this extent, to circumscribe one's own liberty as long as others are prepared to similarly circumscribe theirs (second law); and, then, to accept the means necessary for preserving this compromise (third law) (see also Gauthier, 1982). Morality is a compromise between what individuals most want (the ability with impunity to force others to satisfy their desires) and what individuals least want (being forced to satisfy the desires of others without compensation or revenge). Hobbes's myth of man in a state of nature is, in this respect, similar to Freud's (1913b) myth of the primal horde, the brothers in which were forced to adopt the first, primitive form of justice and social regulation because they realized that what they had done— murdered their father to gain his position, power, and privileges for themselves—each was prepared to do to any other for the same reason. The safety of each, therefore, depended upon the willingness of all to accept a rough equality among themselves. Morality is an artifact. It does not have constitutional roots in human nature. It is the fundamental artifact insofar as it makes possible all other artifacts of society, of culture, and of science, by regulating intraspecific aggression and making cooperation possible in the tasks of ameliorating the human condition. In Hobbes's view, this indispensable artifact depends for its existence and effective operation upon the creation of a sovereign, a Leviathan, of whatever sort, with an unqualified right to make moral rules and social regulations and with the backing of unlimited power to enforce them. Hobbes evidently had two reasons for adopting this view. First, there is no constitutional foundation for morality in man: Morality depends upon experience and causal reasoning. Second, the anxiety that leads the way to morality does not bring about any internal, subjective alterations of a sufficiently reliable nature to reduce the anxiety to tolerable levels. An external alteration of society, therefore, is the only available remedy. A sovereign must be created with the power necessary to exact compliance with moral and civil law from everyone. The exercise of this power by the sovereign is sanctioned, according to Hobbes's theory, by the legitimate fear each has of every other.

Mill (1863), like Hobbes, based morality on the pleasure (good) or pain (evil) that an action yields, directly or consequentially: ". . . the Greatest Happiness Principle, holds that actions are right in proportion as they tend to promote happiness, wrong as they tend to produce the reverse of happiness" (p. 157). Unlike Hobbes, Mill thought that moral conduct is sanctioned by diverse motives (causes), which he classified into two types, external and internal. External sanctions are the wish for reward and the fear of punishment by other persons, whether natural or divine (real or imaginary). The principle of internal sanction is the fear of incurring one's own displeasure (conscience), supported by sympathy, love, religious feeling, childhood memories, or self-esteem, as well as by egoistical motives such as hope of gain. Thus, for our purposes, a distinctive feature of Mill's moral thought is his conviction that there is a potential in men and women, usually although not always realized in their development, for the formation of a conscience that sanctions moral behavior independently of any external sanctions. Mill claimed this to be an observable fact of human nature, but he did not offer any explanation of it:

> The internal sanction of duty, whatever our standard of duty may be, is one and the same—a feeling in our own mind: a pain, more or less intense, attendant on violation of duty which in properly cultivated natures rises, in the more serious cases, into shrinking from it as an impossibility. (1863, p. 184)

Thus, Mill would say that the pleasure we would otherwise take in plundering a neighbor of his possessions, even if we could get away with it, could be and usually is eclipsed by the greater pain of doing a wrongful act. Thus, the limitless egoistical aggression postulated by Hobbes was thought by Mill to be capable of being bound by conscience. As Hamlet said, "Conscience does make cowards of us all": It causes us to shrink from actions that we deem to be morally wrong. Thus, Mill's moral theory requires neither Hobbes's social contract nor a socially constituted sanction for morality except for those who have failed to develop the capacity to react with pain to the thought of wrongdoing. Stated positively, conscience causes us to take pleasure in actions that yield benefit and happiness no less to others than to ourselves:

> the happiness which forms the utilitarian standard of what is right in conduct, is not the agent's own happiness, but that of all concerned. . . . To do as we would be done by, and to love one's neighbour as oneself, constitute the ideal perfection of utilitarian morality. (1863, p. 170)

Whether or not utilitarianism and contractualism can be correctly classified as emotivist theories in the philosophical sense, it would be an error to so classify the moral theory inherent in psychoanalysis. In addition to the role played by affects such as anxiety (which motivate actions that run counter to demands for immediate instinctual pleasure) and the cognitive role played by the perception of reality and the calculation of consequences, there is, in psychoanalytic theory, the role played by identification, which sets up strongly sanctioned imperatives of both a negative (prohibitive) and a positive (aspirational) nature. It is its recognition of the process of identification in the formation of conscience that enables psychoanalysis to provide a naturalistic explanation both for Mill's moral affects and for Kant's categorical imperative. Psychoanalysis recognizes three broad types of affect according to the structural and functional differentiations in psychological processes. These are id affects, which are caused by direct drive discharge, such as sexual pleasure or pleasure in competition; ego affects, such as frustration or pleasure in success; and superego affects, such as guilt or self-righteousness. Certain of these affects, such as sexual pleasure, may be experienced as naturalistic, whereas others, such as guilt, may be experienced as antinaturalistic, which could lead one, mistakenly, to think of them in this way. In fact, guilt has a no less natural explanation and function than has sexual pleasure.

Now as a matter of fact Freud (1930) did not think highly of the golden rule that Mill used to define the essence of the principle of utility. Freud asked: "What is the point of a precept enunciated with so much solemnity if its fulfilment cannot be recommended by reason?" (p. 110). If "neighbor" is to refer to humanity in general, Freud asked, am I not entitled to retain a larger measure of love for myself than the paltry sum that each of millions of others could receive from me if it were parceled out to them? Do not my family, friends, and close associates deserve the preference of my love more than some stranger who may, in any case, be prepared to do me harm? And, tragically, history has proven Freud correct. Christian European communities supposedly committed to the yet more radical injunction not only to love others as themselves but also to love their enemies, nevertheless collaborated with or passively accepted ·Nazi violence against their Jewish neighbors of a kind that Freud had not imagined in the darkest reflections of Civilization and Its Discontents.

Nevertheless, in certain respects Mill's ideas are consistent with psychoanalysis. In the first place, Mill had a realistic view of the individual's capacity to be motivated by considerations of the greatest happiness for the greatest number. Loved ones, children, extended family, close friends, rather than mankind at large, for the most part, define the scope of the application of the utilitarian rule or the golden rule. Relatively few individuals in relatively few circumstances (presumably Mill had in mind those with political power) are in a position to take actions whose consequences have larger scope. With this view Freud would not have had cause to quarrel. The psychoanalytic theory of psychic defense (Freud, 1926) explains the origins of aim-inhibited libido. By means of reaction formation, sadism toward people is replaced by pity for their suffering. By means of repression and sublimation, perverse sexual drives are turned into sympathy, interest, affection, neighborliness, curiosity. These are the affections that sanction behavior toward others, which answers to the requirements of Mill's utilitarianism. Psychoanalysis has shown how identifications with others in whom we find likenesses of ourselves as we are, or who seem to us to have realized in themselves what we would like to be, release affection that makes us want to ensure their happiness as far as we are able. Certain crucial and fundamental identifications with parents bring about the formation of the conscience, which causes us to take pleasure in doing what is right and to experience the pain of guilt and shame when we do or contemplate doing what is wrong. The development of the capacity for this pain and pleasure, which Mill identified as the essential subjective sanction of morality, was studied by Freud (1926) through its stages and forms: beginning with the fear of the loss of the object (i.e., the mother and father on whom the child depends); followed by fear of the loss of the love of the parents experienced as shame; followed by castration fear (for the male the ultimate external sanction insofar as it represents the end of sexual pleasure); and finally fear of the loss of self-approval, which is experienced as guilt at the thought of wrongdoing. These stages of affect development provide for a transition from dependency to obedience to autonomy. It is on the issue of autonomy that Mill and psychoanalysis depart from Hobbes. Freud, Mill, and Hobbes are, however, in agreement on two fundamental points: Morality is acquired, and pleasure and pain are the criteria of good and evil, including moral good and evil.

Although Kant preceded Mill, the logical order of this exposition places him last because I am classifying these moral theories according to the importance they attach to internal moral sanctions. Kant was the high priest of the autonomous conscience. Kant (1785) totally repudiated the consequences of an action in evaluating its moral worth. Only the motive of an action merits our consideration. An action is moral insofar, and only insofar, as it is performed for the sake of duty alone. Pleasure, pain, and all egoistical satisfactions must be excluded entirely from the estimation of the moral worth of an action. Thus, in these two respects, the repudiation of consequences and the unique emphasis upon duty as a motive, Kant's moral theory is at odds with the theories of Hobbes and Mill. In Kant's view, for example, a marriage is moral not because a man and woman take pleasure in each other but only because they conceive themselves to have a duty to treat each other with respect and to preserve the marriage. A marriage based on love and mutual enjoyment is, at best, amoral—not actual wrongdoing, but not a demonstrable moral good either. Kant recognized that in reality motives are often mixed: Many individuals who act dutifully are also motivated by the pursuit of self-interest, but insofar as an action is motivated other than by duty it is without moral worth. Only insofar as it is motivated by duty can it be said to have moral worth. The discrimination of the relative weights of mixed motives is difficult to make. It is actions that run counter to self-interest that can unequivocally be said to have genuine moral worth (see Broad, 1930).

Hensen (1979) has attempted in an ingenious way to defend Kant against the criticism that, for example, a moral marriage in Kant's view would be one in which each spouse had an aversion to the other but was dutifully kind, whereas a couple who took only pleasure in each other would be at best amoral. A difficulty of one aspect of Hensen's argument involves his "battle-citation model," which implies that ideal parenting could, in principle, render morality in this sense unnecessary. This is not an implication that Kant could have viewed with equanimity. From a psychoanalytic point of view, Kant is right and Hensen is mistaken. The genesis of adult morality out of the resolution of the Oedipus complex accounts for the lasting relation of the morality of duty to intrapsychic conflict. No parenting could be good enough to eradicate this psychic conflict, because it owes its origins to spontaneous drive development.

Kant formulated these moral ideas in terms of a basic distinction he drew between categorical imperatives and hypothetical imperatives (Broad, 1952, pp. 224–240). Hypothetical imperatives take the form: "If I wish to get ahead in business and prosper, then I had better be honest in my dealings with others." It is a materialistic, egoistical ambition that motivates the honesty of this hypothetical imperative. A categorical imperative takes the form: "I ought to be honest because I have a duty to be honest whether it is in my interest to be so or not." Kant gave the categorical imperative two fundamental formulations, which he considered to be general criteria in deciding what is and what is not a moral duty. First, a moral action can be universalized; and second, any moral action must treat other persons as ends in themselves, never merely as means. The first rules out any self-serving exceptions in one's own case when circumstances and morality require the renunciation of egoistical or instinctual wants; the second rules out all forms of manipulation of others or the use of others, whatever their circumstances—for instance, however helpless and vulnerable—for one's own purposes.

Kant's philosophy holds up altruism as the *sine qua non* of morality. The severity, one is tempted to say masochism, of this ideal is well illustrated by his veneration of military heroism. In his aesthetics Kant (1790) considered the question Should the general who leads youth into a war or the statesman who negotiates the peace be honored by a statue in the public square? The author of *Perpetual Peace: A Philosophi-*

cal Essay (Kant, 1795) answered that it is the general who merits the honor. Why? Because it is he who provides youth with the opportunity to risk their lives for the sake of duty. What could be more selfless than the sacrifice of one's life in the course of duty? The general is the symbol of the categorical imperative and the highest achievements of morality, whereas the statesman who negotiates a treaty to end the war is, in his pursuit of the merely political, social, and economic interests of peace, the symbol of the hypothetical imperative.

Kant believed that the sanction for moral duty is to be found in a will that is free to choose between duty and egoistical inclination whenever a conflict might arise. This will is a force unto itself. It is not subject to any causality of body, mind, society, or nature. It does not depend upon any motivation from outside itself. The will causes actions that have consequences, but an act of will does not itself have any causal antecedents. It is entirely spontaneous; thus, each individual is obliged, according to Kant, to freely choose the motive for his actions—to choose duty or interest. Kant's moral theory postulates for morality an absolute internal sanction that is altogether independent of any external force or authority. Kant traced the source of his moral will to human subjectivity conceived as a "thing-in-itself." Ontologically, mankind is a kingdom of ends beyond nature and the laws of nature.

In *The Ego and the Id* Freud (1923a) claimed that through his formulation of his theory of the genesis and functions of the superego (conscience) he had, at last, been able to construct a psychoanalytic understanding of morality. He drew attention to a parallel between his conception of the superego and Kant's categorical imperative. Freud (1924a) asserted that "Kant's Categorical Imperative is thus the direct heir of the Oedipus Complex" (p. 167). The superego does, in effect, make it a duty to repudiate the aggressive pleasure of triumphing over the father in order to have the mother to oneself. Here a severely imposed duty is set over and against powerfully charged aggressive and libidinal wishes and egoistical ambitions.

Psychological Foundations of Morality

Can psychoanalysis reconcile the differences among the moral philosophies of Hobbes, Mill, and Kant and construct an integrated, consistent moral theory? A problem is posed by the question itself: These three moral theories are mutually inconsistent. Nevertheless, we have been able to trace similarities, or to note similarities identified as such by Freud, between the moral theories of each of these philosophers and

psychoanalytic ideas about morality. Does it not follow that psychoanalytic theorizing about morality must be a hodge-podge of inconsistent
ideas that could scarcely be of use for the construction of a coherent
ethical theory?

This very question, however, points out the key to its answer.
Psychoanalysis is a theory that accounts for human behavior as compo-
sitions—compromise formations (Brenner, 1982) of the contending
forces of three psychic agencies: the instinctual unconscious, the ego,
and the superego. The inconsistencies among the three moral theories
under consideration arise from their exaggerations of the importance of
one or another of these conflicting agencies. Hobbes exaggerated the
role of the id and the ego at the expense of the superego; Mill exaggerated the role of the ego and superego at the expense of the id; and
Kant exaggerated the importance of the superego at the expense of
both the ego and the id. An understanding that integrated the contributions of each agency by recognizing the fact of intrapsychic conflict
could, in principle, provide a basis for a unifying theory that would
draw upon the legitimate insights of each of the philosophical theories.
It would also follow that, along with points of similarity between each
of these moral theories and psychoanalysis, there would also be important differences.

Let us then consider these agreements and disagreements in some
detail. If one can identify the severity and impersonality of the superego and its capacity for opposition to egoistical or sensual pleasure with
the categorical imperative, one must then proceed to recognize these
differences: The concept of the superego does not require any special
ontological assumptions such as the Kantian "thing-in-itself"; the formation of the superego is a natural human development; it is unnecessary to postulate an uncaused will as the motive force behind altruistic
acts; the work of the superego is subject to psychological causation:
Specifically, it sanctions its prohibitions and prescriptions by the fear
of loss of self-respect and the appeal of self-approval, the narcissistic
satisfaction that replaces the egoistical or instinctual pleasure that must
be forgone when altruism is required.

Then does it not follow that Mill's account of duty and altruism is
the one that is consistent with the findings of psychoanalysis? High on
Mill's hierarchy of pleasures (see Mill, 1863, Chap. 1) is the capacity to
take pleasure in dutiful and altruistic acts. What psychoanalysis would
add is that this pleasure is a form of moral narcissism—a pleasure that
one takes in one's own activities independently of the approval of others. But there are differences between Freud's thought and Mill's as well.

Freud (1930) recognized that our civilized hierarchy of pleasures is
in certain respects an artifact—a necessary adaptive artifact, to be sure,

but an artifact nonetheless. Human beings, however civilized, still remain at best rational animals. It is the direct, convulsive gratification of our instinctual drive life that provides us with our deepest and most complete pleasures. A large measure of the good we do and receive is bound up with our physical life. The most valued pleasures are sensual ones. There is a more elementary, unconscious hierarchy of pleasures, unrecognized by Mill's theory and the reverse of the one he postulates, which attaches the highest values to intellectual and spiritual pleasures—to sublimations. Nor are the pleasures that Mill most valued autonomous, either as to motives or as to what is good. For example, one aspect of beauty in nature and art derives from repressed and sublimated infantile sensual longings for the mother, just as the love of the awesome in nature derives from repressed and sublimated infantile fear of the strength and anger of the father. This is not to say that these experiences and the value attached to them are nothing more than their infantile precursors. Obviously they are different, but the value that comes to be attached to our enjoyment of beauty is psychologically more complex than is recognized by Mill's utilitarian account of pleasure. This value has three sources: the intrinsic pleasure of the experience; the pleasure derived from its unconscious defensive functions, insofar as it guards us from consciousness of our unwanted wishes; and the gratification of these same wishes in a guiltless form.

Accordingly, Mill's moral theory fails, no less than does Kant's, to acknowledge the corruptibility of conscience and to understand the origins of this corruptibility. During World War II German SS men were awarded medals for overcoming their antipathy toward rounding up and killing helpless civilians. This was a case of a will to perform a duty rising above and suppressing a human impulse that, in this instance, was a better guide to moral decency than the performance of duty for its own sake. But neither are pain and pleasure, in themselves, reliable guides to moral conduct. The committing of atrocities can also yield pleasure: A malignant unconscious identification can link the helpless victims of the present to objects of sadistic hostility from the perpetrator's past. The helplessness of reason before real moral dilemmas is evident in the fact that the Nazis could have rationalized their atrocities against Jews, Gypsies, and Slavs on the principles of either Kant or Mill. Nazis would not have hesitated to universalize their brutality toward these people: They did not include them in the "kingdom of ends," whose citizens should be treated only as "ends-in-themselves" and never merely as means. Citizenship in the "kingdom of ends" was available only to members of the "master race." Similarly, a Nazi would argue that it was for the greater good of the greater number that inferior races must be exterminated or enslaved. The treatment generally of conquered native peoples by white Europeans and North Americans guided by their "higher" Christian morality has been different (if at all) only in the degree of its savagery. Examples abound on every continent.

This corruptibility of moral values makes one want to turn back to Hobbes for the comfort, even if cold comfort, of a realistic assessment of man's moral predicament. Perhaps Hobbes's pessimistic cynicism contains more truth than either Mill's naïve optimism or Kant's grandiose idealism. Hobbes advanced two ideas with which psychoanalytic observations have obliged Freud to agree. First, morality is no more innate to human beings than is a knowledge of the world. Morality is a developmental, historical, cultural achievement. Human beings remain perfectly capable of killing one another and even, as Hobbes was well aware, of exulting in violence as though it were a magnificent achievement. In man there seems to be no genetically inherited prohibition against killing one's own kind. It is this genetically unbound nature of aggression that contributes to the intensity of ambivalence in humans. The inherited capacities for the mastery by the individual of his own aggression have to be nourished by adequate early object ties. Therefore, aggression in human beings acts as a spontaneous motivating force, whether it is conceived of as a death instinct (Freud, 1920) or as an object-related spontaneous instinct (Freud, 1905b) or as a reactive instinct (Hanly, 1978). In fact, Hobbes conceived of aggression as a reactive instinct insofar as it is released by the need for the secure possession of goods, in the face of their scarcity and vulnerability to theft by others, and by the insatiable narcissistic demands for superiority over others that Hobbes called vainglory. It is these fundamental shared perceptions of the human condition that have caused numerous commentators to remark upon the affinity between Hobbes and Freud, especially Freud's ideas in Civilization and Its Discontents—an affinity that is more profound than the one Freud himself saw between his idea of the superego and Kant's categorical imperative.

Nevertheless, the similarity cannot be pressed beyond this point. Hobbes believed that morality could be established and maintained only by an external social agent (the sovereign) made authoritative and absolute by his overwhelming power to coerce. That submission to the coercion is made voluntary by self-interest consequent upon the anxiety aroused by the thought of the alternative does not mitigate its infantilizing effect. In psychoanalytic terms, Hobbes's ethical theory would seem to envisage the human situation as though the Oedipus complex must continue to flourish without any possibility of an inner resolution in the life of the individual: Consequently mankind must be permanently satisfied, as the price of survival, with an essentially infantilized relation to an external authority's coercive power. The problem the individual cannot solve on his own must be solved by the group.

This pessimistic view is not consistent with psychoanalysis. Freud (1923a) provided us with an understanding of the processes whereby the subjective resolution of the Oedipus complex is brought about—processes that are normal for individuals with normal endowments, living in normal conditions. The motive for the resolution of the Oedipus complex does not depend upon external intimidation. It is brought about, even when parents are kind and unpunishing, by the development of castration anxiety in boys and fear of the loss of the love of the mother and her revenge in girls, both of which cause the kindest parents to be experienced as dangerous. The imprisoning and poisoning witch is no less frightening to girls than the bogeyman is to boys, and no less capable of generating guilt at the thought of injuring the mother, once an intensification of the girl's identification with her has occurred.

The normal resolution of the Oedipus complex imposed by intolerable fear of the parent of the same sex consists of a withdrawal of libido (incestuous wishes) from the parent of the opposite sex and its investment in the *image* of the parent of the same sex. This investment intensifies the identification with that parent, who now becomes, because of it, an ego ideal instead of a dangerous rival. This ego ideal constitutes a force in the life of the child as a consequence of the now highly charged wish to be like the parent of the same sex. The earlier fear of the parent has now changed into the fear of the disapproval of the ego ideal—the "parent" within—which is now part of the self and is included in the child's own identity. This fear is experienced as guilt. It is this identification with the parents that prohibits wrongful actions and that sanctions rightful actions with self-approval, self-esteem, and pride. Whereas the child was dependent before upon the approval of the parents for self-esteem and upon their disapproval for self-criticism, the child is now able to supply these building blocks of morality for himself and by himself. Now he *can be* and *has to be* good whether his parents are looking or not. Psychoanalysis has provided an understanding, to put it philosophically, of the psychological foundations of the possibility of moral experience. It is this autonomous moral capacity in individuals that Hobbes failed to take into account, a capacity that is autonomous but also rooted in instinctual pleasure seeking made realistic.

Psychoanalysis is thus able, by selectively integrating the partial insights of moral philosophy, to provide the basis for a unified moral theory. In relation to Kant, psychoanalysis is able to explain the nature and genesis of duty for the sake of duty as a moral precept. When all else has failed, when taking pleasure in doing good for others has vanished, when fear of the loss of the respect and approval of others is gone, then subjectively generated fear of wrongdoing—guilt—which internally enforces duty for its own sake with the consolation of moral narcissism, is the last, although scarcely reliable, hope that decency has. Yet psychoanalysis can certainly agree with Mill that the most effective motive for altruism is a well-developed capacity to take pleasure in actions that aim at some good for others, while accepting that the hope of some return of a like good for oneself does not diminish its worth. The points of connection with Hobbes's moral theory have already been identified above: the "abnormality" of morality, the fact of an instinct of aggression that can be at best only imperfectly mastered, and the intrinsic vulnerability of morality to an insidious corruption that can make evil take on the appearance of good.

Concerning the Corruptibility and Creativity of Conscience

It is this corruptibility of conscience that should, and in part does, haunt contemporary moral thought in consequence of the moral regression to barbarity in our century. What bulwark is there that can protect individuals and groups from such regressions? If the psychoanalytic theory of the psychogenesis of morality is correct, this bulwark, frail and uncertain as it is, must reside in part in the contribution parents make to the identifications out of which the individual's superego is formed. These identifications are partly formed out of the subjective vicissitudes of the child's instinct life, but they are also partly formed out of the child's experience of the impact of the parents' total personalities (rather than of deliberate parental teaching) including especially their unconscious wishes, anxieties, ideals, and attitudes. It is not what a parent wishes to be for his child but, rather, what he actually is without even knowing it that will exercise the most decisive influence upon the formation of the child's ego-ideal. It is this involuntary and largely unconscious transaction between generations that carries forward, arrests, or reverses the work of civilization.

These identifications transmit from generation to generation the values of the community filtered through the lives and being of the parents. The individual is partly at their mercy and partly not: The balance will depend in part upon the extent to which the questioning of prohibitions, permissions, and encouragements are themselves prohibited or permitted by the parents in their own conduct, and hence in the value-creating identifications formed by their offspring. But each individual life also brings resources of its own to the task. The images of the parents that compose the nuclear identification around which conscience crystallizes are those of a 4–7-year-old child, modified by the fantasies that express the child's drive life; as the child matures he will have a motive and opportunities, if his continuing relations with his parents are reasonably benign, to test the fantasy elements of his parental images against their reality. A major component of the motivation is the wish to reduce the anxiety associated with parents and to replace fear with love as the mainspring of obedience.

With the onset of puberty the youth is able to, as it were, own his own ego and assume responsibility for what he is, even though he is not and never will be his own unique author. This stage of ego development often releases, in self-aware individuals, an "I-experience" that is only less exhilarating than the burgeoning adolescent sexuality. Reactivated ambivalent feelings animate this new determination to be oneself with the ambition to be and to do better than the parents. Adolescent rebellion, which is at once the search for independence and a reaction formation against the threat of resurgent oedipal feelings, is also a sublimated attempt to find and live by different and sometimes better values than those experienced by the adolescent as having been handed down by the parents. An essential part of this search is the formation of new identifications aimed at modifying the original parental ones. This search can produce disaster, violence, and moral regression; it can end in futile imitation of the parental originals, whose influence is never in any case altogether eclipsed; or it can lead to some measure of moral creativity. It is upon those individuals who can bring about such advances in their lives that the progress of civilization depends. Further examination of these issues will have to await the concluding chapters.

chapter five

Psychoanalysis
and Aesthetics

A psychoanalytic study of aesthetics might explore, as the previous chapter has done in relation to moral theories, the conflicting theories of art advanced by philosophers in order to see to what extent a critical unification of their psychological assumptions could be achieved in this area as well. Many are the divergences of philosophers concerning the nature of art (Sparshott, 1963). This study, however, will confine itself to one: their differences concerning the respective values of form and content. The burden of the argument is that psychoanalysis, contrary to the opinions of some of its critics, can do justice to both form and content and to their integration in the greatest works of art.

The method of the argument combines theoretical and philosophical analysis with the use of interpretive sketches based on works rather than upon the biographies of the artists.

Aesthetic Controversy about Form
and Content

Opposed estimations of the relative values of form and content have been the source of one of the perennial controversies in aesthetics. Bell (1914), for example, has placed paramount importance upon form as the crucial factor in aesthetic experience:

> . . . he who contemplates a work of art, inhabit(s) a world with an intense and peculiar significance of its own; that significance is unrelated to the significance of life. In this world the emotions of life find no place. It is a world with emotions of its own.

and again,

> . . . if a representative form has value, it is as form, not as representation. The representative element in a work of art may or may not be harmful;

86

always it is irrelevant. For to appreciate a work of art we need bring with us nothing from life, no knowledge of its ideas and affairs, no familiarity with its emotions. Art transports us from the world of man's activity to a world of aesthetic exultation.

Among other aestheticians who have subscribed to this view are Carpenter (1921), Parker (1924), and Fry (1924). Tolstoy (1896), on the other hand, devalued form and sought to limit the idea of great art to stories (descriptive painting and plastic representations, by extension) that could arouse strong feelings in simple, unsophisticated people:

> Art is a human activity, consisting in this, that one man consciously, by means of certain external signs, hands on to others feelings he has lived through, and that other people are infected by these feelings, and also experience them.

Similar views have been advocated by Véron (1878) and Hirn (1900). An ostensibly intermediate position that allows for an equal value for form and content in aesthetic experience has been advocated by Frye (1957). Yet Frye's critical theory ends in an aestheticism insofar as it severs art from experience and nature and removes it to a self-contained universe of its own where like the Epicurean gods it can be admired but where it cannot cause any more trouble. The referent of a word in a poem is not some person's experience of life or nature but a word in some other poem. The content of poetry has, in a sense, been formalized and contained within the bounds of a self-referential language. An alternative intermediate position would be one in which form and content were each assigned appropriate values and also linked to their sources and functions in individual experience and the quest for a happier and truer life. We would like to know where psychoanalysis is properly located among these alternatives.

The Problem of Form in Psychoanalysis

At first blush, it would appear that Freud's ideas in aesthetic experience must classify him with Tolstoy in favor of an aesthetics of the arousal of primitive affect irrespective of the means. It is true that although Freud had a highly educated passion for literature and the arts, he placed no greater value than did Tolstoy on a "refined sensibility" or on art for art's sake. And although Freud's (1907) analysis of the dream structure of Jensen's Gradiva is complex and sophisticated, the story itself is more romantically complicated than profound. The novel is not by any means what one would call great literature. Freud's study of the novel is more interesting than the work itself. Moreover, *Creative Writers and Day-Dreaming* (Freud, 1908) does advance the view that the enjoyment of art arises primarily out of the vicarious gratification of otherwise repressed affects. If form, style, and structure are assigned a role in this, it is only as a purely formal pleasure that charms the repressive agencies of the ego and puts them off their guard so that the waking ego, in broad daylight, can experience the pleasure of tasting the forbidden fruit of its unconscious life. The formal beauty of art is the siren's song, which lulls the anxiously guarding ego into a more tolerant experience of its own impulse and affect life. But the core of the aesthetic experience is pleasure in the vicarious gratification of suitably disguised impulses and affects that may be ugly, perverse, destructive, dangerous, immoral, and infantile in themselves and, hence, not enjoyable in any other form.

Rose (1980) has criticized Freud's aesthetics on this very score. He attacks Freud for reducing "form and beauty to resistance and defence—form sugar-coats an offensive content, bribing the critical powers with aesthetic pleasure—and detouring the normal sexual aims into voyeurism or exhibitionism" (p. 7). In this Rose thinks that there is a devaluation of art; "art becomes trivialized as a diversion with the inner structure of perversion" (p. 8). This criticism is a common one. Trilling (1950), who was on the whole sympathetic to psychoanalysis, claimed that "Freud speaks of art with what one must indeed call contempt" (p. 42).

Two questions are posed by this criticism. First, did Freud, despite his own cultivated appreciation of literature and art, nevertheless, as a psychoanalyst advocate an essentially Philistine aesthetics that lacks any criteria for differentiating what is great from what is pedestrian in art? Second, does psychoanalysis actually entail such an aesthetics? The first is a historical question that, in the end, is not of fundamental concern. The second is a theoretical question of first importance for the field of applied psychoanalysis. Our primary concern will be with the second question. If some light can be shed on the first one as we proceed with the second, so much the better.

Ancient Controversy about the Nature of Art

One can mitigate the force of the criticism from two directions. The cathartic function of aesthetic experience was not an idea that Freud invented in order to create a bridgehead for psychoanalysis in the field of aesthetics. It is one that can be traced among poets and artists. It was first formulated by Aristotle (Poetics). Plato (Republic, X) advocated the suppression of all of the great literature of ancient Greece: the works of Homer, Hesiod, Aeschylus, Sophocles, and Euripides. Among his reasons for doing so was his moral fear that the portrayals of sexual lust and aggressive violence on the part of gods and heroes in this poetry would inflame similar latent impulses in their audience resulting in disharmony of soul and, its consequences: individual, familial, and social disorder. The poet must "moralize his song" on behalf of idealized representations of gods and heroes whose conduct would manifest the virtues of justice, wisdom, courage, and temperance. The truth must be sacrificed to moral propaganda. Yet Plato had misgivings. His conclusion must have contradicted his own aesthetic preferences. He may have wondered about the intensity of his own fear of the drives—a fear that informs the argument. His own creative imagination must have protested against its indictment. In any case, Plato asked for a vindication of poetry and art that he could not himself discover.

Aristotle's Poetics can be seen as a response to Plato's petition. Aristotle thought that tragedy provides for a catharsis of feelings, which preserves and strengthens the civilized personality by discharging emotions that could otherwise lead to destructive, aggressive, or wrongful sexual conduct. The catharsis of tragedy protects, rather than enervates, the life of reason and morality. There is an obscurity concerning the emotions selected by Aristotle for this cathartic remedy. They are pity and fear. This obscurity may result from the fact that Aristotle did not understand the unconscious thoughts and affects aroused by tragedy and, in a qualified sense, gratified (abreacted). It is these unconscious thoughts and affects that terminate in a conscious feeling of pity for the tragic hero who suffers a calamity and a fear lest we ourselves suffer a like calamity. These conscious feelings of pity and fear are released in us by an unconscious identification with the tragic hero that arises from the activation of our own repressed memories and fantasies. The catharsis is of these unconscious drive constellations rather than of the pity and fear. The capacity for pity is extended and strengthened in the process not purged, and thus it promotes tolerance and generosity of feeling; the capacity for moral resignation is enlivened by the fearful realization of the consequences that flow from the pursuit of inappropriate wants. In these ways the experience that tragedy works in us is both humanizing and civilizing.

Aesthetic experience is, on account of its cathartic effect, similar to dreams in the homeostatic function that it performs. But it accomplishes two things that dreams cannot. Aesthetic experience is public and general, whereas dream experience is private and individual. Hence, aesthetic experience is able to correct the depressing and isolating feeling of being an outsider, a criminal, a pariah or outcast among one's fellow man. Aesthetic experience provides for a certain preconscious or conscious realization: "If I identify with Oedipus in his crimes and suffering so does my brother, father, friend, neighbor"; "If my life and character have been carved out of a conflicted human nature, it is a human nature that belongs to others as well as to me." In this awareness there is, for the individual, a salutary realism; the superego is encouraged to be more tolerant.

This aspect of aesthetic experience has its source in the public nature of the experience itself. It is nurtured, that is, by the creative genius of the artist who is able to transform thoughts and memories of his own into characters, scenes, and actions that acquire an objectivity that enables them to arouse an intense interest in many people (Freud, 1908). Part of the great artist's genius is his capacity to select from his own experience and from his intuitive knowledge of the lives of others, the derivatives of those psychic conflicts that form our common humanity. The great artist expresses what Johnson (1765b) called general human nature in his art.

Aesthetic experience thus helps to liberate us from an alienating subjectivity (Arlow, 1982). Psychoanalysis has been criticized for degrading art by its preoccupation with content. The issue involved can also be clarified by a reflection on the controversy between Plato and Aristotle. Plato attacked art for being merely an imitation of an imitation of reality. Art, in Plato's view, was both epistemologically and ontologically a degraded object, lacking both intelligibility and reality. In reply, Aristotle set out a concept of poetic truth. A knowledge of the reality of the human condition can be given expression by the poet as a consequence of his ability and entitlement as artist (unlike, e.g., the historian) to disregard the accidental and adventitious in human affairs in order to focus our attention on what is essential and fundamental.

Aesthetic form is the vehicle through which this "focus" is achieved. Aristotle considered *Oedipus Rex* to be the most perfect of the tragedies. Aristotle's choice of this play was no doubt based, in part, on the beauty with which it realizes the unities of time, place, and action, thought by Aristotle to be necessary to formal excellence in drama, and at the same time because the play expresses something fundamental and universal in the human condition. As Aristotle already implicitly realized in *Poetics*, the efficacy of tragedy for psychic re-creation is dependent upon its themes. In this there is no trivialization of art.

The themes of the extant Greek tragedies concern the calamities that arise in family life, in the exercise of power, and in the relations to the gods. In all of these themes there is evident either directly or indirectly the struggle with the fatefulness of the instincts, circumstance, or nature. If we interpret Aristotle's definition of tragedy as "an imitation . . . of action and life, of happiness and misfortune" (*Poetics,* p. 13) empirically—a procedure of which he would have approved—and apply it to the great ancient and modern plays, we are impressed by the extent to which the actions thus imitated are those that lead to repetitions in one form or another of the dreaded calamities of early life that give permanent shape to our most profound anxieties: the loss of the object, the loss of the love of the object, castration, the loss of self-approval. These are also the calamities that must move us to pity and fear. Of the extant plays, those in which these themes are central exert a perennial fascination: the plays concerning the house of Atreus; Oedipus and his children; Alcestes; Medea; and Hippolytus. The same holds true of the tragedies of Shakespeare and Racine. In the great modern novels of Dostoyevski, Dickens, Hardy, Lawrence, Balzac, Stendhal, Mann, and Faulkner, conflicts of family life in their various derivatives and complications are explored again and again. Over many centuries writers have shared in the struggle to find expression for what is most operative and least expressible in the lives of men and women, ancient and modern. Psychoanalysis has helped us to understand how these themes exercise such an influence upon our imaginations and why their expression in literature plays such an important part in the search for self-understanding. Psychoanalysis provides for a clear differentiation between great art and lesser art in terms of its capacity to focus these essential conflicts. Great art will always concern itself with the forces in human nature that decide the outcome of life whether for good or ill. In this psychoanalytic view, formal excellence consists of, at least, these five elements: the focus given to the great conflicts of the thematic material; the modulation into intersubjectivity and universality of presentation; a homeostatic balance of thematic disguise and revelation that is sensitive to levels of anxiety; poetic justice; and facility and felicity. Here there is no derogation of art any more than there is a derogation of art by Aristotle in his *Poetics.*

In one sense *Oedipus Tyrannus* is a detective story. The plot concerns the search for the identity of the murderer of Laius. Part of the interest of the play consists in solving this mystery. But even the most brilliantly ingenious detective stories, such as Poe's *The Purloined Letter,* offer a different and lesser aesthetic experience. Even if we unconsciously identify with the clever criminal and wait with mingled disappointment and relief to be exposed by the yet more brilliant detective (who is, after all, also identified with oneself) and then experience a vicarious expiation of unconscious guilt, an experience of a different order is generated by the realization in the tragedy that the detective is going to make the discovery that he is himself the murderer of his own father. The dilemma of Oedipus goes beyond the dilemmas that artistic ingenuity can create: It is a dilemma of the human condition itself. I, therefore, cannot agree with the criticism that Freud, because of his interest in the content of art (its psychological meaning) "clarified everything concerning art but art itself" (Hacker, 1953, p. 129) or that there is "no distinction between good and bad art" (Langer, 1942, p. 207) inherent in Freud's understanding of artistic meaning. This distinction between great and pedestrian art can be grounded in part on the latter's powerful evocation of meaning and truth in which a recognition of formal excellence is implicit. It is an error (into which Freud did not fall) to assume, as Hacker does, that "art itself" concerns only form and does not include meaning or content. Freud's concept of the affective significance of art does not involve the naïvely puritanical idea of Tolstoy that would reject Shakespeare in favor of stories that would arouse simple, unconflicted affects and thoughts. The concept of artistic meaning bequeathed by Freud to psychoanalysis is not Philistine. It makes an essential contribution to any aesthetic theory that is adequate to its object.

The same fundamental point applies to conceptions of art as the expression of emotions (e.g., Langer, 1953; Siomapolous, 1977). But art *would* be trivialized if no distinctions were made concerning the nature of the affects in question and the nature of their objects. Multiple violent deaths are characteristic of Shakespeare's plays as they are of Jacobean drama. But the effect of death upon our feelings is very different because of the meaning of the lives and deaths of Shakespeare's characters as compared with those of Webster, Turner, Ford, and Middleton. The emotional effect of Jacobean drama is melodramatic; death in Shakespeare's plays is tragic. There are, at least, two reasons for this difference. Shakespeare connects violent death with the perennial psychic conflicts of life. He presents these conflicts in the characters in such a way as to facilitate our unconscious identifications with them. We are not permitted to be detached, excited, thrilled, fascinated vicarious observers; instead, we are drawn into the world of the drama as vicarious participants. Hence, our affective responses, even when humorous, possess a quality of seriousness that is absent from our responses to lesser theater. The source for this deeper affective engagement with the work must be traced to Shakespeare's capacity to give expression in his art to the unconscious fantasies that shape our destinies (cf. Arlow & Beres, 1974).

Psychoanalytic Controversy about Form and Content

But we must not forget the fact that sympathetic (Trilling, 1945; Noy, 1979) as well as unsympathetic (Storr, 1972; Pruyser, 1983) critics have argued that Freud failed to appreciate fully the unique contribution of form to aesthetic experience. But before turning to a more direct consideration of form, I would like first to consider the inherence of form in content or, stated differently, the contribution of primary process thought activity to the creation of form. The notion has developed that Freud devalued form because of his early necessary preoccupation with the instinctual unconscious. And although Freud later developed the psychology of the ego, he did not then use its resources to update psychoanalytic aesthetics (e.g., Noy, 1979). But ego psychology has tended to devalue the contribution of primary process thought activity to artistic creativity. There has been a strong emphasis upon the role of secondary narcissism from which the ego is able to draw resources for creative activities through sublimation (Giovacchini, 1960; Coltrera, 1965; Kohut, 1966). At first glance this emphasis is warranted by Freud's (1923a) hypothesis that the conversion of object libido into narcissistic libido involved in identification is the first stage in sublimation. If, then, sublimation is the essential factor in artistic creativity (a proposition first put forward by Plato in the *Symposium*), the centrality of narcissism is established. Creativity becomes primarily a function of the ego. But such a view is not tenable for a number of reasons.

The ego, however well stocked with narcissism, could not invent the themes in art that fascinate and affect us. But perhaps it does not need to. It could discover them in the lives of men and women either directly or indirectly in stories, legends, myths, histories, and the tradition of the art. Do not writers, even the greatest of them (e.g., Sophocles, Shakespeare, and Racine) draw upon themes already in existence? Of course they do, but in doing so they modify and revive them to create a fresh version (e.g., Shakespeare reworked the sources of all his plays and as a result gave to them a psychological depth their originals did not have; Wangh, 1950, examined this process in relation to *Othello*). There is a metaphysical principle stated by Descartes (1641) to the effect that it takes no less power to maintain nature in existence than to create it in the first place *ex nihilo*—a principle used against the creationist thesis that only a *creatio ex nihilo* is commensurate with infinite power. One might similarly argue that it takes no less creative genius to revive an old story than to invent a new one. In any case, it is to the instincts, their vicissitudes, and their derivatives that one must trace the original thematic material of great literature. Moreover, the ego does not have the resources to synthesize scenes and characters to give to them that ego alien, strange, verisimilitude that alone can command the willing suspension of disbelief. What the primary process thought activity accomplishes in each one of us in the production of dreams must be available to artists for the creation of works of art. Aesthetic judgment is sensitive to this factor in the greater value that it attaches to Aeschylus's *Oresteia* as compared with O'Neill's trilogy on the same theme. As paradoxical as it may seem, blind primary process thought is better able to create artistic verisimilitude than secondary process thought, even though the latter has fresh perception of real persons and places available to it. An exploration of this paradox would be a digression here (but see Chapter Seven). Suffice it to say that great art depends upon primary process synthesis for the simultaneous achievement of verisimilitude and psychic depth (overdetermination). To achieve this richness, images, experiences, stories, indeed, any material that is to be shaped into art, even though it has an external origin, must undertake a sojourn through the id (see also Noy, 1972).

Contributions of Primary Process Thought to Artistic Form

Lacan (1966) reminds us that the roots of two of the basic form-generating devices of art are to be found in primary process thought, although Lacan incorrectly linked condensation to metaphor and displacement to metonymy. Condensation is the root of metonymy in both the narrow and the broad sense just as displacement is the root of simile, metaphor, and symbolism. It is the business of primary process thought activity to generate these formal elements in new constellations of images richly endowed with meaning through many associative connections.

Arlow (1979) has demonstrated the fundamental role of metaphor in the psychoanalytic situation. We daily observe in our analytic work how the ego, exploiting its capacity for expression in language, is able to achieve a remarkable richness and precision of expression because it is subject to the influence of the preverbal synthesis of primary process thinking. The creation of metaphors and similes in art and in life is a contribution of primary process thought activity to the work of the ego.

But the synthetic activity of primary process thought has a further striking and unexpected contribution to make to the creation and appreciation of art: Although it is a function of the ego to test reality, the instinctual unconscious makes an indispensable contribution to verisimilitude in art. The imagination acting under the aegis of primary process thought is able to create a likeness to the life of real persons and places that it could not achieve if it were guided only by realistic perceptions. The synthesis of primary process thought is guided with an astonishing sureness and aptness of expression by affective meanings that operate unconsciously; whereas the intellectual synthesis of secondary process thought activity is less overdetermined, more rational but less able to evoke a vital impression of reality. This affective synthesis is indispensable to artistic creativity. It allows the universal unconscious themes of conflict and calamity to find implicit yet coherent expression in artistic forms (e.g., in the multiple interconnections of plot, metaphor, and character in a good novel or play).

Consider these lines from *Hamlet*:

> O, most wicked speed, to post
> With such dexterity to incestuous sheets!
> (I, 2, 156–157)

That secondary process thought does not dominate the choice of words is evident from the fact that the sentence is incomplete and, apart from the superficially incongruous allusion to travel by horse, there are the displaced adjectives of "wicked speed" and "incestuous sheets." These implicit metaphors are the handiwork of primary process thought. The choice of words and their combination are guided preconsciously by displacements that enormously enrich their evocative power. The choice of "post" with its sexual symbolism adds to the effect. These displacements of the implied metaphors and the symbol avoid a crude assault on the imagination while conceding nothing to the demands of a superficial, moralistic propriety. The exclamation thus expresses Hamlet's disenchantment, horror, and hurt at his mother's sexuality, which caused her to betray his father; and it also hints at the feelings of jealous rage that then give rise to the incipient melancholia of the very next lines:

> It is not, nor it cannot come to good.
> But break my heart, for I must hold my tongue.

The genius of the artist does not reside in the ego. It pervades all three of the great agencies of the mind (Waelder, 1965).

The role of affective synthesis in great music has already been well articulated by Noy (1979). The phenomena of inspiration first discussed by Plato in the *Ion* in terms of divine madness and often experienced by artists as the compulsion to create is clearly related to unconscious libidinal sources (Kris, 1952). Artists often feel driven toward the resolution of a problem (knowing that a particular end is inevitable without knowing what it will be) or feel despair that the resolution will not come about. In all of this there is a certain passive receptivity of the ego to a comprehension and an intention that lies beyond its grasp. It was to this affective synthesis of the instinctual unconscious that Freud (1908) was referring when he described how memories come to be organized through common affective significances. "Thus past, present and future are strung together, as it were, on the thread of the wish that runs through them" (p. 148). It is an error to think of form as though it were imposed on an unorganized, raw thematic, and affective material—to assume that content is only Dionysian and form only Apollonian.

A Psychoanalytic Approach to Understanding Form

Neither must psychoanalysis entirely lay down its arms before the formal aspects of art considered separately and in their own right. As Freud (1908) pointed out it is the task of the ego to remove enough of what is idiosyncratic in the artist's inspiration to render it accessible to many people. There are two requirements here, however. The artist must be able to tolerate what is universal in himself—that is to say, the calamities all people share. The artist must be able, in his secondary elaboration of these experiences and fantasies, to find in and for them an impersonal form. This form, in art that transcends entertainment and decoration, must do more than offer a "bribe of pleasure"; it must provide an order that allows the ego to tolerate the exploration of identities and experiences that would otherwise be denied to it. Form promises an alternative to action or repression as a means of mastering anxiety-provoking experiences. To be sure, the connection with play inherent in aesthetic experience and its vicarious nature contributes to this freedom from the superego's restrictions. But the deeper, more powerful forms of aesthetic experience reactivate memories of a time when thought and deed, fantasy and reality were not yet securely differentiated, both because of the conflicts of that time that are momentous for individual destiny and because the aesthetic experience itself demands a regression to a state of mind in which an appearance can function "as if it were" a reality: that is, in which there is a willing suspension of disbelief. Artistic form allows us the freedom to explore vicariously experiences that otherwise would be denied to us by repression.

Artistic forms no less than moral rules are part of the cultural inheritance transmitted in the most elementary ways through early identifications. But they are also, like moral rules, a subject for the artist to imitate, study, master, modify, and then discard for new ones. The creation of form is not itself free from the struggle to master the powerful affects generated by instinct life and relations with objects. For this reason artistic form can in a more explicit way, as the "shape of the content," be illuminated by psychoanalysis. Although form can be considered separately in the work of art, in aesthetic experience it is intrinsically related to content. There follow three brief illustrative explorations.

Of Cézanne it has been said that it was the purpose of his work "to join the erring hands of nature" (Bernard, 1920). His landscapes, portraits, and still lifes with their subtle geometrization of objects seem to exhibit a deeper law for the organization of nature than ordinary observation is able to detect. Yet the very formalization of the landscapes suggests a dissatisfaction and unease with the casual permissive untidiness of nature. These qualities are renounced, delicately brushed aside by the gentle vagueness of things and the detached sensuality of their colors. Cézanne's geometric formalization serves as a defense against the provocative, proliferate fecundity of mother nature. Cézanne has caught in subtle chains the primitive earth mother Gaia just as Zeus once chained the Titans. The formal quality of Cézanne's paintings reminds one of the Kantian idea that the mind itself spatializes its experience of nature and thus imposes a formal order on it. Feuer (1970) has shown the relation of this concept of space in Kant's philosophy to his fear of "lawless, uncontrollable sensation" (p. 80). The choice of form in Cézanne is the expression of a defensive struggle.

The exploration of geometry in Cézanne's work created a style that was eventually developed into cubism. Picasso's *Les Demoiselles d'Avignon* is generally held to have been a seminal work, after Cézanne, in the development of cubism (Golding, 1959). This painting is still expressive of individual human qualities in its subjects, although the variations in portraiture lead toward African mask disguise; but it is in transition toward an anonymity made possible by the geometrical destruction of objects. On its figures, already partly distorted by the reorganization of their planes into a single two-dimensional surface, via the intermediary of the African mask, there is still expressed a curious blend of exhibitionism and modesty that Picasso either saw in or projected upon the prostitutes of his painting. At the same time, the faces are reduced to a striking similarity. All of them bear a remarkable similarity (with their wide, surprised eyes) to the self-portrait of the artist from the same period. It would appear that the defenses at work in the cubistic distortions leading Picasso toward the pure spatial anonymity of cubism allowed him an impression in this painting of the feminine identifications out of which part of his own nature was

formed. The "mask" of cubistic form facilitated the expression of identifications otherwise repressed.

It is also possible to pursue the relation of psychological defense
into the domain of content, something that must remind us of the
essential unity of content and form in art. There is a defense implicitly
at work contributing both to the choice of subject, style of painting,
and treatment of form in the school of impressionism out of which
Cézanne himself evolved. The impressionists sought to dissolve form
into color and light. They selected themes of pastoral tranquility, high
culture and society, and prosperous, pleasant bourgeois life. The result
was canvases of beauty, gracefulness, and elegance, but also of astonishing naïveté and even blindness to social reality. Monet's *Gare St.
Lazare* illustrates this denial of painful social realities. In the painting
the steam rising from the engines dissolves into mist; the glass of the
station roof protecting passengers from wind and rain mingles with a
foggy morning into a dissolving sunlight and a curious radiance. The
station and its trains are cleansed of their grime in a pastoral idealization. The railroad terminal is romanticized. The physical and socioeco-
nomic reality of these objects is romanticized. No trace is found of the
human and social realities that were contemporaneously being painted
by van Gogh in, for example, *The Potato Eaters*, of the mining, steel
fabrication industries that Marx had illuminated and that were prepar-
ing the political destruction of the social order that had made impressionism possible. There is to be found in the dissolution of physical
objects into color and light characteristic of the elegant beauty of impressionism, a denial and an idealization of life that suppressed painful
social realities. What appears in art as a strictly formal and technical
innovation may nevertheless yield to psychoanalytic interpretation.
The denial of harsh social realities in the impressionist portrait of life
is matched by a denial of the intrapsychic conflicts that find expression
in the work of van Gogh along with his greater social realism. This
conclusion agrees with Devereux's (1970) point of view that the structure of the work of art replicates the organization of the psyche. In the
visual arts as well as in literature one finds the multifaceted relations
between the primary agencies of the human mind—the competing demands of the superego, ego, and id, which strive for harmonization in
its formation.

Form and Content in the Play of Children

I want to conclude this study of the relation between form and
content in psychoanalytic aesthetics by returning once more to the

instructive relationship that Freud drew between the play of children and the play of artists in artistic creation. It was once my privilege to observe the spontaneous creation of a game by three small boys who were children of three of my neighbors. They chanced to have something in common—the birth of a new baby sister or brother. It was this common circumstance that had become the shared motivation for their invention. They lived in adjacent row houses joined by a walk leading down a step to a common cement patio. In their game they had transformed the step into a dock, and the patio had become a sea. They were solemnly and diligently undertaking voyages by boat with much huffing and puffing, revving of engines, blaring of whistles, and shouting of orders. The purpose of their voyages was soon apparent. The boys were taking turns at being captain and crew. Their cargo was a bundle of cloth. When the ship had sailed a sufficient distance the cargo would be flung into the patio with the cry "Baby overboard." The ship would be rapidly brought about and one of the crew would plunge to the rescue and, after valiantly thrashing about, would triumphantly return the baby to the safety of the boat and so be returned to port and to safety by the captain.

The boys had invented the game and designed its rules under the dictates of a shared need to rid themselves of their unwanted sibling (the privilege of the first crew member), then to appease their fear of the loss of the love of their mothers (heroism of the second crew member), and finally to be an observer of the conflict (the captain). The nature of the aggression was ingeniously varied by each boy according to whether his hostility or his anxiety had the upper hand as the fateful moment approached: Sometimes the baby was flung overboard, sometimes it seemed to be accidentally dropped by a busy seaman, and at other times a stealthy hand would make the baby bounce about in the seaman's arms from which it would tumble out as a result of its own naughtiness. The game was repeated over and over again during the course of an afternoon with a remarkable concentration and attention to detail commensurate with the seriousness of the business at hand. The boys took turns at playing the different roles.

Art and the Human Condition

It has been asserted that art seeks to change the appearance of the world, whereas science by means of technology seeks to alter it to make it safer, more convenient, and more habitable. Freud (1933) seems to adhere to this view when he stated that art "does not seek to be anything but an illusion" (p. 160). But although this statement is true in itself, it is also seriously incomplete, for art, in order to achieve its affect, must be able to get us to treat its illusion as "true" for the time being. What is omitted by the distinction between art and science as Freud drew it is the recognition that the play of children and the creation of art, although not enlisted in the task of changing the world to make it better serve ourselves, may be enlisted in the work of changing ourselves in order to make us better able to serve ourselves and the world. There is something more than the simple, vicarious discharge of otherwise undischargeable impulses in the play of the children. To be sure, discharge and improved homeostasis are present. But there is also the exercise of defense mechanisms and the building up of psychic structure by means of trial identifications and the search for pathways for sublimations, all of which are part of the ongoing struggle for maturation (Freud, 1920; Winnicott, 1953). Freud tended to overlook, in his theoretical formulations, this second aspect of play and of art. Consequently, he tended to treat aesthetic experience in an Aristotelian way as only catharsis—as repetition but never as remembering or as working through. Yet there is no inherent reason for circumscribing psychoanalytic aesthetics in this way.

In fact, Freud (1908) pointed out the maturational strivings in the play of children; but because of the economic focus of his argument, he did not emphasize the equivalent of this function in adult aesthetic experience. This aspect of art was, nevertheless, perfectly familiar to Freud, for he recognized that the truth of the most fateful conflicts of childhood was revealed in an ancient tragedy from which he derived its name. It was to Shakespeare's *Hamlet* that Freud (1900) turned to illustrate the Oedipus complex in *The Interpretation of Dreams*. The unification of form and content in great art, which arouses our admiration, corresponds to a quest for psychic integration in creator and appreciator.

But to emphasize this aspect of play, of form, of mastery and integration to the neglect of the need for the affective synthesis provided only by primary process thinking involves an equal and opposite imbalance and a loss of insight into both the travail of creation and its appreciation (cf. Winnicott, 1971). The experience of great art can yield both insight and an adaptive inner reconciliation to the reality of self, others, and world. The affects that signal this reconciliation in addition to Aristotle's pity and fear are sadness, remorse, rue, resignation, forgiveness, tolerance, forbearance, patience. Play, form, mastery, and integration must of necessity not only take drive life into account, it must be aided and abetted by it.

Psychoanalytic Values in the Evaluation of Art

It is true that in *The Creative Writer and Day-Dreaming* Freud (1908) did not introduce distinctions between types of identification involved in aesthetic experience that could have allowed him to have formulated a more adequate criterion of artistic excellence than simply romantic wish fulfillment. It is also true that Freud had not yet explicitly investigated the complexities of identificatory processes and their relation to drives. By exploiting his later work (Freud, 1923a) we can say that there are two different types of identification that may engage us in the enjoyment of a work of art. There is an identification with what we would like to be but are not. These are typical of the romantic wish-fulfilling heroes and heroines of Freud's (1908) rather egoistical wish-fulfillment theory and as exemplified by the characters of Sir Water Scott's *Ivanhoe*. In them there is to be found elements of the ideal ego (Hanly, 1984) as well as of relatively unconflicted drive demands. Danger does not lead to calamity; it recedes, giving way to triumph and safety or, at least, to the promise of tranquil gratification and success. But there is also an identification in art with what we are but do not wish to be, with what we were but still wish we had not been, or, at the least, with what we might have been and still fear we could be. These are the somber bonds we establish with the heroes and heroines of tragedy. In them there are to be found elements of the ego ideal (Hanly, 1984) in conflict with powerful drive demands that result in calamity—destruction and death. Between these polarities are to be found the range of works of art from romance and comedy to tragedy excluding only the purely decorative, which yields only a pleasure of the purely formal kind. Within individual works of literature we find characters from various points along this spectrum. For example, in *King Lear* Cordelia represents an ideal of womanliness, whereas Kent represents an ideal of masculine loyalty, and Goneril, Regan, and Edmund represent female and male evil. It is not only in the modern psychological novel that the conflicting tendencies of the ego of the artist—the clash of drive demands and ego ideals—come to be represented in characters and plots.

I have argued that there is nothing in psychoanalytic theory that requires it to devalue form for the sake of content in art. Form, no less than content, may be clarified by means of psychoanalytic study. The view that there is an intrinsic relation between form and content that, after all, is the dominant view of aestheticians and critics (as it is the implicit sense of our primary prereflective engagement with art when we allow ourselves to become lost in its enjoyment) is also the point of view proper to psychoanalytic aesthetics. The integrity of form and content in art needs to be understood in the light of what we have learned about all three agencies of the psyche. This integrity cannot, for example, be understood adequately in terms either of ego functions alone or of primary process alone. When viewed from a multifaceted perspective the function of art can be recognized to include not only catharsis but also, as in the play of children, the quest for maturation, reparation, restoration, and psychic integration.

chapter six

Lear and His Daughters

An inconsistency or contradiction in conscious, deliberative, secondary process thought can be the handiwork of a conflict promoted by unconscious primary process thought. Ambiguity in speech or writing may be used intentionally in order to exploit the deeper ambiguities to which psychic conflicts give rise (Freud, 1905a, p. 65, n. 1; 1907, pp. 84–86). The presence of an unexpressed and unexpected trend of wishful thought can be revealed by the emotional emphasis of the expressed contrary thought: When a dignified elderly lady concludes her denunciation of a philandering local reprobate with the declaration that she would certainly be afraid to meet up with Mr. X in an alley late at night, the listener may appropriately wonder what stirring of what fantasy of exciting sexual molestation sought satisfaction in the shadows cast by her indignation (see also Freud, 1910a; 1925). Freud has pointed out the importance of an inconsistency in the reporting of a dream—a second version, as it were, of a dream episode, character, scene, and so forth. The inconsistency identifies that portion of the dream that is least well defended and that can be most expediently used as an access to its unconscious determinants. Inconsistencies, contradictions, vagueness, ambiguities are often useful points of departure for psychological inquiry.

Such points of departure are presented in applied psychoanalysis by contradictory interpretations or evaluations of works of literature. Leites (1947) in a study of Camus's (1942) *The Stranger* took as his starting point the tendency of critics of the novel to adopt one or other of two antithetical views of it: either its hero Merseault is intelligible as the representative of the author's existentialist understanding of the human condition, or he is unintelligible, without a credible character or plausible motives for any of his actions including his murder of an Arab. Of course, Camus's existentialist ideas, like Sartre's, deny the efficacy of motives and character. Any act, even a murder, is an *acte gratuit*. Human existence is absurd. Meaning and purpose is a *creatio ex nihilo*. Leites proceeds to escape between the horns of the dilemma posed by these antithetical evaluations of the novel. He uses psychoanalysis to show that, contrary to Camus's philosophical intention, he has created in the novel a character who appears to be affectless and without motive because of the dangerous hostility and anxiety that dominates his life. His apparent indifference both masks and expresses wishes to frustrate and disappoint. Thus, Leites's psychoanalytic interpretation makes Merseault and his actions intelligible, not as the incarnation of existential principles but as a representative of a psychologically flawed human nature.

In this respect Camus, like Sartre, is a writer whose creative imagination grasped more of individual human nature and of the human condition than did his abstract philosophical ideas. One is reminded of Freud's (1905a) comment:

> When I set myself the task of bringing to light what human beings keep hidden within them, not by the compelling power of hypnosis, but by observing what they say and what they show, I thought the task was a harder one than it really is. He that has eyes to see and ears to hear may convince himself that no mortal can keep a secret. If his lips are silent, he chatters with his finger-tips; betrayal oozes out of him at every pore. (pp. 77–78)

The creative writer's imaginative descriptions may disclose more than can be grasped by means of his own preferred intellectual categories. From Camus's descriptions of Merseault there "ooze" the very motives that Camus's philosophy denies. Camus's descriptions of Merseault's object relations support Leites's interpretation. For example, Merseault's treatment of his girlfriend "chatters" of his passive aggression. She is obliged to ask him if he would marry her. He replies that he will, if she wants him to. The girl's anxiety at this reply leads her to inquire whether he would have consented to such a proposal if it had come from someone else. Merseault's reply is that he guesses he would. A similar paradoxical quality is to be found in Sartre's novels. His characters make speeches according to the premises of his existentialist philosophy; but his portrayals of them and of their actions disclose the very motives (causes) at work in their lives that his existentialist premises deny. There is more of the reality of the human condition in the novels of these writers than in their philosophy.

Critical Inconsistencies and Psychoanalytic Criticism

The study of *King Lear* that follows was inspired by the discovery of two inconsistencies in the work of one of the great Shakespeare critics, Coleridge. Coleridge considered *King Lear* to be Shakespeare's greatest play, yet he also thought it to be seriously flawed in its form— in the unity and plausibility of the action it portrays. Even if one rejoices in the extent to which and in the ways in which Elizabethan drama escaped from the unnecessarily restricting confines of Aristotle's requirements of unity of time, place, and action, one must consider it a flaw in the play of a great psychological writer such as Shakespeare if the scene that initiates the action of the play is without an intrinsic connection to what follows and is not essential to its understanding. Yet such was Coleridge's view. Further, Coleridge offered an insightful psychological account of Edmund's evil but failed to extend any comparable understanding to the evil of Goneril and Regan, even though the structure of the main plot and subplot in Shakespeare's drama would warrant it.

This study of *Lear* seeks to exhibit the psychological unity of the play and its action by extending Coleridge's understanding of Edmund to Goneril and Regan. Psychoanalysis provides the basis for doing so and for using the result to gain a better understanding of Lear and the tragedy that befalls him, and one more faithful to Shakespeare's text.

As I have insisted above, any adequate psychoanalytic interpretation of a work of literature must be based on the details of specific, identifiable texts, must be consistent with everything else in the text, and must illuminate the text in a way that no other account is able to do. The crucial texts must not only be able to bear the interpretation, they must require it. The light that it thus sheds should also answer questions or solve puzzles about other important elements in the work. For example, the psychoanalytic understanding of the division of the kingdom scene that initiates the action of *King Lear* also enables us to understand the fatal love of Goneril and Regan for Edmund—an element in the play that might otherwise seem to be a gratuitously contrived retribution. A coherent psychoanalytic "reading" of the play is not enough. It provides nothing better that Ricoeur's (1981) requirement that "a good psychoanalytic explanation . . . must conform to Freud's psychoanalytic system" (p. 271). A good psychoanalytic explanation must rather conform to the demands of the object. It is an advantage if it can also solve problems, clear up difficulties, and render intelligible aspects of the work that would otherwise remain obscure and incomprehensible. Psychoanalysis may, as in this case, enhance our appreciation of the aesthetic form of the work and of the genius of its author as it deepens our understanding of the play and its characters, as it deepens our affective comprehension of their tragedy. Correct psychoanalytic interpretations are not reductions. They do not destroy the meaning of a work of literature by reducing it to a few simplistic theorems: They enrich and enhance its meaning.

The method employed here is that of psychoanalytically informed textually based criticism. Refutations or corroborations of the interpretation of the play must rest upon textual evidence: For example, my interpretation would be damaged if Kent did not support Cordelia or if, having supported her, he were subsequently revealed to have had an ulterior motive in doing so. On the other hand, the understanding of the unity of the play does not depend upon the interpretation I have given of Lear's character at the end of the play. Shengold (1974) takes the view that Lear, in the end, is redeemed by his suffering: "In his suffering Lear learns to value the love of and for Cordelia" and "He [Lear] has attained a full sense of what it is to love—and thus can feel its loss as a man and not as an infant" (p. 118). This interpretation is less bleak, but also less tragic, than mine. In the end the text must decide the question. If the text cannot, then the question must remain unanswered.

Inconsistencies in Traditional King Lear Criticism

King Lear has long been held by both critics and theater-goers to be Shakespeare's greatest achievement (Johnson, 1765a; Lamb, 1808; Hazlitt, 1817; Coleridge, 1818; Swinburne, 1876; Bradley, 1904; Hunter, 1972). Coleridge, who held this view of the play, nevertheless considered it to lack dramatic formal unity. He thought that the principal action of the first scene, Lear's division of his kingdom among his daughters, was a psychological deus ex machina, an action unintelligibly artificial in itself but from which everything else follows with tragic rigor:

> Let the first scene of this play have been lost, and let it only be understood that a fond father had been duped by hypocritical professions of love and duty on the part of two daughters to disinherit the third, previously and deservedly, more dear to him;—and all the rest of the tragedy would retain its interest undiminished, and perfectly intelligible. (p. 330)

The greatness of Shakespeare's greatest play, in Coleridge's view, consists of the extraordinary *tour de force* by which the playwright's powerful language is able to win from us an acquiescence in the originating cause of the tragedy despite its improbability; but, although the language of the play can in fact create complex effects, can it be that Shakespeare's greatest play is an aesthetic failure, that it lacks unity? Can it be that the poet who conceived of his art as "holding a mirror up to nature" could rest content with an arbitrary action as the motor of a play that had brought his genius to its greatest height?

That is not to say that Coleridge's perception of the play is universally shared by critics and scholars; however, less defined versions of it are to be found among contemporary scholars. One view is that, having rejected the political and personal reasons of the earlier *King Leir* from which he worked, Shakespeare offers no motive at all for Lear's division of the kingdom; that Shakespeare made Lear's action intelligible only insofar as it was willful and arbitrary (Hunter, 1972). But Shakespeare has Lear reveal that his action is indeed motivated: "Meantime we shall express our darker purpose." This "darker purpose" is only slowly revealed in the unfolding of the play: It is a "darker purpose" than Lear knew.

King Lear, despite its political theme, is a tragedy of family life. Johnson (1765a) believed the soul of the play to be Lear as father: "Lear would move our compassion but little, did we not rather consider the injured father than the degraded king" (p. 162). The relations between a father and his daughters, a father and his sons, and of sisters and brothers are at the heart of the play. Shakespeare uses Lear's madness as a device for stripping away the narcissistic illusory aspects of royalty in order to try to lay bare what is essential to the human condition. It is this very narcissistic illusion, which Shakespeare was concerned to penetrate, that many critics have found it necessary to preserve in their idealization of Lear. Lear's exercise of political authority has often received comment, but the calamity of Lear's exercise of parental authority has largely been passed over in silence. It is in the further analysis of the play as a tragedy of familial relations that Lear's "darker purpose" is to be found.

A Psychoanalytic Explanation of Lear and His Daughters

Freud (1913a) did not do justice to Lear's daughters or to Lear's relations with them. Freud took it for granted that Lear's contract with them, even if tragically misguided, can be fully comprehended in terms of Lear's failing struggle to accept decline and death. This perception is sound as far as it goes; but Freud treated Lear's daughters merely as abstractions—as symbolic representatives of the fates from whom Lear cannot escape—not as dramatic characters in their own right. Freud's interpretation of the daughters as fates is inconsistent with Cordelia's efforts to save and protect her father and with the fact that Lear is indirectly responsible for Cordelia's death. Freud passed over what is in my opinion a crucial psychoanalytic perception of the play and its central and secondary themes and characters, a perception that reveals the play's dramatic unity.

Freud was not alone in treating Lear's daughters as abstract symbols, although this treatment is more usually limited to Goneril and Regan, who not infrequently have been treated as personifications of ingratitude rather than as plausible, if horrifying, personalities. Although Coleridge (1818) showed that Shakespeare had taken pains to prevent evil in Edmund "from passing into utter monstrosity," he did not attempt any similar understanding of the characterization of Goneril and Regan. Although Freud gave them the dignity of being representatives of the Fates, critics before and after him have considered them simply inhuman. Goneril and Regan are, according to these critics, too monstrous to be human, their actions too evil to be explained; and yet there is no foundation for this treatment of Goneril and Regan in Shakespeare's language. On the contrary, Shakespeare has Lear treat his daughter Goneril very much as a woman when, in his rage at her refusal to entertain his knights, he curses her with barrenness. Shakespeare treats them as manipulative, evil, scheming women, but as women nonetheless. The intellectual denial of humanity to Goneril and Regan is instrumental to the psychological denial that they really are Lear's daughters. This denial, as we shall see, is part of a failure to come to terms with the psychological meaning of the opening scene of the play, which consequently is experienced as lacking in verisimilitude.

The play opens with a simple yet powerful conversation between Kent and Gloucester. We learn that Lear equally esteems his two sons-in-law, Albany and Cornwall. Gloucester discloses that he is ashamed of one of his two sons, his bastard son, Edmund, despite the fact that nature has given him physical and mental strengths at least equal to those of the legitimate son, Edgar. As the action of the play unfolds we realize that Lear has been blind to the grave differences in the characters of his sons-in-law—Albany decent but weak, Cornwall weak and cowardly but vicious. Similarly we discover how unreliable is Gloucester's judgment. In Edmund's presence he speaks wittily, sensually, but degradingly of Edmund's mother and the circumstances of his conception. Because of Edmund's illegitimacy, Gloucester has deprived Edmund of any stable, continuing relationship to himself and of the beneficial influence of a father on a son. Out of shame, Gloucester has maintained Edmund in a condition of exile from himself and informs Edmund and Kent that this deprivation is to continue:

> He hath been out nine years, and away he
> shall again. The king is coming.
>
> (I, 1, 31–32)

Lear's appearance in Act I, scene 1, is announced by Gloucester in conjunction with this rather brutal dismissal of his son. Moments later we will hear Lear's scarcely veiled though unconscious insults to Goneril and Regan and his enraged, brutal disowning of Cordelia. The themes of the subplot and the main plot of the play are tied together at the outset by Shakespeare. With the sure psychological instinct of the great dramatist he taps into the logic of free associations in his use of contiguities and juxtapositions such as this one while simultaneously elaborating his themes according to the logic of historical exposition. Unconscious, implicit connections and meanings are integrated with conscious, explicitly elaborated themes.

Coleridge, astute psychologist that he could be, was sensitive to the provocation and rejection inherent in Gloucester's treatment of Edmund. He saw that it could arouse in him a desperate, vengeful rage that could subvert his ambitions (which were consonant with his exceptional endowments) through the choice of violent means for their realization. As Coleridge (1818) put it:

> all the kindly counteractions to the mischievous feelings of shame, which might have been derived from co-domestication with Edgar and their common father, had been cut off by his absence from home, and a foreign education from boyhood to the present time, and a prospect of its continuance, as if to preclude all risk of his interference with the father's views for the elder and legitimate son. . . . (p. 336)

To this one might add that Gloucester's attitude to Edmund deprived the son of any affection for his father, and thus of the positive side of the ambivalence that could have helped him to accept and identify with his father's authority and hence with the authority of just law and self-restraint. His lack of any legitimate hope of advancement commensurate with his capacities neutralized in him the anxiety that might otherwise have imposed some constraint on him in his choice of means. Coleridge has demanded of us that we appreciate the dilemma of the defiant prayer by which Edmund steels himself in his plan to have Edgar exiled and not himself: "Now, gods, stand up for bastards!" (I, 2, 22). Edmund is exposed to overpowering feelings of sibling jealousy. Edmund's ambitions mount as fresh opportunities present themselves, but his first intent was bred out of sibling jealousy: to turn the tables on his legitimate and preferred brother:

> Well then,
> Legitimate Edgar, I must have your land:
> Our father's love is to the bastard Edmund
> As to the legitimate: fine word, "legitimate"!
> Well, my legitimate, if this letter speed
> And my invention thrive, Edmund the base
> Shall top the legitimate. I grow; I prosper.
> (I, 2, 15–21)

If the subplot is in fact dramatically bound to the main action by repetition of theme and variation, we would expect to find something of this "preference and rivalry" in the relations of Lear and his daughters.

With few exceptions the critics have found the subplot of the play to be essential to it precisely because it does reflect the characters and actions of the main story. Johnson (1765a) defended the place of Edmund in the play for the opportunity afforded "the poet of combining perfidy with perfidy, and connecting the wicked son with the wicked daughters, to impress this important moral, that villainy is never at a stop, that crimes lead to crimes, and at last terminate in ruin" (p. 61; cf. Warton, 1754). The duplication of plots, according to Bradley (1904), "startles and terrifies by suggesting that the folly of Lear and the ingratitude of his daughters are no accidents or merely individual aberrations, but that in that dark cold world some fateful malignant influence is abroad" (p. 262). But, although entirely agreeing with the critics concerning the dramatic and aesthetic importance of the relation of the subplot to the main story, I do not believe that the nature of this relationship has been either adequately or completely understood; indeed, it has been partly misunderstood insofar as it has involved the dehumanization of Goneril and Regan and the idealization of Lear. What is this fateful, malignant influence? Where does it spring from? Why invoke Satan or the gods or unredeemed animality? What if the poet's combining of perfidy with perfidy includes the fathers as well as the son and daughters? After all, Gloucester is not so "unsuspicious" as Bradley would have him; otherwise, how could Edmund have so easily aroused suspicions and fear of Edgar in his father? May not similar tragic flaws appear in Lear's relations to his daughters, if, indeed, the two plots reflect each other as it is agreed they do? Like Gloucester, Lear is deceived by his faithless daughters and repudiates his true daughter. Moreover, Lear is active whereas Gloucester is only reactive. Lear invites Goneril and Regan into the situation in which they deceive him with false promises of fidelity. Gloucester submits to deception; Lear invites it.

By these repetitions with variations Shakespeare holds up to the characters and actions of Lear and his daughters a mirror that dramatically illuminates, without verbalizing, the nature of Lear's "darker purpose" in the division of his kingdom. Coleridge went halfway toward grasping this crucial relation within the play in his analysis of the character of Edmund, but then was stopped short by his own idealization of Lear and corresponding fear of Goneril and Regan. Let us, then, extend to Goneril and Regan Coleridge's insights into the character and motives of Edmund and see what understanding of the main story and its great protagonist is offered by that vantage point: Lear's treatment of Goneril and Regan in Act I is no less provocative than Gloucester's treatment of Edmund.

If Edmund was driven by jealous rage against his brother to take by deceit what had been denied to him by his father, can less be said of Goneril and Regan? Lear makes his preference for Cordelia over her sisters naïvely and harshly clear:

> Now, our joy,
> Although the last, not least, to whose young love
> The vines of France and milk of Burgundy
> Strive to be interess'd, what can you say to draw
> A third more opulent than your sisters?
> (I, 1, 82–86)

And again:

> I loved her most, and thought to set my rest
> On her kind nursery.
> (I, 1, 123–124)

Goneril and Regan have been placed in a situation of severe humiliation by their father. They are invited to compete with each other for the richest portion of their father's gift, in the knowledge that they must lose to their father's favorite, Cordelia. Could it be that the deceitfulness and coldness they exhibit come from their own chilling realization that nothing they can do or say could win for them an equal place in their father's heart? The tendency of some critics to hold that the play has no past—only the improbable present of Act I, scene 1, from which the tragedy follows, can be understood as the consequence of the denial that Lear is the father of Goneril and Regan as well as of Cordelia. If her father's love provided a fertile soil in which her goodness could grow, then the absence of genuine fatherly feeling must have been the barren ground from which the deceit and hate of Goneril and Regan have sprung. In fact, one of Lear's tragic flaws revealed in the opening scene is his demand for a show of love so narcissistically invested that he is filled with rage at Cordelia's refusal to comply. When one attends to the psychology of the relations between and among Lear's daughters, the scene's roots in the past come clearly into evidence: It is a fateful repetition at the end of Lear's life of character-forming episodes in the past.

In this connection one must underline once more Freud's (1913a) astonishing psychological purblindness to this dimension of the play, "the relationship of a father to his children, which might be a fruitful source of many dramatic situations, is not turned to further account" (p. 301)—other, that is, than to regard the daughters as symbolic representatives of the Three Fates. Freud (1901) saw with perfect clarity the oedipal theme in Shakespeare's Hamlet, but from his (1913a) reading of King Lear this awareness is entirely absent, even explicitly denied. In 1934, however, Freud corrected this earlier misreading of the play, without abandoning his allegorical interpretation. In a letter to Bransom cited by Jones (1957) Freud treated Cordelia's silence and her repudiation of her father's demand as a reaction against "her love for him . . . her holy secret" (p. 487). But there is also strength and courage, which Freud does not note: a wish to be free of her infantile attachment to her father, "to love him according to her bond" so that she can leave him to love a husband.

The rage that causes Lear to unleash the series of events leading to the final scene of destruction is a reaction to Cordelia's perfectly healthy, decent, and honest refusal of his demand for an avowal that she love only him. Shakespeare's language is simple, direct, unequivocal, and extraordinarily powerful in its assertion of a fundamental emotional truth:

> Haply, when I shall wed,
> That lord whose hand must take my plight shall carry
> Half my love with him, half my care and duty:
> Sure, I shall never marry like my sisters,
> To love my father all.
>   (I, 1, 100–104)

Shakespeare confirms Cordelia in two ways: by having Kent, who is utterly honest and entirely loyal to Lear, come to her defense; and by having Cordelia chosen by France, who loves her for her own sake, after Burgundy rejects her because she has lost her dowry and has been disowned by her royal father. These are the very values and truths that make life worthwhile in the face of an indifferent universe and death—values for which Lear gropes in his madness. Lear's folly is not merely that he decided to divide his kingdom and resign his authority and power to his daughters and their husbands, nor is it merely that he failed to anticipate the ingratitude of Goneril and Regan; it is rather that he undertook all this in a way that imposed a demand for falsehood and emotional disorder on his daughters without knowing what he was doing.

Lear declares that one of the purposes of dividing his kingdom is so "that future strife/May be prevented now" (I, 1, 44–45). But his method of carrying out the division, with its inherent preference for Cordelia, must set her sisters against her and, in effect, could only avoid future strife by precipitating it in the present. His other purpose is to find relief from the cares and responsibilities of his great office:

> . . . *and 'tis our fast intent*
> *To shake all cares and business from our age,*
> *Conferring them on younger strengths, while we*
> *Unburdened crawl toward death. . . .*
>
> *(I, 1, 48–51)*

There is a profound irony in this statement because Lear is altogether unaware of how "unburdened" he will in fact become, but there is also a profound deception in him caused by his denial of death.

Lear's Narcissism

Although Lear seems to accept the reality of his death, the details of the contract he forces upon his daughters reveal his narcissistic conflict. The effect of these arrangements, had they succeeded, would have been to re-create for Lear the emotional conditions of adolescence—carefree, without responsibilities, surrounded by his chosen companions—and also of early childhood with its omnipotent illusion of being cared for by an all-loving and all-powerful mother who is able to protect her child from all dangers and who needs nothing from the child herself. Lear's division of the kingdom was neither an accident nor an unmotivated act nor the dramatically unintegrated residue of an ancient tale. Shakespeare has made the division of the kingdom psychologically inevitable because Lear had to divest himself of the responsibilities that bound him to reality, and thus to mortality, in his attempt to give "objectivity" to the narcissistic illusion to which he unconsciously clings (Hanly, 1984). He has to make himself helpless in order to reassure himself that he enjoys the unconditional love of his daughter–mothers.

Lear nevertheless proposes to retain 100 knights, to be sustained by his daughters, as well as the title but not the power of a king. His folly, insofar as it consists of believing that he could possess the dignity of office after having handed over its powers and prerogatives, has not escaped the critics (Colie, 1974), nor has his folly in trusting himself to Goneril and Regan while disavowing Cordelia. What has not been well perceived, if at all, is the libidinally provocative contract he proposes to make with his daughters. In exchange for their shares of his kingdom Lear considers himself entitled to demand of them what no mature daughter can or ought to give. The overpowering force of Lear's rage reaction to Cordelia's clear perception of the nature of this demand, and her refusal of it, is Shakespeare's way of embodying this meaning in dramatic action. Lear rages at Cordelia because she has touched on the sensitive core of his folly; she has no alternative if she is to remain loyal to herself, to the truth, and to him.

The Evil Sisters

Thus, it is that by playing upon their father's narcissism—and by acting upon the maxim of their own damaged pride, "if I cannot have his love I shall get whatever of his power and property I can"—Goneril and Regan manage to do to Cordelia, without trying, what Edmund by scheming does to Edgar: They dispossess her of her inheritance and secure her exile. In this way Shakespeare prepares through the opening scene for the fateful intertwining of the subplot and the main story, which leads to the catastrophic conclusion of the play. Goneril and Regan both fall in love with Edmund. Freud (1921) has pointed out that the most primitive attachment is one of identification. There is a psychological inevitability in Goneril and Regan's attachment to Edmund because they share with him both the common circumstance of paternal devaluation and a criminality that in part results from it. Edmund is the masculine incarnation, rendered effective by his martial strength, his ruthless commitment to the pursuit of power at any cost, and his courage, of their own bitter, vengeful hatred. Regan has already found something of such a man in Cornwall, but his cruelty is cowardly and he is killed by one of Gloucester's servants who tries to stop him from trampling out his master's eyes with his spurs. As for Albany,

Goneril's husband, he is both decent and weak and hence of no real interest to her. Thus, it is that Edmund is offered by the sisters an opportunity far beyond his original hopes: to make himself king by defeating the French forces brought by Cordelia to rescue Lear; and thus it is that Edmund, having gained the upper hand in battle and having captured Lear and Cordelia, gives the order for their deaths and becomes the vehicle for the final realization of the parricidal and fratricidal wishes of Goneril and Regan, wishes he shares with them.

Pauncz (1952) and Donnelly (1953) have pointed out the incestuous nature of Lear's attachments to his daughters. To demand all the love of a daughter is a thinly veiled repetition of the child's possessive, incestuous love for his mother. Lear's apparent acceptance of old age and death is in reality a rejection of it. His plan is to be regal without responsibility, at ease and carefree surrounded by his retainers and completely cared for and doted on by Cordelia. Lear greets the prospect of being stripped by death of his monarchy, his pleasures, and his life, with a narcissistic refusal, and hence with the pursuit of a magical return to boyish vigor and irresponsibility, to infantile erotic possession, and to the status of "his majesty the infant" who is the unique recipient of selfless love. The unconscious magical idea that is inherent in this regression to early stages of narcissism, before death acquires its full meaning and reality for the ego, is the psychological core of Lear's "darker purpose" in the division of his realm.

Donnelly (1953) pointed out that it is inadequate parents who accuse their children of ingratitude: Adequate parents are able to take satisfaction in a child's independence and autonomy. Lear's narcissism does not permit him to know these satisfactions, which are one of the healthy sources of consolation in face of old age and death. His accusations of ingratitude, although in one respect justified by his daughters' callous behavior toward him, are also expressions of his denial of his own threatening and impossible demands on them. Nothing could be more threatening to a daughter than the demand Lear makes. Nothing is more psychologically damaging to a daughter than to submit to the demand. Goneril and Regan, whose mastery of their hostility is precarious at best, are confronted by a father whose love for them, inferior though it is to his love for Cordelia, is eroticized. (This is not to say that Lear consciously desired sexual intercourse with his daughters, any more than a 5-year-old boy at the height of his oedipal passion would plan the sexual seduction of his mother in the the adult sense: In fact, nothing could be more disturbing to a child than the attempt of a parent to realize these wishes by a real seduction.) Lear's speech and conduct give expression at the conscious level to reactive infantile fantasies that are at once oedipal and pre-oedipal, and it is because his emotional life is thus governed by fantasies that one is entitled to emphasize his narcissism. It is these same fantasies that cause Lear to act toward his daughters as though he expected them to mother him:

> I loved her most, and thought to set my rest
> On her kind nursery.
>
> (I, 1, 123–124)

The reaction of Goneril and Regan is compliance on the surface and a cold hatred and fear of their father underneath. Hatred of their father has become their only defense against the instinctual calamity that would otherwise confront them. It is this hatred that makes sense of the sisters' determination to rid their father of his knights and render him helpless, dependent, and subject to their control. Their destructiveness is motivated by the repetition of an anal sadistic, regressive recoil from Lear's inappropriate demands. Their actions manifest an anal sadistic, manipulative hatred that seeks the possession of power and objects and the vengeful degradation or destruction of persons. (The anal sadomasochistic aspect of Lear's relation to Goneril and Regan has been touched on by Sharpe, 1946, although for the most part she has missed the psychological significance of the relation between Lear and his daughters. Like Freud and some of the nonpsychoanalytic writers, she treats Goneril and Regan as symbolic rather than as dramatic characters.)

Lear's narcissism makes him blind to the reality of the situation, which has been brought about by this same narcissism. He is unaware of the fear and hatred Goneril and Regan have for him as a consequence of his preference for Cordelia. He is, therefore, unable to sense their own coldly calculating manipulation of him by their false declarations of love. Nor is he able to respond to the honesty, loyalty, and appropriate love of Cordelia and Kent; instead, he imperiously dismisses Cordelia as worthless now that she has lost his favor and her dowry, and he exiles Kent for trying to make him see what he is doing. Then, having rendered himself all but defenseless, he turns to Goneril and Regan for succor. Shakespeare presents them as being aware of the surface of Lear's folly, and as being afraid of it:

> GONERIL: The best and soundest of his time hath been but rash; then must we look to receive from his age, not alone the imperfections of long ingrafted condition, but therewithal the unruly waywardness that infirm and choleric years bring with them.
>
> REGAN: Such unconstant starts are we like to have from him as this of Kent's banishment.
>
> (I, 1, 294–300)

There is an irony in the cold, detached, calculating attitude the two sisters have to their father—an attitude that echoes something of his attitude to them, inasmuch as they exist for his convenience, whereas Cordelia was his "joy." They appear to be completely detached from Lear, as though he were to them only a rather threatening, deteriorating old man from whom they had to protect themselves; and yet they are bound to him sadistically by having submitted to him masochistically by (falsely) promising the fulfillment of his wishes. They fear that he may become dangerously out of control. They believe themselves free to manipulate him at will because they do not really love him; but at a deeper level they are driven by their own erotic fear of him into a sadistic determination to strip him of his "riotous," "disordered" knights and to take pleasure in rendering him completely helpless.

This sadomasochistic bondage to Lear repeats itself in the loves of Goneril and Regan for Edmund. The sisters must fall in love with Edmund for the reasons above, but also because his reckless daring, his lusty determination to have his way, his self-willed purposes indifferent to the needs of others or to the law, all cause him to appear to Goneril and Regan as the youthful embodiment of their father's reckless imperiousness. They are fascinated by him. They wish to submit to him emotionally and sexually. Their sadomasochistic love of their father thus returns to haunt them in the person of Edmund, and he, like their father, treats them as mere conveniences for his own purposes:

> To both these sisters have I sworn my love;
> Each jealous of the other, as the stung
> Are of the adder. Which of them shall I take?
> Both? one? or neither? Neither can be enjoy'd,
> If both remain alive.
>
> (V, 1, 56–59)

Goneril and Regan had thought themselves to be indifferent to the ordinary filial bonds and affections. So they are, but their indifference, their capacity for cold manipulation, is rooted in their sadomasochistic bondage to their father. So it is that they are fascinated by Edmund's virile willfulness, which causes them to be as womanly as they are capable of being; and so it is that their suspicious, envious rage and destructiveness are turned against each other.

Lear's narcissistic blindness—the source of his folly, which sets the tragedy in motion—persists to the end. He could not bear the truth Cordelia had to tell at the beginning of the play. He was not able to learn it from the catastrophe he suffered. The insights that take Lear's mind by storm concern the reality of the human condition when the narcissistic supports of office, privilege, wealth, and power have been stripped away, but he remains as blind as ever to Cordelia's needs, to her separate existence, to the end:

> CORDELIA: We are not the first
> Who with best meaning have incurr'd the worst.
> For thee, oppressed King, am I cast down;
> Myself could else out-frown false fortune's frown.
> Shall we not see these daughters and these sisters?
> LEAR: No, no, no, no! Come, let's away to prison:
> We two alone will sing like birds i' the cage:
> When thou dost ask me blessing, I'll kneel down
> And ask of thee forgiveness: so we'll live,
> And pray, and sing, and tell old tales, and laugh
> At gilded butterflies, and hear poor rogues
> Talk of court news. . . .
>
> (V, 3, 4–14)

Cordelia is angered by her defeat at her sisters' hands; she is aware that she is "cast down"; prison is no "nursery" for her. She is a young woman, married to a man who loves her. She wishes to be engaged in life and not a mere spectator of it. Lear is content to have her back, to have her all to himself to serve his old age, to comfort and amuse him. He demonstrates no awareness of the devastating sacrifice this situation would involve for his daughter. Cordelia is nature's martyr: She is among the truest and best of all the personalities that people Shakespeare's plays; but Shakespeare's comprehension of life was never, at its best, compromised by idealizing distortions. The love "according to her bond" that gave Cordelia the freedom, denied her sisters, to live and love independently of her father also bound her to him. She had to return from France to try to rescue him from her sisters, and to be hanged.

Lear's Blindness

The tragedy of Lear is the tragedy of his narcissism and his violent search for a love that cannot flourish or succeed, because it is contrary to nature. In this respect as well the subplot echoed the great themes of the main story. Edmund, as he dies, consoles himself with the appalling testimony of Goneril and Regan's love for him:

> Yet Edmund was beloved:
> The one the other poison'd for my sake,
> And after slew herself.
> (V, 3, 237–238)

It is this desperate assurance that he was loved that releases in Edmund the will to try to prevent the murder of Cordelia and Lear. Gloucester's real, physical blinding also echoes and illuminates Lear's blindness. Gloucester, during his blinding, learns the truth about Edmund's treachery and his own injustice to Edgar. His physical suffering is overtaken by his remorse and his wish to make amends to his loyal son for his mistrust and mistreatment of him. Lear betrays no equivalent realization of his folly or of his mistreatment of Cordelia. The harsh truth of *King Lear* is that so much suffering could result in so little insight, correction, or amelioration. In the end there is violence, despair, and death. Lear comforts himself with the thought that he has killed Cordelia's hangman. He knows what he has lost, but he scarcely knows the daughter he has lost. His despair can be softened only by the delusional uncertainty as to whether Cordelia is alive or dead. Shakespeare expresses in Lear a despairing longing that clings to reality and to unreality all at once:

> *She's gone for ever!*
> *I know when one is dead and when one lives;*
> *She's dead as earth. Lend me a looking-glass;*
> *If that her breath will mist or stain the stone,*
> *Why, then she lives.*
>
> *(V, 3, 258–261)*

Lear dies uncomprehending as he lived. (See also Stompfer, 1960; Brooke, 1963; Gardner, 1967; Goldberg, 1974; Zak, 1984.)

An understanding of narcissism and its relation to sadism helps us to see the opening scene for all it reveals of Lear's family relations. The aesthetic unity of the play can be grasped in a new way if Lear's "darker purpose" in the first scene is understood both as an essential part of the tragic flaw in his character and as the spring that sets the action of the play in motion. The division of the kingdom is not merely a modified borrowing from a received legend, an extraneous act Shakespeare used as an artifice to set the action going; on the contrary, he wrote the scene to make it, by its psychological depth, reverberate with the past and portend the future. Heraclitus said that "character is fate." Shakespeare uses the division of the kingdom to convey implicitly, in affective language and action, the character of Lear and his daughters and the misfortune to which they are exposed by the gift and what Lear wants from it.

The Unity of the Play

The linkages that the best critics have always seen between the main story and the subplot are enriched by extending Coleridge's understanding of the character and motivation of Edmund to Goneril and Regan; Coleridge's inability to do this derives from a need to maintain his idealization of fathers, and hence of King Lear—the royal father. Coleridge (1818) gave eloquent expression to this idealization and its consequences:

> All Lear's faults increase our pity for him. We refuse to know them otherwise than as means of his sufferings and aggravations of his daughters. (p. 340)

What is this refusal but a denial of the impact of Lear's character and his actions upon his ungrateful daughters who, as a result, are supposed to be responsible for his faults? Coleridge, for his own dark reasons, has identified with Lear's attitude to women.

The idealization of Lear is nowhere more fervently expressed than in Kitteredge (1940):

> But in Shakespeare Lear becomes colossal. His character defies analysis because it needs none. He is a man; he is a father; he is a king—and he is old. That is the whole account. (p. xiv)

And there is attendant upon this idealization the inevitable derogation of the daughters, even of Cordelia:

> Eminent critics have done their best to reconcile Cordelia's character with her refusal to compete with her sisters' lies by speaking the truth her father longs to hear. . . . If Shakespeare had changed the tale here, his tragedy would have come to a happy ending in the first act. (p. xiii)

Once this idealization is modified, Goneril and Regan are able to assume human proportions as women, daughters, and sisters made evil by jealous rage, hatred, and sadomasochistic sexual desires. At the same time, Lear's contribution to their violence is brought into view. Our pity is mingled with fear. Goneril and Regan can take their place with Lady Macbeth as part of Shakespeare's struggle to understand and articulate the origin of evil in women. Seen and understood in this way King Lear assumes its pride of place as a great artistic achievement and a profound evocation of the tragedy of family life.

chapter seven

Autobiography and Creativity

A Case Study

This chapter takes up a group of interconnected problems in literature and art: the relation of the imaginary to the real; the relation of dreaming to the imaginary real; the relation of the life of the writer to his creations; and the universal in the particular in art. The art of the writer consists, in part, in the ability to create out of the real an imaginary world of characters and their lives that is, in a sense, more real (more true) and hence more engaging than the reality used as a point of departure for its creation. The life of the criminal upon whom Dostoyevski (1866) based his character Raskolnikov in *Crime and Punishment* was of but passing interest and edification by comparison with the enduring fascination aroused in generations of readers by his imaginary surrogate. Raskolnikov occupies an imaginary space that, unlike the space of the original criminal, allows a measure of tolerance of and interest in evil not only in the object but in ourselves. This imaginary space is not in a world of literature and art detached from life: It is an imaginary space that is continuous with the world of dreams, no matter how carefully it imitates reality. It is for this reason that good literature is able to imitate psychic reality.

Freud (1907) showed how dream psychology can illuminate the way in which a novel is built up out of condensations, displacements, plastic representations, and symbolization. This idea is exploited here to explore the relationship between imagination and artistic verisimilitude, and that exploration is then used to identify the inevitably autobiographical elements in any artistic work. It is argued that it is precisely these elements that constitute what is universal in the particularity of the work. It is the link with the unconscious life of the writer and of the reader that justifies our treating these imaginary characters of fiction as though they were real in our interpretation of them.

The basis of these arguments, apart from the theoretical considerations involved, is an interpretative study of the short story "Fits" by Munro (1986), a Canadian writer.

The Imaginary and the Real

I shall begin the argument with a paradox: *It is the imaginary rather than the naturalistic elements in art that cause the willing suspension of disbelief.* Can such an idea serve as a premise for a study of the contribution of autobiography to the art of Munro? Does it not contradict the sensible notion that we are invited into the world of the writer by the reality-bound impressions included in the descriptions, characters, scenes, and actions? Moreover, Munro's art appears, at first glance, to be on the side of common sense.

One need only consider Munro's style. Her sentences are brief and crisp. Her prose has a certain no-nonsense quality about it; it is down to earth, matter-of-fact. We are left with the impression of ordinary happenings in an everyday world supported by a fine sense of detail. Even when her themes are dark they are composed with the clarity of a cloudless western Ontario winter day. In this respect Munro seems to defy Aristotle's claim that literature is closer to truth than history because the writer can disregard the contingencies of actual events and center intuition upon what is essential in the human condition reflected in imaginary or legendary characters and events. Yet Munro's style is but the bezel in which the jewel of her art is set. It is, to use Freud's (1908) metaphor, her "bribe . . . of a purely formal, that is, aesthetic pleasure in the presentation of [her] phantasies" (p. 153). And, as we shall see, this "bribe" is more than a bribe. Nor is it simply formal. It is also communicative and meaningful.

By what alchemy does the imaginary acquire a greater potential to evoke the real than the realistic? Here, some psychoanalytic considerations can be of help. Our approach shall be via what Freud called the royal road to the unconscious—dreams. Certain dreams involve unusually intense anxiety, which causes us to awaken; others involve unusually intense pleasure, which causes us to want not to awaken and, when we do, to want to return to the dream. These dreams shed light upon the nature of the imaginative alchemy that brings it about that something subjective comes to assume the character of something real and objective.

An example of a nightmare will serve the purpose of illustration. The dreamer, a patient in analysis, finds himself in some kind of public building from which he is being ushered by somber men. They escort him through silent streets to a railway station where, to his relief, he is able to catch a train as though to make his escape. The train draws out of the station and begins to gather speed. The train goes faster and faster as the dreamer becomes increasingly terrified. His terror becomes overwhelming as he realizes that he is alone in a train that has no destination. It is typical of anxiety dreams that the dreamer is roused into wakefulness in order to assure himself that the dream is not real and that he is safely at home in his own bed. This fact is a measure of the degree to which such dreams are able to achieve a suspension of disbelief. It is in this respect that dreams reveal a psychotic-like process in each of us—an ability to lose ourselves in the world of imagination, which becomes more real than reality. The difference between a psychotic state and a normal dream state is that in the psychotic state the sufferer cannot awaken and regain access to reality. He is already awake. We can enter into the imaginary world of the great writer because we can always put the book down or remind ourselves that we are in the theater.

This astonishing work is done by primary process thought activity that includes condensation, displacement, symbolization, dramatization, and secondary revision. The potential for creative synthesis of these processes can be illustrated from the dream. Analysis revealed that the stern, ominous figures who appeared as complete strangers to the dreamer, and who were unlike anyone he could remember ever having seen, had been constructed out of facets of various male authority figures from his past life. Their clothes were derived from the garb of priests; their severe demeanor and bearing had been borrowed from army officers; the belts with large buckles that they wore led via associations to the father's belt of his childhood, which he had feared on account of its use to punish him. These elements had been selected by way of a common affective significance attached to the persons from whom they were drawn: the dreamer's fear of male—ultimately paternal—authority. By this same affect the images were invested with life and the capacity for action apparently independent of, and even contrary to, the dreamer's will: Thus, in dreams there arise images of ego-alien strangers with characters and lives of their own.

A displacement, in cooperation with condensation, created the imposing public building from which the dreamer found himself being escorted. The building represented a municipal building. It was drawn from a day residue: The dreamer had visited such a building in order to conduct some routine business in connection with his professional work. Like other such buildings in small municipalities, it housed a county court facility that had nothing to do with the business transacted by the dreamer but that, as a result of displacement, gave the building in the dream the aura of a courthouse. The building was also associated with a hospital. The displacement, combined with this condensation, then became tantamount to the idea of a hospital as the place in which the dreamer was to be found guilty of some crime and be punished for it.

The nature and meaning of the punishment could be deciphered from the associations that shed light upon the symbolic element of the dream—the voyage by train. During this same business trip (by train, to a small town about an hour from the city) the dreamer had been obliged to take a break when the offices closed for an hour at lunch. After lunch he had spent his free time wandering in a church graveyard near the municipal offices, studying the gravestones and meditating on the lives of the dead whose graves they marked. The symbolic connection between a voyage and death, so frequently exploited in folklore, myths, and literature, and indicated here by the dreamer's associations, suggested that the punishment was to be some kind of death sentence.

As the dream was progressively interpreted, the dreamer was able, for the first time, to acknowledge to his analyst that he had become anxious about a lump that had been developing on his chest. He had already sought medical attention and had been advised to have it removed surgically. He was now in a state of increasing anxiety as the date of the surgery approached (in the dream the dangerous acceleration of the train had represented the all too rapidly approaching date of the surgery). He had become convinced that the growth was a terminally malignant cancer, hence the overdetermined and, realistically speaking, inappropriate identification in the dream of a hospital with a courthouse.

But are not latent dream thoughts supposed to be unconscious? Of these thoughts of death the dreamer was all too well aware. The intensity of his fear, the obsessionality of his belief in the cancer, and his secretiveness about it were remarkable yet, given the dread aroused by the mere possibility of a diagnosis of cancer, comprehensible enough. But the dreamer was also feeling guilt, which found expression in the vague but unmistakable theme of punishment.

The associations of the patient to his real-life predicament revealed the true nature of the unconscious thoughts. Associated to the lump on his chest there was the unconscious fantasy, now made conscious in the analysis, that he was in the process of being transformed into a woman—the lump growing on his chest was the first beginning of a breast, itself the first sign of his metamorphosis. This fear substituted for a yet greater fear of punishment by castration. That anxiety in turn was maintained in him by a fixated wish to triumph over his father and, later, over his father's substitutes. The father's latest substitutes in the patient's life were the surgeon who was to operate on him and the analyst who was analyzing him. He now feared that the surgeon/analyst had surmised his hostile wishes and would revenge himself on him in the hospital. Instead of going into hospital to have removed what happily turned out to be a benign growth, the dreamer unconsciously feared that he was going there to be subjected to sex-change surgery that would complete a calamitous process already latently at work.

We thus have the following situation: An individual has the perfectly uneventful and satisfying experience of a trip by train to a nearby town where he transacts some ordinary business at an office in the local municipal building. Consciously at play in his thoughts during part of the day were his worries about his health, which had aroused his interest in the graveyard and had given rise to an hour of melancholy brooding. These thoughts and feelings then had become linked to unconscious guilt-provoking sexual and aggressive aims, to a homosexual defense against them, and hence to the unconscious transsexual fantasy. This fantasy, burdened as it was by tendencies repugnant to the dreamer's ego, could not become conscious or find direct means of discharge except in some substitute and altered form. In its pursuit of discharge, the fantasy exploits the primary process thought activity of symbolization, condensation, displacement, and dramatization and, in doing so, forces upon consciousness a new version of the business trip in which it is transformed into an allegorical punishment for unknown crimes. By means of dramatization (in this case by representing the dreaded punishment as actually about to occur) and because of the strength of the affects that unconsciously invested the dream scenes, figures, and actions, this new dream version of events is able to achieve such a degree of hallucinatory vividness that it assumes the character of reality. It is in this way that imagination, when it is under the influence of "blind" primary process thought activity, can sometimes create a more convincing reality than it can when it is guided only by conscious memories and perceptions. It is only in this way that imagination can come so close to vying successfully with normal waking perceptions in capturing our sense of reality. One important aspect of the genius of the writer involves his capacity to use language to arouse this very process in the reader so that his primary process thought activity can bring to life the scenes, characters, words, and actions of the poem, story, or play.

Munro has said that she draws bits of her stories from real experiences, either of her own or of others, but that in the telling she modifies them. It is argued here that in modifying this material Munro, like other creative writers, makes these experiences her own (no matter whether they were originally hers or others') by bringing them into relation with her own character and life-shaping unconscious memories and fantasies. These memories and fantasies determine the fundamental modifications that are to be wrought in the original material. These memories and fantasies and the primary process thought activities that transform them are the psychological wellspring traditionally called inspiration. This involuntary process guides the work of creation with an unseen hand. It is here that we come upon the inevitable autobiographical factor in literature and art.

But before turning to this aspect of the subject, let us first explore the idea of artistic realism in relation to one of Munro's stories. Before taking this step we need to take into account two further considerations. The dream that is dreamed is not always exactly the same as the dream that is remembered upon waking. A final effort is made, upon waking, to render the dream more congenial to conscious thought activity by making it more thematically organized, more intelligible, less amoral, more logical, than its original version, and hence even more disguised. This working over of the dream was referred to by Freud as secondary elaboration. In the creative literary imagination, the reworking of the derivatives of the unconscious life of the writer is usually carried even further in an effort to render them at once more impersonal and more accessible to readers. It is also carried out more skillfully because of the writer's special gift for formal expression. This process of objectification is furthered by the synthesis of personal emotion-laden material with neutral, objective descriptions (elements that offer the same psychological reassurance within the aesthetic experience as does waking from a nightmare) and by the artistic form of the work that frames the world of the story.

A Psychoanalytic Account of
Munro's "Fits"

In the story "Fits" Munro uses a town's reaction to a murder—suicide as the backdrop for exploring the meaning of the reaction of one woman, Peg, the victims' neighbor, and the response of Peg's husband Robert to her reaction to the grisly scene she chanced upon. At first, Peg's constrained, calm, matter-of-fact attitude to the event sheds a critical light upon the town's morbid craving for details and explanations. Munro has used certain strengths of Peg's character to create an implicit social commentary. Munro then gradually unfolds the irony of the story. These strengths in Peg's character cover over something else.

We learn that Peg sensed that something was badly wrong before she made the turn at the top of the stair to the neighbors' bedroom but did not retreat to call upon anyone for help, that when she knew what was wrong she had to get a good look even though to do it she had to walk in fresh blood and to get blood on her coat, presumably from a wall or doorframe. Despite this experience she carried on throughout the day as though nothing out of the ordinary had happened; she even chose to prepare spaghetti with tomato sauce for dinner that evening.

In the practice of psychoanalysis one is always alerted by any inconsistency in, for example, a patient's account of a dream, because the detail over which the inconsistency arose will always be linked to significant unconscious thoughts. Robert, who married Peg because there were things that he "absolutely and eternally want[ed] to forget about" (Munro, 1986, p. 128) and who believed that Peg's matter-of-fact, orderly ways would enable him to do that, is forced to abandon his idealization of Peg by such an inconsistency. Peg, at last, gives her account to him of what she saw. She tells him that she saw Weeble's foot—the one that still had the shoe on it—protruding through the doorway. But for all of her calm factuality, Robert knows that this is not what she has in fact seen, because the town policeman has already told him that Weeble blew himself backward through the door and that what was left of his head and torso was lying in the hall. It was into the bedroom that the suicide's foot protruded, not into the hall, as Peg claimed.

Peg has already altered her memory of what she has seen, not in order to make what she saw better than it was but in order to make why she had to see it better than it was. Neither does Robert want to acknowledge what her motive and her pleasure might have been. Peg's son, Clayton, who is still a virgin, is reminded by the murder–suicide of the violent quarrels he witnessed between Peg and his father (Peg's first husband, who had drifted off to the Arctic); he is further reminded of his fear that Peg or his father might come and kill him with a knife. Peg tries to use her maternal authority to get Clayton to deny that he ever had such a fear. Robert insists that such violent happenings are like an earthquake or a volcano, a kind of fit, a freak occurrence. But Clayton's cruel adolescent passion for truth is not to be deflected: " 'Earthquakes and volcanoes aren't freaks,' said Clayton, with a certain dry pleasure. 'If you want to call that a fit, you'd have to call it a periodic fit. Such as people have, married people have' " (Munro, 1986, p. 126)—a western Ontario way of saying that although sex may involve love, it may also involve violence in its periodic, convulsive demand for gratification. Robert is obliged to acknowledge something in Peg at once unknown and painful. He looks to her for assurance that she and he do not have "periodic fits" but she,

> who always seems pale and silky and assenting, but hard to follow as a watermark in fine paper, looked dried out, chalky, her outlines fixed in steady, helpless, unapologetic pain. (Munro, 1986, p. 126)

During a late-night walk over snow-crusted fields, Robert is driven to remember and acknowledge to himself the latent hatred and sexual violence that eventually erupted and destroyed his relationship with the woman he had known before Peg. But he also knows that he cannot ever ask Peg about the discrepancy in her story, nor dare to understand its meaning or explain her to their neighbors. Instead, he distracts himself with a comforting rationalization and hopes to distract her with his account of the magical miniature cityscape or battle scene he had seen in the moonlit frozen woods, but that turned out to be only a pile of old cars: distraction, repression, forgetfulness. Munro has her characters draw a discreet veil of silence over the disturbing event, its meaning, and its meaning to them. They are going to carry on as though nothing has happened. Whether they can is the disquieting question the story raises and chooses not to answer.

Peg's character centers on her orderly, matter-of-fact, reliable focus upon and attachment to the ebb and flow of everyday life. Her affective life appears to be as steady, reliable, and tranquil as a Sunday afternoon in Huron County. But secure as this surface is, it is only that—the surface. The fact that Peg had to distort what she saw tells us indirectly, in the syntax of primary process thought (displacement), that there was something she needed to cover up in herself. Her subsequent behavior is a compound of denial, splitting, and counterphobic reactions. These processes defend conscious ego life from an awareness of unpleasant realities. Munro's writing reveals an intuitive sense of these character-forming "mechanisms of defence." Fitzpatrick (1984) has demonstrated the way in which Munro in other stories has unwittingly (inspirationally) exploited the defense mechanism of projection as a device for revealing features of character and hidden motives. Defense mechanisms in general render thoughts, memories, and affects unconscious, and they bar impulses from access to behavior. Denial does this by substituting a fantasy for an unpleasant reality, isolation by detaching the affect from the idea, and counterphobic reactions by forcing a person to act in a way that is contrary to the real fear or aversion.

Peg's lie is a denial. Her memory of what she saw is a fantasy that makes what she thinks she saw a little less appalling than what she actually saw—not the shattered, grisly head but the "indicative leg, whole and decent in its trousers. . . ." (Munro, 1986, p. 131). Isolation of affect and counterphobic reaction are evident in Peg's act of morbid scopophilia. She calmly stepped over Weeble's shattered body to go into the room to get a good look at what Weeble had done to his wife and how it had been done. She remained as calm as though she had been inspecting a dress and the clever stitching that was used by the seamstress to hide the seams. Her report to the police, her preferring not to mention what she had seen to her clerk at the store, her attitude that, well, this was just another day, her choice of menu for the evening meal (spaghetti with tomato sauce), and her account of her experience to Robert are all of them behaviors that have been controlled and modified, given their shape and quality, by these defenses. But how does such an interpretation square with Munro's affirmations in several places, and especially through Robert, that Peg is not reacting to a trauma?

> Peg lifted a strand of spaghetti to try it. Robert was watching her from time to time. He would have said he was watching to see if she was in any kind of trouble, if she seemed numb, or strange, or showed a quiver, if she dropped things or made the pots clatter. But in fact he was watching her just because there was no sign of such difficulty and because he knew there wouldn't be. She was preparing an ordinary meal. (p. 124)

Munro's character Peg is psychologically consistent. These defenses were not mobilized by the trauma of her experience in order to deal with a crisis: They had become characterological through persistent, long, and necessary use. She will not become "her real self" again after the effects of a trauma have been worked through. She is only and already being "her real self." Nor will she change as a result of the painful insight forced upon her by Clayton's reminder of his fear of her and of the violence that existed between her and her first husband. That man withdrew into the safety of the Arctic. Robert walks off across the frozen fields. He will return, but only to help Peg patch over the temporary rent in her character armor and to ease her pain with distractions and forgetting.

In a culture that has lost its innocence along with its ignorance as a result of psychoanalysis, one has to be even more cautious about making interpretations beyond the point we have already reached. For example, there are whiffs of cannibalism in the preoccupation with food and drink in the story and of the primitive envy that gives rise to it. But modern writers, after Freud, are at liberty to play jokes on us as never before. For example, in *The Stranger* Camus (1942) introduces a "Freudian" newspaper story about a mother who killed her son as a result of mistaken identity in order to tease the reader into attempting a psychological explanation of Merseault's *acte gratuit*. If, however, as I have supposed, the creative imagination depends in part upon primary process thought activity, there is a limit to deliberate artifice of this sort. Leites (1963) has convincingly demonstrated that the novel in fact possesses the very psychological depth that Camus wished to deny with this teasing joke. The choice of artifice is itself meaningful, and every disguise must also reveal, even though we may not be able to plumb its secret, because primary process thought activity cannot, in the end, either lose its innocence or abandon its guile, for it is governed by the pleasure principle. Thus, we may venture a little farther, even over the protests of the author, let alone those of some critics and scholars, as long as we are fully aware that we are dealing with conjectures and probabilities. Although we cannot accept the stricture of those who claim that it is an irredeemable error to treat characters in stories as though they were real characters just because the willing suspension of disbelief induced by all good literature compels us to do so, the stricture nevertheless contains this grain of truth: that such interpretations of character and motive cannot be clinically confirmed.

Clinical psychoanalysis has by now well demonstrated the ubiquity of primal-scene fantasies in the lives of children. Parental intercourse, whether witnessed or imagined, is the object of intense curiosity, excitement, and fear on the part of the child. The fear is the result of the impression of violence given when intercourse is observed, as a consequence both of the convulsive quality of orgasm and of the sadomasochism characteristic of the sexuality of small children. There is a phase-appropriate sadomasochism in children that causes them, for example, to dismember insects or offer to poke out parents' eyes without remorse and to inflict painful pleasure upon themselves through exaggerated bowel and bladder control. Psychoanalysis has called this naturally and inevitably occurring stage of psychosexual development the anal stage. Characteristic of it is an active–passive, sadistic–masochistic auto–erotic pleasurable anal play consisting of retention and expulsion of feces. This psychosexual organization informs the perception or imagination of parental intercourse. Its active, sadistic component is identified with the father (seen or imagined); its passive, masochistic component is identified with the mother (seen or imagined). The child's own phase-appropriate sexual experience governs the sense and significance of the real or imaginary scene. He can neither perceive nor imagine how the sexual activities of his father could be other than destructive—a violent use of force—or how his mother's activities could be other than a submission to pain.

The Central Scene in Fantasy and Story

What Peg saw at the Weebles' was the most extreme reality of the violent aspect of this fantasy. But what basis is there for supposing that the real gist of the story hinges upon an implicit yet powerful motivation in Peg to witness such a scene? There is a basis. Peg is certain before she goes up the Weebles' stairs that no intruder who might still be lurking in the house has caused them harm. This certainty could have no basis in fact. It is based on some inner conviction of her own, such as that inspired by an upsurge of an old intense curiosity to see something forbidden. The one reality-bound social motive would have been concern for the safety of her neighbors, and the one reality-bound motive for getting a closer look by going into the bedroom would have been concern for Mrs. Weeble, who might still have been alive. It is the conspicuous absence of these ordinary fears and concerns that raises a doubt whether Peg's otherwise conspicuous attempt to cling to the ordinariness of everything does not reveal a hidden motive. The space in imagination created by this doubt is occupied by the bedroom scene that Peg had to see.

The theme of sexual violence returns during the crisis of the story when Clayton reminds Peg of her quarrels with his father and of his fantasy that she or his father might come and kill him with a knife. Then, after all other explanations concocted by village gossip have turned out to be false, Clayton is able to speak the truth: The Weebles were overcome by a ". . . periodic fit. Such as people have, married people have" (Munro, 1986, p. 126). But, of course, the periodic sexual convulsions and ecstasies married—or unmarried—people have are not supposed to be violent. The truth of Clayton's utterance does not refer to reality but to fantasies that give expression to dangerous sadomasochistic impulses. These impulses are real even though the fantasies they cause do not adequately represent reality. Moreover, they can and do erupt into acts of real sexual violence, and they are more generously distributed than we like to think in human nature, where they make their influence felt in myriad variations of the domesticated war between the sexes that is found in neurotic and in ordinary lives. It is this poetic truth that the story artfully conveys through the powerful image of Peg's "unapologetic pain" (p. 126). It is through this play with fantasy and reality that the story acquires its access to the primary process thought activity of the reader, which contributes in an essential way to the willing suspension of disbelief that allows us into the world of the story to find aspects of ourselves in imaginary others.

Autobiography and Creativity in Literature

The autobiographical content of literature does not, I suggest, consist of the repressed memories and fantasies of the writer. It consists, rather, of their derivatives. The autobiographical content of literature, no less than the manifest content of dreams, expresses the life of the writer only in a disguised form. Writers need have no greater grasp of their own inner lives than others. They need only have an unusual ability to give expression to their unconscious lives in a form that enables others to achieve a similarly disguised, tolerable self-realization. Writing, like the imaginative experience it gives rise to, is not a curative process; it is cathartic. This state of affairs is brilliantly conveyed by Munro in "Fits".

I do not know whether a real episode of murder–suicide was the occasion for the creation of the story. It does not matter, because, whether based on a real or an imagined happening, the basic details of the murder–suicide are presented as being real and unambiguous. If imagined, these events are imagined as taking place in the world of publicly verifiable objects. From the point of view of dream psychology, this material is the functional equivalent of a day residue (the trip by train of our earlier example). It is in relation to her account of Peg's distortion of the facts that Munro opens up for us the ambiguous, overdetermined world of the subjective experience and motives of a character who is, at the same time, placed firmly in that publicly verifiable object world. If the story was based on a real incident this element—the distortion—was introduced or seized upon by Munro's creative imagination and her instinct for subjective, psychological realities. The exploration of what it could mean for a woman to have to disguise what she had seen when she was called upon by circumstances to witness such a scene could then be guided by the primary process thought activities of the author—processes that need be no more conscious in the author than they are in the dreamer. She may become conscious of the derivatives of these processes only as the story gradually emerges into words and images that can eventually be crafted and reworked after the fashion of the secondary elaboration of dreams: that is, still under the influence of the need for disguised disclosure.

If my hypothesis is correct, there should be evidence in the text itself of the relation of the author to the story, and it should be identifiable independently of biographical knowledge of the author. No one would argue with the thesis that authors' styles are their own, each style the product of diverse influences. We have already commented, as have others, upon the sparse, factual, descriptive style of Munro's prose. Her fine sense of detail, so simple as to be at once ordinary and elegant, and a brilliant economy of words allow her to go beyond what is either ordinary or elegant to what is mysterious, disturbing, and frightening: Her style is to literature what the style of magic realism of Colville or Danby is to painting. In fact, her prose illuminates the surface of an experience so brilliantly that it causes the surface meanings to become overdetermined. Munro's prose style is crystallized, expressed, incarnated in the character of Peg in "Fits." Peg's controlled matter-of-factness (e.g., her attention to how Weeble managed to pull the trigger when he shot himself) is the characterological equivalent of the factuality of Munro's prose style. The autobiographical signature of an author upon her work is made in diverse ways. In this story, it takes the form of the inscription of Munro's prose style on the character of the leading figure in the story.

In saying this, I am not saying that the character of Peg is an autobiographical portrait of Munro any more than the characters of Raskolnikov (in *Crime and Punishment*) or Smerdiakov (in *The Brothers Karamazov*) are autobiographical portraits of Dostoyevski. Peg is an intensification of certain character traits of the writer that also find expression in her prose style. Peg is more akin to the author as she might appear to herself in a dream: the bearer of the derivatives of still-intense memories from childhood that also, in a diminished and contained way, find a place for themselves in the adult character and life of the writer. The character of Peg reveals the inner life of her author insofar as she also disguises it. The artistically important autobiographical component of literature is the unconscious autobiography of the writer—those aspects of the author's life that he knows in the disguised forms provided by creative imagination and that, accordingly, he also does not know.

Philosophers have often puzzled about the universal in the particular or the concrete universal. I do not think that such phenomena are to be found in nature, but they are to be found in the worlds created by good literature, for, in a sense that we can now define, a work of literature becomes more universal as it is able to express what is most profound, individual, and unconscious in the life of the artist. Artistic creativity does not find its way to universality by means of generalizations about human nature. The writer's capacity to illuminate "general human nature" (Johnson, 1779) or to discover what is essential in the human condition does not and could not depend upon ratiocination (Aristotle, *Poetics*). Such discovery is achieved by the capacity of the writer to submit his imagination to the influence of primary process thought activity in order to give expression to the unconscious fantasies and memories that have shaped diverse aspects of his life and that shape in different ways and in different degrees the lives of everyone.

chapter eight

An Unconscious Irony in Plato's *Republic*

At a crucial stage of his argument concerning the nature of justice in the *Republic*, Plato introduces the story of Gyges the Lydian to make a philosophical point about the predisposition to injustice in men and women. There is an irony in Plato's use of this story. The nature of the irony depends upon its source. If, as I shall argue, the story of Gyges was Plato's own invention, the irony lies in his having unconsciously contributed to the literature he would banish from his ideal republic; if he was retelling a received legend, it lies in his having been deceived by the disguise in which the oedipal themes of the story were cloaked.

Two Versions of the Gyges Legend

The story of Gyges the Lydian was first set down by Herodotus (*Herodotus*, I, 8–13). Plato's version, as we shall see, differs significantly from that of Herodotus. According to Plato, Gyges was a shepherd. One night, during a violent storm, a chasm opened in the earth. Gyges descended into the chasm where he found a bronze horse with the huge body of a man inside it. From a finger of the body Gyges removed a ring, which he subsequently discovered to have the power to render him invisible whenever he turned its jewel inward to the palm of his hand. He arranged to be sent to court, where he demonstrated the magical power of his ring to the queen, seduced her, and conspired with her to murder the king and take the throne. Plato tells the story initially in the context of an argument concerning the nature of justice. Farther on in the *Republic* he uses it again in greater detail to illustrate Glaucon's thesis that, should anyone have the opportunity to perpetrate injustice without any danger of retribution, he would do so without restraint (*Republic*, II, 359–360).

Let us now compare Plato's version of this story with that of Herodotus. In Herodotus's version Gyges, a courtier, was required by a narcissistic king to view, in secret, the naked charms of his queen, so that the king's boasts of her beauty could be corroborated to his retainers. Against his better judgment, Gyges complied. The queen detected the intruder in her bedchamber. She did not let the king know that she had discovered his plot, but in obedience to an ancient code of modesty, she presented Gyges with the alternatives of killing the king or being killed himself. Reluctantly, Gyges conspired with her to murder the king and to take his place. He was eventually exonerated by an oracle on the condition that retribution would be exacted in the fifth generation of the dynasty he had established.

The Platonic version differs from Herodotus in several important respects. In Plato's account the provocations of the king and queen that bring about the murder are replaced by the force of spontaneous, internal motivation—instead of being the victim of circumstances Gyges becomes a self-appointed regicide. In the Herodotus story exposure leads to the crime; in Plato's account just the opposite occurs. Secrecy, the ability to go undetected, is its condition: The acquisition of the power of invisibility leads to the crime. According to Herodotus the woman involved, the queen, is prompted by a moral code to seek revenge on her husband, the king. Plato, on the other hand, portrays a woman who is susceptible to the sexual seductions of the man who wears the ring. Her sexual hunger for him quickly alters her loyalties and makes her a willing conspirator with him in a plot to murder her husband. Plato's version omits any reference to the confirmation of Gyges' reign by the Delphic oracle or to a revenge to be carried out by the descendants of the murdered king in the fifth generation of Gyges' dynasty. Finally, the mysterious circumstances in which Gyges acquires the ring, and even the ring itself, are absent from Herodotus's version of the story. Thus, a number of new themes are present in Plato's version of the story: the storm, the cave, the body in the bronze horse, the ring with its mysterious powers, and the sexually dangerous woman: And the element of retribution is absent.

Plato had philosophical reasons for wanting these changes in the story, reasons that can easily be inferred from the context in the argument of the *Republic* in which he first used it: in illustration of Glaucon's thesis that justice is a compromise between what we most want (to do injustice with impunity) and what we least want (to suffer

injustice without redress). Herodotus's version will not serve this purpose: Herodotus's Gyges is a reluctant regicide incited to act by force of
circumstance and by the wish to save his own life. Plato needed a man
who was internally motivated to murder a king, and he needed a device—the ring—to protect the criminal from retribution by keeping
the deed secret. No one but Gyges and the queen could know who
committed the regicide. If he had used Herodotus's story as a starting
point Plato would therefore have had to modify it very considerably to
make it suit his philosophical purpose as illustration of the view that
every man would so act were he to have Gyges' ring, and that every
woman would so cooperate were she to be so seduced.

Here, however, we come upon a methodological issue. The exposition employs comparison of a version of the Gyges story apparently
invented by Plato with the version recorded by Herodotus. There is
some disagreement among scholars as to whether the Gyges of Plato
was intended to be the same person as the Gyges of Herodotus. If they
are not the same, and if there was a legend that antedated Plato about
an earlier Gyges, and if Plato knew of it, then the differences between
Plato's version and Herodotus's cannot be used as evidence that Plato's
version is the work of his own creative imagination. Although some
scholars consider the two Gyges to be one and the same, Adam (1902),
for example, argued that there is "no solid reason for connecting the
Gyges of [Plato's] proverb with the historical Gyges" (p. 126). Adam
based this view on the existence of the differences, and he is supported
by some internal evidence in Plato's text (assuming that the text we
have is accurate): Plato does refer to the "ancestor of Gyges the
Lydian," rather than to "Gyges the Lydian."

Supporting the identity view is the ingenuity with which Plato's
version has been tailored to the requirements of his philosophical argument—which one could hardly expect to find in a legend handed
down about a much earlier king of Lydia of the same name and family.
In favor of Adam's view are Plato's inclusion of so many extraordinary
magical details, logically unnecessary for his philosophical purpose—the
magic ring, the miraculous storm, the cavern and its contents—which
give the story the quality of a legend or fairy tale. Do they not suggest
that Plato was drawing from a source other than Herodotus?

Clearly Herodotus was not the source of such details. The first
question, therefore, is whether they came from an oral legend about an
ancestor of Herodotus's Gyges that was known to Plato and his contemporaries, or from a lost written account. Because there is no extant
documentary evidence for the existence of such a legend prior to
Plato's use of it, the second question is whether the source of the tale
may not have been Plato himself.

Several considerations favor the assumption that the story in Book II of the *Republic* is Plato's invention. The lack of references to it prior to Plato, and the fact that all subsequent references are to Plato's version, provides external evidence of his authorship. There are also three internal factors leading to the same conclusion. First, Plato's imagination seems to have been occupied with the theme of the cave and its symbolism: His allegory of the cave—the central metaphor for his ontology, epistemology, and anthropology—appears in the *Republic* (VII, 514–518). Second, Plato's mind during this period was in a state of flexible repression such as would be required for the creation of a story involving derivatives of unconscious fantasies. The evidence for this is his intuitive grasp of components of the Oedipus complex (*Republic*, IX, 571). Third, Plato had a fertile imagination, which enabled him to create his own versions of both old myths and new myths that gave more concrete expression to certain of his ideas than did his abstract philosophical theories. One of these, the myth of Er, concludes the *Republic* (X, 614–621).

On balance, then, unless scholarly evidence of an earlier legend comes to light, it is not unreasonable to assume that Plato created rather than borrowed his tale of Gyges the Lydian. This study adopts the premise that Plato used the story recounted by Herodotus as the starting point for a creation of his own that he cast yet farther back in time by inventing an ancestor of the historical Gyges who had done on his own initiative what the historical Gyges had been obliged by circumstance to do.

If Plato's Gyges was indeed his own creation, we are entitled to study it for indications of Plato's unconscious fantasy life and the influence this may have had upon his experience of life and upon his philosophical ideas. If on the other hand new evidence shows that the tale was not original with Plato, then it cannot be used, as it is here, to interpret other Platonic texts. On the contrary, other Platonic texts would be required to interpret the Gyges tale, for if Plato took it from an earlier source because of its suitability for his philosophical purpose, that explanation would in itself be sufficient. Such an explanation does not rule out the possibility of Plato's unconscious affinity for the legend, but this would have to be established on other evidence.

Plato rejected the idea of justice put forward by Glaucon in the Gyges tale, and assigns to Socrates the idea that committing injustice makes the miscreant miserable whereas the just life is a happy one despite social and personal misfortune. Herodotus's version of the tale thus must be altered in one further respect. The Gyges of Herodotus, having killed a king and married his queen, nevertheless is exonerated by an oracle and is able to found a dynasty. He appears to have a happy life, his crime having been excused by the gods. Such a conclusion is contrary to Plato's view of the connection between the just life and happiness, and he not only omits it but in doing so provides a different reading of Gyges' life that is consistent with his own views. In making this omission Plato commits what we might call the moralistic fallacy: He derives the proposition that those who commit injustices *are* miserable from the moral premise that those who commit injustices *ought* not to be happy.

Although Plato's argument as such remains philosophically fallacious because it attempts to derive a factual statement from a normative statement, it nevertheless embodies an important psychological insight. Individuals who commit evil acts are punished for them by the anxiety (guilt) aroused within themselves even when their acts go undetected and unpunished by external authority. Shakespeare illustrates this mechanism when Macbeth and Lady Macbeth begin to suffer the consequences of their crime long before they are punished for it. Although the theme of retribution is absent from the Gyges story as it appears in the *Republic*, I believe that this absence is psychologically significant and paves the way for its reintroduction in another context.

A Psychoanalytic Interpretation of Plato's Gyges Legend

The foregoing provides an analysis of Plato's philosophical reasons for modifying the Gyges story; but no account of the philosophical reasons, however exhaustive, can provide a sufficient understanding of the story itself. The philosophical reasons require a protagonist who has his own motive for committing the crime and a means of avoiding retribution, but the significance of all the details in Plato's version is left unexplained. A second, psychological layer of significance in the story is pointed to by these details: the mysterious circumstances that provided Gyges with the ring and set him on the path that led through seduction and murder to the throne.

At this point one must have recourse to psychoanalytic interpretation and construction in order to proceed further. The need for an apt illustration of a philosophical idea seems to have stimulated Plato's powers of imagination to rework the tale of Gyges the Lydian into a form suitable for his philosophical purpose; but did unconscious ideas and fantasies also play a part in motivating him to choose to alter the story precisely as he did?

The tale consists of a series of episodes that, if they occurred in a dream, could be interpreted as having unconscious significance, and knowledge of dream symbolism can therefore be used to interpret Plato's alterations of it. To be sure, the Gyges story is not a dream but a waking poetic fiction. Nevertheless, one may assume that, as in other poetic fictions, unconscious processes contribute to its formation just as they do in the production of manifest dreams.

In Plato's tale, therefore, the cave can be taken to symbolize the womb, and Gyges' descent into it might then be understood as representing his birth. What then could this tell us about Gyges' birth? In the cave Gyges comes upon the massive body of an unidentified man from whom he takes the magic ring. The massiveness of this body and its entombment in the bronze horse suggest the majesty of a regal personage—indeed, none other than the king. His ring, falling into the hands of Gyges, could symbolize Gyges' acquisition of the king's potency as well as of its sexual object, the queen. Dodds (1963) has discussed the symbolic phallic significance of the ring in Greek culture in connection with Aristides' dream prescriptions (p. 116). These symbolic elements might tell us that Gyges was the prince—the son of the king—whose birth was accompanied by the prophecy that he was fated to murder his father and marry his mother. In terms of ancient dream lore this event in Plato's version of the Gyges tale can be construed as a symbolic preenactment of the course it will follow. The storm and earthquake that set the atmosphere of the story and cause the rending of the earth seem to confirm that we are being presented with the account of a royal birth; in the animistic world of folklore, nature customarily reverberates with storms and quakes at such events. Shakespeare exploited this association in *Henry IV, Part I*, when he had the Welsh rebel Glendower express his pretentiousness by claiming:

> . . . *at my birth*
> *The frame and huge foundation of the earth*
> *Shaked like a coward.*
> *(III, 1)*

I propose that the content of the Gyges tale as presented by Plato is a symbolically disguised version of the Oedipus legend. Even Plato's making Gyges a shepherd points in that direction: The infant Oedipus was abandoned in the rough countryside to die, only to be found by shepherds who saved and raised him. Rank (1909) has shown that identity disguised by reversal of social status is a recurrent theme in folklore. Altering Gyges' status from that of a member of the king's bodyguard, as in Herodotus's version, to that of a lowly shepherd can be viewed as effecting such a disguise by way of opposites. The ring with the magical power of invisibility occurs in association with oedipal material in other cultures as well. The ancient Indian play *Avimar-aka* (see Masson & Kosambi, 1970, p. 92ff.) contains a variant in which the invisibility induced by a ring is used to commit a forbidden libidinal act, as Gyges' ring makes it possible for him to hide his criminality and escape retribution. Thus, Plato's version of the oedipal theme differs significantly from that of Sophocles: In the Gyges tale parricide and incest go undetected and unpunished.

In Sophocles' *Oedipus Rex* Jocasta counsels her son against pressing his search for the murderer of Laius:

> Nor need this mother-marrying frighten you;
> Many a man has dreamt as much. Such things
> Must be forgotten, if life is to be endured.
> (p. 52)

But Oedipus does not heed her. In contrast, Plato's Gyges was spared the self-righteous arrogance followed by fearful doubts that led Oedipus to seek out his true identity. The ring that makes Gyges invisible to others makes his true identity invisible to himself. Gyges can be seen as a prototype of the kind of person whose character and life have been shaped by an oedipal triumph in childhood—an individual who has "dispatched the king" and has gotten away with it.

Such an individual may have had parents who cooperated with his oedipal strivings. The father may have been a weak, unsuccessful man and the mother a dominating, frustrated, angry woman who made no secret of her dissatisfaction with her husband and placed her hopes for fulfillment upon her son; or the father may have died when the son was still living in an animistic world and could not be realistic about his rivalrous hostility toward his father. The father's death would enhance the son's belief that he had vanquished him, leading to the formation of an identificatory alliance with his mother and possibly to the development of homosexuality. Such individuals can develop a profoundly derogated image of their fathers that enables them to deny the fathers' importance in their lives and at the same time to deny their anxiety (guilt). As a further defense against their anxiety they can develop the fantasy that they do not owe their origin to the debased and vanquished father but to some other, more perfect being who guides their destiny.

Plato's tale of Gyges has been interpreted as a homosexual version of the Oedipus legend, and it is worth evaluating the credibility of the interpretation in relation to other independent evidence. For example, if the interpretation is correct, one could expect to find evidence of a strong homosexual preference in Plato's interests, relationships, thought, and values, as well as thematic recurrences. Does such evidence exist? Do the Platonic texts confirm the predictions one would make on the basis of this interpretation of Plato's Gyges legend?

Textual Evidence

Let us turn to Plato's self-revelations in his philosophic writings. In an early dialogue, the *Charmides*, Socrates' homosexual attraction to the youthful soldier Charmides is vividly described. Plato has Socrates report how he was "caught on fire" by what he saw "inside his [Charmides'] cloak" (155.D) and how he felt quite beside himself, scarcely able to speak. In the middle dialogues, the *Symposium* and the *Phaedrus*, homosexuality is still preferred to what Plato takes to be the meanest form of loving, heterosexuality, although homosexual love must in its turn yield primacy to its sublimation in intellectual pursuits and mystical experience. In the *Phaedrus* the idea is developed that a blissful celestial afterlife awaits those who, having been consumed by a homosexual passion, suppress their desires for sexual gratification and intellectualize their love in philosophical pursuits (*Phaedrus*, 254–257).

Plato intuitively grasps the source of the anxiety that motivates such a partial sublimation: the threat of sadistic aggression toward the homosexual partner, which is a cause of the instability of such relationships (*Phaedrus*, 239–241). As one might expect, Plato's idea of intellectual activity seems to be shaped in part by repressed conflicts. In these dialogues and others we find descriptions that suggest displacement of the procreative urge from psychophysical organization into intellectual life. Plato grounds his philosophical dialectics in a partially sublimated homosexual relationship between mentor and pupil, and his favorite metaphor for this relationship compares it to procreation. The older man makes the youth pregnant with his brain children—his ideas; Socrates is portrayed as a midwife who helps the ideas to be born. A passage in *Epistle VII* seems to refer to just such a grounding by Plato of philosophical activity in sublimated homosexual intimacy:

> For this knowledge is not something that can be put into words like other sciences; but only after long-continued intercourse between teacher and pupil, in joint pursuit of the subject, suddenly like light flashing forth when a fire is kindled, it is born in the soul and straightway nourishes itself. (341)

We know little of Plato's life. His father, Aristo, who is said to have been descended from the kings of Athens, died when Plato was still a boy. Plato's mother remarried (her uncle Pyrilampes), but Plato may not have accepted his step-father. In any case it was Socrates, whom he met at about the age of 20, who became the ruling influence in his life. Plato had two older brothers, Adeimantus and Glaucon. It is to Glaucon that Plato attributes the telling of the story of Gyges in the *Republic*, and it is Glaucon who is made the advocate of a concept of justice that Plato rejects. It is possible that disavowal is at work: "It is not I but my brother who invents such tales!"

Unconscious Irony

We then come to the unconscious irony in the *Republic*, referred to above. The philosophical argument seeks to justify a severe censorship of literature and the exile of the poets from the ideal state. Concerning censorship Plato says:

> Well, firstly, the poet, who told the greatest falsehoods of the greatest of being, told a falsehood with no beauty in it, when he said that Ouranos did what Hesiod said he did, and that Kronos took vengeance on him. And as for the deeds of Kronos, and what he suffered at his sons' hands, even if these stories are true, I should not think we should so lightly repeat them to the young and foolish. It were best to be silent about them or if they had to be told, it should be done under the seal of silence to as few hearers as possible, and after the sacrifice not of the mystic pig but some great and almost unprocurable victim so that very few would hear the story. (*Republic, II, 377–378*)

Finally, in the concluding arguments of the *Republic*, Plato advocates the banishment of poetry from the well-governed city (*Republic, X, 572*). Plato apparently wants to believe that the ideas contained in Hesiod, Homer, and Sophocles take root in the minds of men only by transplantation from other minds.

The irony is that, in the Gyges story, Plato himself introduces into the *Republic* a poetic fantasy that disguises a disturbing psychological truth, thus unconsciously breaking his own rules of censorship. In his arguments on behalf of censorship Plato must of course refer to the forbidden stories, but he is not constrained by logic or by the explicit subject matter of his argument to embellish with a fantasy Glaucon's defense of a concept of justice that is introduced only to be rejected.

It can be assumed that Plato's views on the censorship of literature were formed in part by the work of his superego. The argument of the *Republic* is based on an analogy between society and self. How does the material of the Gyges tale avoid the inner censorship of the author of the *Republic?* First, the manifest meaning of the story is ego-syntonic: It is suited to Plato's conscious philosophical purpose. Second, the manifest meaning disguises in symbols the latent meaning of the story. Third, Plato's dramatic method enables him to transfer the telling of the story to Glaucon, with whom he does not consciously identify.

The notion of an *unconscious* irony has been used to differentiate it from the deliberate and conscious use of irony in the dialogues, including the *Republic*, by Plato's Socrates, who is frequently made to simulate ignorance in order to force others to explain their ideas and thus expose the inherent contradictions they contain. This dialectic is followed by a statement of Plato's own views. When Glaucon recounts the tale of Gyges he does so in response to conscious Socratic irony, but it is Plato who has drawn the character of Glaucon and makes him recount the tale, and it is in this displacement onto Glaucon that we come upon the unconscious irony. Plato tells, without knowing that he has told it, what he says should never be told.

The irony, however, is not yet complete. Plato seems to know unconsciously that the psychological truths contained in the legendary material of the poets have universal application. At a later point in the *Republic* he makes Socrates assert the existence, as revealed in dreams, of a class of "terrible, fierce, and lawless desires" (*IX*, 572) in every man, even in those who have every appearance of being decent. The intense anxiety aroused by this insight—which leads to denial—is evident in the pessimistic cast of Plato's choice of words, suggesting a belief on his part that the instinctual wishes cannot be escaped merely by having their cathexis withdrawn from them. To effect the denial he uses the mental construct of the philosopher-king. This perfectly just, wise, courageous, and temperate man presumably is the individual whose decency is real, not merely apparent. One may ask how Plato thought the purified virtues of the philosopher-king could be wrested from the matrix of the base desires that exist in every man. Plato's conscious thoughts on this subject have long been the matter of detailed philosophical analysis. It is the unconscious thoughts that, we can infer, lie behind them that are the focus of attention here.

Further Textual Evidence

If our conclusions are correct, we should expect to find the latent theme of Plato's version of the Gyges story appearing elsewhere in his work; also, following a suggestion by Arlow (1961), we might expect to find the theme reprised in a second version that conveys the elements of Plato's attempt to resolve the unconscious instinctual conflicts it involves. If our hypothesis that Plato's Gyges tale represents a homosexual's oedipal fantasy is correct, we can expect to find the recurrence of at least five themes: the sexually dangerous woman, paranoia, castration anxiety, rebirth, and narcissism.

The theme of the dangerous woman appears again in Plato's theory of political decay. It is to the destructive influence of women that Plato attributes the deterioration of the timocratic city into the oligarchic, a fall that precipitates a succession of deteriorating psychosocial systems through democracy to tyranny:

> [The son] hears his mother complaining that her husband is not one of the rulers, and that in consequence other women are set above her. Then she sees that her husband does not trouble himself much about money, and does not fight and wrangle in law-suits or in the assembly but takes all these matters very calmly, and she perceives that he is always attending to himself, treating her neither with marked reverence nor marked disrespect. All these things make her angry, and she tells her son that his father is unmanly and utterly casual, and treats him to all the many varied complaints which women love to make on such matters. (*Republic*, VIII, 549–550)

Plato has drawn a portrait of the kind of woman whose behavior might facilitate a conviction in her son that he has achieved an oedipal triumph. The additional feature in this portrayal is the value attached to wealth, which is appropriate to the context of Plato's sociopolitical analysis but, from a psychological point of view, also suggests regression to an anal-sadistic level of organization. The son seeks to win his mother's approval by outdoing his father and fighting to retain and increase the family wealth.

Some women, of course, do answer to Plato's description; the problem is that it must apply to a very large class of women if they are to have the effect on social systems attributed to them in Plato's argument, and it is not likely that there could have been so many women in ancient Greece angry at their husbands and willing to encourage their sons to defeat and destroy them. To be sure, Plato's analysis of the psychological bases of various sociopolitical systems is an abstract model rather than a historical description, but the philosophical adequacy of a model depends on the plausibility of its underlying assumptions and the applicability of its implications. Plato's ideas about the contribution of women to political decay are unrealistic and appear to stem from distorted, unconsciously determined attitudes toward them.

Following Grunberger (1956, p. 202), the concept of the danger-ous woman can be interpreted as a projection of the bad (castrating) mother. Such an interpretation can shed light upon the "seduction" by Gyges of the queen, who then helps him to murder the king. From this perspective, it is not a genital sexual wish that Gyges seeks to gratify in the seduction but rather an anal-sadistic wish to castrate the king (father) and thereby gain possession of his power. Grunberger has pointed out the operation of such a pre-oedipal wish in the dynamics of masochism. Plato's puritanism probably derived in part from moral masochism, as indicated by his negative attitude to even the vicarious gratifications afforded by the aesthetic emotions aroused by classical tragedy.

The themes of punishment and paranoia reemerge in the context of Plato's political theorizing. In the *Republic* (VIII–IX 544–581), he formulates a theory concerning the connection between political con-stitutions and the characters of those who are assigned by them to exercise political power. Each constitution is correlated with a specific character type. The ideas concerning the dangerous woman discussed above are drawn from this context. In the argument of the *Republic* as a whole, this analysis of constitutions and characters plays a crucial role. In *Republic, II*, in which the Gyges tale is presented, the claim is made that the best man is happiest and the worst man is most misera-ble. Plato's philosophical analysis of constitutions and characters is de-signed to establish this fundamental point. A central psychological issue upon which Plato's philosophical analysis focuses is the identifica-tion of the son with the morally good father; failure to achieve such an identification is a major factor, according to Plato, in the develop-ment of flaws in the character of the son and hence in the decline from a timocratic to an oligarchic constitution and ruler.

Plato ranks political constitutions in descending order from aris-tocracy (rule by a communized intellectual elite), through timocracy (rule by a military elite), oligarchy (rule by the wealthy), and democ-racy (rule by the people) to tyranny (rule by a parricidal despot). A detailed examination of the psychology of Plato's political ideas lies beyond the scope of this chapter; only the theme of punishment and paranoia as they find expression in his account of the tyrant will be examined here.

There are three significant features in Plato's account of the ty-rant. First, it is in this context that Plato makes his famous reference to the impulses underlying dreams. He makes Socrates assert that "a terrible, fierce, and lawless class of desires exists in every man, even in those of us who have every appearance of being decent people. Its existence is revealed in dreams." And in the same context:

[W]hen the rest of the soul, the reasoning, gentle, and ruling part of it, is asleep, then the bestial and savage part, when it has had its fill of food or wine, begins to leap about, pushes sleep aside, and tries to go and gratify its instincts. You know how in such a state it will dare everything, as though it were freed and released from all shame or discernment. It does not shrink from attempting incestual intercourse, in its dream, with a mother or with any man or god or beast. It is ready for any deed of blood, and there is no unhallowed food it will not eat. In a word, it falls short of no extreme of folly or shamelessness. (*Republic*, IX, 572)

Second, the essential character of the tyrant, according to Plato, is that he does in waking life what once he only dreamed of doing:

Once they [forbidden desires] were let loose in sleep when he dreamt, in the time when he was still under the laws of a father. . . . But when Love established his tyranny over him, he became for always, and in waking reality, the man he used occasionally to be in dreams. And now he will stick at no frightful murder, no unhallowed food or dreadful deed, but Love dwells tyrannically within him in all lawlessness and anarchy. (*Republic*, IX, 574–575)

The tyrant as conceived by Plato appears to be essentially an oedipally motivated criminal.

Third, Plato describes the tyrant as one who is constantly tormented by fear.

He has the nature we have described, full of thronging and diverse fears and lusts. He has a greedy soul, and yet he is the only man in the city who may not travel or go to see things which all free men want to see. He lives hidden away in his house for all the world like a woman. (*Republic*, IX, 579)

Even there he is unsafe, because what he has done to his father any soldier in his bodyguard may do to him. Plato's tyrant is not significantly different from the great and wretched god Cronus, who, having castrated his father with his mother's help, lived in terror of his own progeny lest one of them follow his example (Hesiod). Here again we find evidence of the presence of an anxiety-provoking unconscious conflict that makes its way into Plato's philosophical thought under the license provided by a moral condemnation of the figure (the tyrant) who is made the bearer of the theme.

The often-repeated remark that in every delusion there is a kernel of truth can be extended to projection as well. Projection is able to achieve its aim of making an idea and its intrapsychic significance unconscious by selecting an object that has, in itself, a real element of fittingness. The personal element in Plato's idea of the tyrant comes into view once we realize that tyrants in ancient times were not always the criminals Plato makes them out to be in the *Republic*. Herodotus's Gyges was himself a political figure. Other Greeks, among them the classical tragedians, did not share Plato's view of tyrants, and, in an aside, he cites this fact as an additional reason for tragedians to be banished from the city (*Republic, VIII,* 568). Plato's tyrant has all the trappings of opulence, but he is in reality an impoverished beggar who cannot enjoy his own wealth. He accumulates wealth and power only to make himself secure by impoverishing and weakening others. He is a man, we might interpret, who is in the throes of severe castration anxiety: He castrates (impoverishes and weakens) in order to protect himself against castration. The personal element that I see contributing to Plato's concept of the tyrant (the element that deprived him of the capacity to take a more objective look at the men who were political tyrants in ancient times) was his need to ward off, projectively, his own castration anxiety, that is, to vividly imagine these forces operating in another.

Plato makes the brilliantly perceptive remark concerning his tyrant that he is a man who, when he "cannot master himself, must try to rule others" (*Republic, IX,* 579). What is Plato's concept of the psychology of self-mastery? Here again the theme of castration makes its appearance. In the *Phaedrus* Plato elaborates a metaphor of the human psyche in which he likens it to a charioteer driving two horses. The horse on the left is an unruly brute that represents the appetites; the one on the right is a fine, domesticated animal amenable to the guidance of the charioteer (intellect) who represents moral will or spirit as Plato identifies it in the *Republic*. The unruly brute is nourished and grows strong on sensual gratification; it threatens to carry off the charioteer into moral danger. When approaching the beloved object the sinister horse "lowers its head, elevates its tail, takes the bit in its teeth, and pulls shamelessly." The charioteer must have recourse to severe measures: "he jerks back the bit even more violently than before from the teeth of the wanton horse, bespatters its malicious tongue and jaws with blood, forces its legs and haunches to the ground and causes it much pain" (*Phaedrus,* 254). It is my contention that Plato is describing homosexual drives, although he consciously considered heterosexual drives to be even more dangerous to the welfare of the soul. The symbolism of Plato's metaphor suggests that self-castration is the psychological means by which self-mastery is acquired.

Grunberger (1956), in his study of the psychodynamics of sado-masochism, calls attention to a significant characteristic of moral masochism:

> Suffering ennobles and purifies. He who suffers is entitled to veneration, for he is virtuous. Indeed, pleasure being assimilated to castration of the father, it follows that suffering, i.e., being the castrated instead of the castrator, is a proof of innocence and a shelter against the accusations of the superego while, at the same time, permitting introjection at a deeper level. (p. 200)

In my opinion Grunberger's account of moral masochism applies to the psychogenesis of one of Plato's major philosophical formulations in the *Republic*.

The other vantage point that is useful is Arlow's (1961) idea that myths contain two expressions of a single unconscious instinctual derivative, one representing its "raw" form and the other the form it takes after it has been subjected to the defensive operations of the ego, involving sublimation and identification, that is, its connection to the superego. The Gyges tale seems to be representative of the first type in Arlow's classification and the allegory of the cave of the second type.

The themes of the cave and of rebirth reappear in the *Republic* in the allegory of the cave, through which Plato seeks to give an imaginative account of the psychogenesis of the philosopher-king, the man of justice who is fitted to rule the ideal state because he is beyond temptation. The allegory has been subjected to thorough philosophical analysis by Plato scholars, but its psychology has been insufficiently explored.

In his allegory, Plato pictures prisoners chained deep in a cave. Toward the mouth of the cave is a parapet, and on the other side of the parapet a fire burns. On the wall of the cave the chained men see the shadows cast by objects that move along the parapet behind them. They take these shadows to be real. One man manages to turn around and, although blinded at first by the fire, he learns that what initially he had taken to be reality was but the shadows of more substantial objects. Proceeding then to the mouth of the cave, he realizes that the objects on the parapet are themselves only replicas of the entities that make up the real world illuminated by the sun. The philosopher, for such he is, is at last able to look directly into the sun.

Philosophically, the objects and the fire in the cave represent nature and the natural sun; nature and the natural sun in the allegory represent the world of the forms and the Form of the Good (God).

From the psychological point of view the allegory can be seen as describing a far-reaching transformation affecting the philosopher's sense of reality and his values. Plato's description of this transformation is as follows:

> It is just as if the eye could not turn from darkness to light unless the whole body turned with it, so this faculty and instrument must be wheeled around together with the whole soul away from that which is becoming [nature], until it is able to look upon and to endure being and the brightest blaze of being and that we declare to be the good. (Republic, VII, 518)

Whereas before, the world of nature seemed real and the abstract ideas used in constructing knowledge seemed to be only representations of it, now it is the abstract ideas that seem real and the objects of nature appear to be only their replicas. Whereas before, physical gratifications were valuable, now they are demeaning distractions from the pleasures of the life of the intellect and the austere virtues that protect it. Whereas before, life was of primary importance, now death and the preparation for immortality take its place, as evidenced by the myth of Er, which concludes the Republic.

The allegory of the cave appears to reflect a reconstitution of Plato's superego, or a far-reaching modification of it, under the pressure of the conflicts involved in his homosexuality.

Three features of Plato's account are of particular interest. The light of the fire and then of the sun in the allegory are blinding even while illuminating. The philosophical illumination produces a debilitation of the physical sense of sight. Having emerged from the cave, the philosophical hero is destined at last to undergo a blinding intellectual vision of the ultimate source of things—the Form of the Good, symbolized by the sun. This vision supposedly yields intellectual power, but it also produces debility:

> Then do you think it at all surprising, if one who has come from divine visions to human miseries plays a sorry part and appears very ridiculous when, with the eyes still confused and before he has got properly used to the darkness that is round him, he is compelled to contend in law courts or elsewhere concerning the shadows of the just or the images which throw those shadows, or to dispute concerning the manner in which those images are conceived by men who have never seen real justice. (Republic, VII, 517)

The vision of the Good damages the physical senses and impairs the capacity of the philosophical hero to adapt successfully to the realities of social life. He will appear ridiculous and inept when confronted by the demands of the world. The price that the philosophical hero must pay for his intellectual vision of reality is an impairment of natural vision. Reliance on the physical senses must be abandoned in favor of pure thought, for the eyes are corrupt and they are corrupting of knowledge and virtue.

This interpretation leads us to the psychogenetic roots of Platonic antiempiricism. Unlike Oedipus, the philosopher-hero does not have to put out his eyes physically: He puts them out psychologically. It is this act of psychic self-mutilation that Plato believed, without knowing consciously that he believed it, would legitimize the philosopher hero's exercise of power by making him proof against the temptation to abuse it. Psychic self-mutilation is the specific form of suffering that ennobles and purifies in the Platonic scheme of things.

The superego is formed of a further strengthening and internalization of an identification with the parent. To put it another way, it is formed by a shift of cathexis from the object of a relationship to the image or idea of that object that is already part of the self. The identification with the Form of the Good—Plato's deity—is evident because the philosopher-king is to bring order and harmony to the city just as the Form of the Good is the source of order and harmony in the cosmos. But the Form of the Good bears a divine characteristic that betrays the impulse—the wish to castrate, against which the superego is organized. The Form of the Good is without a personality. It does not create; its efficacy is limited to controlling, ordering, organizing. It is an abstract principle—a being beyond being. As such it is proof against Gyges, Prometheus, Cronus, Zeus, and Plato. Plato's concept of being shares this feature of the concept of being that had been elaborated by his predecessor Parmenides (see Hanly, 1970b, pp. 184–185).

Accordingly it can be said that Plato's allegory of the cave represents in disguised form a life history that has failed to resolve the Oedipus complex, one that has been obliged instead to erect defenses against it through modifications of the ego and the organization of its functions. The dialogues that follow the *Republic* bear the consequences of these changes. They become increasingly abstract and devoid of the rich human content of the early and middle dialogues. The conversion of object libido into narcissistic libido can be inferred from Plato's substitution of abstract entities for real things; his conviction of his own immortality (the substitution of the Form of the Good for his earthly parents); his belief in his preexistence, which is derived from the same idea; his sense of superiority over ignorant earthbound mortals; and his own conviction that only he or someone like him is qualified to rule.

A Biographical Construction

The narcissistic idealization of the self that we have been consid-ering did not stop Plato from carrying on a productive philosophical life. It did not break down his contact with reality, as in serious narcis-sistic disorders (e.g., schizophrenia), but preserved his contact with life and reality. The *Weltanschauung* that he created, when it was synthe-sized with Christianity by Augustine, came to dominate several centu-ries of thought in Western civilization. Consequently I cannot agree with the view advanced by Brès (1968) that Plato's thought was psy-chotic in nature. Kris (1952, p. 105) differentiates between the effects of primary process activity on an incapacitated ego and its effects upon an ego that has retained its basic strengths. Perhaps Coltrera (1965) is correct in postulating the existence in creative people of unique narcis-sistic vicissitudes that would be destructive to average minds but that are contained and utilized for creative purposes by the unusually gifted. Perhaps Coltrera is also correct in insisting that "not all motivated processes which produce deviations from veridicality are ineffective from the standpoint of adaptation" (p. 670).

However, we know that Nietzsche's creativity did not spare him in the end. My surmise is that it was a sum of unsublimated and repressed, or only partly sublimated, homosexual object libido that helped Plato's ego to remain attached to the real world of people and things and made of his metaphysical world a consolation for lost and abandoned gratifications in life rather than a delusional system. The evidence for this construction is to be found in the practical regulations the philoso-pher-king, working under the guiding spirit of his vision of the Form of the Good, would impose on society: the censorship of literature to remove all traces of oedipal themes; the destruction of the family; the removal of any social differentiation between men and women; the opportunity for male rulers to fulfill parental roles, both male and fe-male, for selected offspring who are taken at birth from their mothers and placed in state "rearing-pens"; the control of procreation by means of a rigged lottery that would enable the rulers to decide who should mate during state nuptial festivals; and the selection of breeding sea-sons according to magical astrological calculations. These are some of the extraordinary provisions Plato considered necessary for the ideal state. The force of an extreme oedipal anxiety, the need to create opportunities for partially sublimated homosexual needs (parenting without procreation), and regression to magical thinking are evident.

Popper (1966) has commented on the political totalitarianism of these ideas and has shown the connection between Plato's ideas and similar elements in modern totalitarian ideologies. One need not comment here on their obvious psychological destructiveness. The regressiveness of Plato's social thought is evident in a specific reversal of values. He feared individuality. He wanted to create a society of persons that would function as a collective individual: That is, he wanted to bring about a social regression to tribalism. Citizens of the ideal state must all rejoice and grieve at the same time over the same thing. Individual gain or individual loss must not be experienced. It must be acknowledged that his provisions for life in the ideal state are well calculated to achieve this end.

Following Coltrera, it can be said that there is a veracity of a kind and an adaptiveness of a kind in these ideas. They project a social world in which a group of unconscious libidinal, aggressive, and narcissistic gratifications can be achieved. There is an ingenious adaptation of means to these ends. They cannot, however, be said to be the products of a mind that is well adapted to the needs of individuals or to the needs of society. They are ideas that defend against the derivatives of unconscious conflicts and that, in order to accomplish their defensive function, have to make substantial concessions to the demands of the instinctual drive pressures contained in them. Kris (1952) stated that the establishment of certain sublimations can lead to a regressive reactivation of instinctual wishes, the indulgence of which may be permitted. This idea raises the difficult question of what might be the conditions under which such reactivation and gratification can occur and what form they would take. In the case of artistic works and aesthetic responses to them, the gratification seems to be controlled by the aesthetic experience itself, which provides the condition for the gratification. In the case of philosophical ideas that aim at a real alteration in individual and collective life, the issue may be more serious.

The question of whether a significant degree of neutralization can occur in sublimations that do not rest on the resolution of the Oedipus complex is, in my opinion, a real one. Kris (1952) has pointed out that "the degree of neutralization may be low" and yet we may nevertheless "be dealing with secondary processes" and that "while fully under the control of the ego, fully bound, the energy may still have retained the hallmark of libido and aggression" (p. 27). I believe that this formulation applies adequately to Plato's philosophical thought, except that the hallmarks seem to be very prominent and to produce identifiable distortions in the secondary process. What is at issue is the nature and extent of the control the ego is able to exercise in the face of the compromise the ego must make with id demands in the absence of the resolution of the Oedipus complex. There can be no question that Plato developed a highly idealized superego and qualified on that score for Kohut's (1966) encomium of the man of wisdom who views the rabble of common men with disdain (p. 265); but these narcissistic vicissitudes and the idealized superego with which they are connected also bore in Plato the hallmarks of unconscious libidinal and aggressive aims when it came to the crucial task of setting out practical rules for individual and collective life.

A Final Irony

Perhaps one can find a second layer of irony in Plato's thought, related to the one already identified. Plato did not think that his ideal society would ever exist, and he recommended that his followers should only attempt to apply its provisions in their personal lives. When he had the opportunity to try to make a philosopher-king of the tyrant of Syracuse his attempt ended in a disaster from which Plato narrowly escaped with his life. He also had doubts about his attitude toward the poets, and he called for someone to show why they should be admitted to the just society or be given a place in the life of just men—which Aristotle eventually did in "On Poetry and Style" in his *Poetics*. Perhaps the part of Plato that dreamed, that conceived of an imaginative variation on the life of Gyges, that struggled with the severity of his superego, and that found the narcissistic gratifications it afforded him a poor substitute for fulfillments enjoyed by lesser men, wanted us to wonder at but not to imitate his remarkable intellectual odyssey. Such ironic reservations would, more than any of Plato's explicitly formulated philosophical doctrines, locate him in a tradition of thought that eventually led to Freud.

chapter nine

From Animism
to Rationalism

$\mathbf{T}$his chapter is a study of psychological forces at work in cultural history. The transition from an animistic culture to a culture that could sustain rationalism, and even the beginnings of natural science, mathematics, and the arts, more or less as we know them today, was the remarkable achievement of the ancient Greeks. It was accomplished in a relatively short time, roughly equal to the time between the Renaissance and the present. This achievement had a profound influence on subsequent history as a result of its propagation by the Alexandrian and later the Roman conquests and then, during the Renaissance, by the turning back to Greek origins to lay the foundation for modern scientific culture.

For such a historical advance there is no single explanation. The transition from animism to rationalism in ancient Greece can be illuminated from various perspectives: economic, geographic and environmental, technological, political, and sociological. Each of these perspectives can provide knowledge essential to a complete understanding of this transition. Psychoanalysis does not have, nor need it claim, a privileged position among these perspectives; but the psychology of the process is likely to have been an essential factor. Culture is the human creation that creates man. Culture is both rooted in individual psychology and an influence upon individual psychology. The study of the history of ancient Greek culture leaves one with the clear impression that gradually there took place a quite far reaching development in the psychic organization of these remarkable people.

On Method

The method consists of a comparison of certain aspects of the psychic functioning of the Homeric Greeks with that of the Greeks of the fourth and third centuries B.C. This comparison is made at the phenomenological level. Each is then characterized psychoanalytically, and a dynamic hypothesis is advanced to explain the difference between them. The hypothesis is that the crucial factor in the cultural change was the alteration of ego functions brought about by the evolving capacity to form a superego.

How could the argument of this study be falsified? There are several crucial points. Documentary evidence could be found to show that the Homeric Greeks were actually ignorant empiricists who had invented a complex, coherent set of explanations for natural events based on what was most familiar to them—their own motivated behavior and relationships. New observations of childhood development could show that modern children, too, are ignorant empiricists who use psychic metaphors and analogies to try to comprehend the world around them; it would follow that the Homeric poets were simply rendering into vivid imagery and coherent form the best explanatory constructs available to a prescientific culture. The theoretical and explanatory hypothesis can be refuted by evidence showing that the superego does not actually perform the functions presupposed by the hypothesis, and hence that its development cannot account for the alterations in the way self and nature are experienced, which form the core of the cultural transition from animism to rationalism. (For the psychoanalytic view, see Weinshel's [1986] examination of the superego's role in reality testing.) In summary, the argument can be attacked by showing that the cultural change did not occur as described; or that, even if it did, and even if there was a significant psychological factor, the one postulated is not correct.

The Hypothesis

It is my thesis, then, that the cultural transition from animism to rationalism came about in part as a result of a gradual improvement in individual psychic functioning. During a relatively short time the ancient Greeks advanced from an animistic culture in which borderline personalities were normal to a rationalistic culture in which neurotic personalities were normal. This does not imply a unidirectional causality from changes in individual psychology to changes in culture: On the contrary, the relationship is reciprocal. Individuals inherit the accumulated experience of their ancestors not through the genetic transmission of their acquired characteristics (Freud's "archaic inheritance"; 1915, 1923a, 1939) but by means of childhood identifications with the parents and their later surrogates (Freud, 1923a). After his discovery of the fundamental importance of identification in psychic organization and functioning, Freud no longer needed his Lamarckian hypothesis theoretically, although he clung to it for personal reasons: prereflective cultural values and modes of conduct can be transmitted nongenetically through identification with the parents and their generation. Thus, to emphasize the importance of improvements in individual psychic functioning is also to emphasize the importance of the precognitive cumulative experience of previous generations as reflected in the actual lives of each parent generation, and thereby made available to the next one.

Because the concept of a borderline personality will be used in a technical and nonpejorative sense, some definition may be useful. Borderline personalities have a relatively tenuous grasp on reality; they are subject to rapid and extreme mood shifts from omnipotence to terror, from ecstatic hope to despair, from elation to depression; they are impulse driven; their superego functions remain precarious and unreliable; they are vulnerable to paranoid forms of perception and thought; and they rely on projection, denial, and splitting for instinct mastery (see Fenichel, 1945; Frosch, 1970; Kernberg, 1970; Abend, Porder, & Willick, 1983).

To gain an empathic grasp of the borderline personality and its typical forms of experience, it is only necessary to remember emotionally significant experiences of our childhood, for we were, all of us, once borderline personalities. Children may have hallucinatory experiences without being psychotic. They may have "spirit" companions with whom they converse and play. Paranoia is normal in childhood, when (nonexistent) dangerous animals, witches, and bogeymen often appear under beds and at windows. It is normal for children to perceive inanimate objects as having "souls": "Bad table hit Johnny." The parallels between ordinary childhood behavior and adult borderline behavior can be observed by anyone; and just as animism is the natural worldview of modern children, so too animism was the worldview of the Homeric Greeks. Freud has discussed animism from a psychoanalytic perspective in various works (see especially Freud 1913b, 1919b). Animism is the culture that is natural to the borderline personality.

It must be recognized that the parallel is not complete. An adult Homeric Greek was obviously very different, physically and psychologically, from a modern child; but he was also, at least psychologically, very different from a modern adult whose personality is borderline in the clinical sense. The cultural environment of the ancient Greeks was congruent with and congenial to the borderline personality: For them it was the norm. A modern general would (one hopes) be relieved of his command and hospitalized if he advised a council of war to consult a prophet, a priest, or a dream interpreter to learn why a campaign was going badly, yet Achilles' advice to that effect was considered perfectly sensible by his Homeric contemporaries. The ancient Greeks were not surrounded by a social environment in which borderline personalities were at a disadvantage and that constantly reminded them that there was something amiss with them, and hence they were able to act with as much force, confidence, and dignity as any 20th-century adult, even though their actions and their reasons for taking them were, by any modern standard, dangerously out of touch with reality.

At the same time, it must be appreciated that remnants of animism not only continued to play an active part in the lives of the more rational fourth-century Greeks, as they do in the lives of children today. But they still have their place in the lives of contemporary adults as well. Some of our contemporaries, for example, faced with the uncertainty that remains after they have consulted scientific authorities, turn to dowsers to decide where to dig their wells. William Lyon Mackenzie King, Canada's most successful politician (if success is measured by length of tenure in the highest public office) regularly consulted a medium to obtain the advice of the dead on important matters of state as well as on personal matters, although he felt it prudent to confide this practice only to his diaries and to trusted associates. One would like to think that the substance of his decisions were the result of normal consultations and realistic considerations; if so, his seances would have been used to deal with residual uncertainties and doubts. The well-known reliance of President Ronald Reagan on the advice of an astrologer (although there is no conclusive evidence that he followed her advice in matters of state) is another case in point, and there are many more. These practices would seem to serve the same function in the lives of statesmen that water witching serves among country people. They are vestiges of animism preserved in our century to patch over the anxieties left by gaps in knowledge and technology. The greatest of these vestiges is, of course, religion.

In two respects individual and collective life are similar. Just as an individual retains the residues of his infantile modes of psychic functioning (e.g., in dreaming), and, in consequence, so too civilizations retain the residues of their earlier forms; and just as individuals may, under conditions of severe anxiety, regress to more infantile modes of functioning, so too a society, however advanced its culture, acquires no immunity to regression to more primitive forms.

Nevertheless, there is good evidence that civilization has advanced: that the cultural anthropology of Levy-Bruhl (1910), which allows for real and fundamental cultural change (without denying its reversibility), is truer to the human condition than the cultural anthropology of his successor Levi-Strauss (1962), which proposes that there is no fundamental cultural change. The thesis of this chapter is that a basic cultural advance was accomplished by the ancient Greeks, in whose debt we moderns remain insofar as we are its beneficiaries. An explanation of the psychological factors that were at work in that advance will be proposed. The focus will be on the psychological changes that were connected with the cultural change, using a series of contrasts between the Homeric Greeks and their fifth-and fourth-century B.C. descendants.

Projection in the Perceptual Life of the Pre-Homeric Greeks

The perceptual life of the Homeric Greeks was unable to penetrate beyond the global projections that invested it to the inanimate world of physical objects, and as a result they lived in a world that was overdetermined. No objects were simply material. No forces were simply physical. No events were simply mechanically or chemically produced. When the string of Teucer's bow broke he replaced it with another carefully selected for its physical strength; but the Homeric hero would also experience the event as the consequence of some psychic intervention—a recalcitrance on the part of the bowstring's animate being, or the intervention of a demon or a god (*Iliad* 28; see Dodds's 1963 comment, p. 12). A Homeric Greek might simultaneously use all his acumen as a bowman to select a sturdy replacement and care for it properly, and also undertake the ritual precautions needed to make it obedient to his purposes. (Teucer, in fact, is described as having abandoned his bow for a spear.) Of these preparations the magical ones would have been deemed by the Homeric Greek to be the most important.

The central action of the *Iliad* is initiated by a plague. To learn what is causing it, Achilles recommends consulting a dream interpreter; he speculates that Apollo has been offended by a broken vow or a ritual failure. Achilles' hunch turns out to be wrong in detail but not in principle: As Homer tells the story, the plague was "in fact" caused by Agamemnon's insult to a priest of Apollo. In the Homeric account no consideration is given to any realistic efforts to contain the plague, but only to ritual and magical solutions. It is reasonable to suppose that, when knowledge was scarce and anxiety was high, recourse to omnipotence of thought was high as well.

The whole of nature was overdetermined for the ancients. They suffered, as it were, from "hypergnosia," distorting experience by reading more meaning into it than is objectively present (Waelder, 1926). Natural events had an ominous character. For example, during the Trojan counterattack the Trojan soldiers see an eagle with a snake in its talons flying over their positions. Suddenly the snake manages to free itself and falls among the soldiers. They draw back from it in horror, not primarily from physical fear of it but because they see it as an evil omen. That it is portentous they have no doubt: They need a priest only to tell them what it portends. The priest reports that the eagle represents Hector and the snake, Agamemnon; the failure of the eagle to keep its prey in its talons means that Hector will fail in his efforts to take the Greek camp (Homer, *Iliad*, pp. 226–227). The natural world and its events were experienced as though invested with the hidden purposes of the gods.

The psychic experience involved in such an episode is not difficult to reconstruct. Made too anxious by their fear of failure to experience that fear in themselves, they projected it onto a suitable natural event in which they could become aware of it as something ominous that endangered them. By means of a culturally sanctioned interpretation the meaning of their fear could be made known, and at the same time legitimized. This elaborate detour by way of projection is evidence of an ego life lacking in stability and strength and dominated by the terror of shame—shame, that is, at being seen to have fears or anxieties deemed cowardly by the soldiers. This type of projection should not be considered as itself the source of the animism of these primitive men: Projections of this kind exploited, and were facilitated by, a more profound, global structure of experience, a structure of a paranoid type, which I have elsewhere called narcissistic schematization (Hanly, 1987).

This paranoid structure is evident in the mental events, character, and volition of the Homeric Greeks as well as in their experience of natural events. It dominates their perception of one another and their self-awareness as well. Psychic interventions experienced as alien to the ego were experienced as the source of special emotional states, of dreams, and of exceptional achievements, follies, and failures. Hector contemptuously rejects the prophecy of his failure to destroy the Achaeans because he has received, in a vision or visionary dream sent by Zeus, a promise of victory (*Iliad*, p. 227). Agamemnon has already had a similar dream of opposite import. An *ate* (a mental lapse, from a momentary inattention or carelessness to outright madness) was experienced as the handiwork of an alien psychic agency: Zeus, *moira*, or the Erinyes. It is an *ate* that causes Odysseus to fall asleep and thus fail to prevent his retainers from killing a tabooed ox (see Dodds, 1963, p. 608). A *menos* is an exceptional emotional state that gives rise to extraordinary deeds. Diomedes, wounded by Pandarus, receives a *menos* from Athena so that he fights with phenomenal ferocity and bravery to revenge his injury and wreak general havoc upon the Trojans (Homer, *Iliad*, p. 95). Hector is inspired with a *menos* of manic triumph: He foams at the mouth and his eyes burn with a strange fire when he puts on the armour of Achilles after having killed Patroclus (pp. 321–322). Aias is similarly inspired by Poseidon on the Achaean side, and he is certain that the priest Calchas, who had encouraged him, was an apparition of the gods, for it was "not hard to recognize a god" (p. 236). Thus, the highly volatile shifts of mood, attitude, and behavior characteristic of Homeric man were attributed by him to interventions by gods and demons over which he had no control—or at best a magical control:

> But the thoughts of Zeus outstrip the thoughts of men. In a moment the god can make a brave man run away and lose a battle; and the next day he will spur him on to fight. (*Iliad*, p. 311)

Thoumos (a counseling interior voice seated in the chest or midriff) was commonly experienced as independent of the ego even when it was not felt to be acting under the influence of a god. The inner as well as the outer landscape of Homeric man was experienced as being regularly subject to alien psychic intervention.

The struggle with strong conflicting passions, which in modern man takes place within the self, could be experienced by Homeric man as a struggle between himself and a constraining god. When Agamemnon punishes Achilles for his arrogance by insisting on taking Briseis from him for himself, the enraged Achilles is about to kill Agamemnon, but Athena appears to him and persuades him to desist. The description is of a hallucination. Achilles can see and hear the goddess but the others present cannot (p. 28). Evidently the superego of Homeric man was not yet a secure, internal acquisition. In conditions of crisis ego ideals made themselves felt as hallucinations, projections of the archaic parental images. We do not have to look any farther than these hallucinatory experiences to find the origins in individual experience for the Olympian gods, the collectively edited and elaborated versions of archaic parental images projected onto an outer scene.

Among classical scholars there has been a debate between those who see Homer's descriptions of the gods as an allegorical poetic mechanism without substantive roots in the life experience of ancient men and those, like Dodds (1963) and Cornford (1957), for example, who treat Homer's accounts as having been, in their essentials, literal descriptions of the psychic lives of the Homeric Greeks. Psychoanalysis supports the latter position. No other understanding can do justice to the antiquity of Homeric man or appreciate his achievement. If the Homeric Greeks were really no different psychologically from the Greeks of the classical period, and hence scarcely different from modern Western man but for their lack of science and an industrial technology, then one of mankind's greatest cultural achievements—the gradual conquest of animism by rationalism—would have to be attributed to some yet earlier people. The evidence for that, however, would have to be the same sort of evidence we find in the Homeric and Hesiodic legends, and the same argument that these accounts are merely literary devices would apply equally well ad infinitum. Finally, the argument that the gods were "literary" rather than "real" for the Greeks would lead us to postulate the creation of an original homo sapiens not essentially different from ourselves. The "literary" theory would seem to be based on a narcissistic denial that homo sapiens (as he now is) was once a nonrational being who in consequence of evolutionary pressure and genetic accident became the precariously civilized (although inventive) creature of today. Such a denial would protect us from the anxiety-provoking realization that, because what has been accomplished by "civilized man" is not guaranteed by instinct, genetic endowment, or the environment, it can also be undone and therefore needs to be assiduously preserved.

From Homer's descriptions in the Iliad it is evident that the Greeks were subject to severe shifts in mood. Agamemnon goes from exultant confidence to tearful despair. Achilles goes from arrogant challenging of Agamemnon to tearful grief at his public humiliation when he is obliged to accede to Agamemnon's demand for Briseis, and then to sullen, suspicious, vengeful rage. Impulse mastery was precarious. Agamemnon's knowledge that the safety of his enterprise, let alone its success, depends on Achilles and his men is lost in his determination to humiliate Achilles. Realistic considerations of state or of military strategy are constantly at the mercy of impulsive responses carried immediately into action. Mood shifts are sometimes occasioned by the course of battle between the Achaeans and the Trojans, but more often it is the outcome of the fighting that is determined by mood shifts from despair to manic triumph in the leading warriors on one side or the other. These "inspirations" are always perceived as the handiwork of a god. To the fear of defeat there is added dread of the loss of divine favor; to the hope of victory is added exultation in divine sanction and support.

Homeric man's morality was governed by five factors: fear of superior physical force, fear of superior guile, lust after wealth, the pursuit of sexual pleasure, and fear of the loss of reputation. To the extent that Homeric Greeks were able to master impulse, affect, and behavior, that mastery was accomplished by shame reactions—by the fear that the contemplated action would result in loss of esteem in the eyes of others—and these are the reactions to which the Achaean and Trojan commanders appeal in their exhortations to their comrades and to the ranks of their followers. In consequence, when there is no danger of being recognized no actions are constrained; fear of the loss of self-respect, which is the source of a sense of duty, plays no significant part in the psychology of Homer's Greeks. In the absence of an internalized conscience their actions are ultimately sanctioned by physical intimidation and psychic projection. The gods behave no differently from men. When Zeus was absent from Olympus it was the fear of his unquestionable physical superiority that constrained the lesser gods to obedience. When mortal commanders were unable to compel their troops to action by invoking shame and the prospect of triumph, booty, and women, they threatened them with death.

Fifth-Century Greek Rationalism

By the fifth century B.C. some fundamental changes had occurred. The psychic structure of the characters who populate Plato's dialogues allows us to recognize them as fundamentally akin to ourselves. The archaic mystery and grandeur of Homeric man's paranoid, narcissistic psychic organization had been brought under cultivation and subjected to maturation: Plato attempted to demonstrate the correctness of his tripartite division of the soul, for example, by appealing to the universality of psychic conflict, the nature of which he illustrated by the example of Leontius, who, having chanced upon the bodies of some recently executed criminals, found that despite his best efforts he could not restrain himself from looking at them with an excited, morbid fascination. Leontius is inescapably aware that it is his own necrophilic impulse that drives his conduct, curse his eyes for their lust as he may (Plato, Republic, IV, 439–440). Even unwanted, inconvenient, guilt-provoking, and calamitous impulses are accepted as belonging to the self. To be sure, they are alienated from the rational and moral self and assigned to the sphere of a degraded and degrading body; but nevertheless the instinctual, affective, and moral activities of the psyche have been largely withdrawn from the world into the self, and the self has been transformed in the process.

In contrast, Homeric Agamemnon, as part of his reconciliation with Achilles, found it necessary to declare solemnly that it was Zeus who had caused him to act vengefully toward Achilles. In place of

remorse or self-criticism there is the experience of having been a passive vehicle for the machinations of an external psychic agency, the
god, against whose force no mortal could struggle successfully.

> It was Zeus and Fate and the Fury who walks in the dark that blinded
> my judgement that day at the meeting. . . . What could I do? At such
> moments there is a Power that takes complete command, Ate, the eldest
> Daughter of Zeus, who blinds us all, accursed spirit that she is . . .
> flitting through men's heads, corrupting them, and bringing this one or
> the other down. (*Iliad*, p. 356)

Numerous other illustrations of the changed experience of self and
nature can be found in Plato's dialogues alone. Although Plato's version of the crime of the ancestor of Gyges the Lydian is replete with
magical descriptions and symbolism, at its core is the idea of a character whose oedipal criminality is the expression of his own hidden desires (*Republic*, II, 359–360). When Socrates (*Republic*, IX, 572)
wanted to establish that evil impulses exist in even the most decent
among us he appealed to the evidence of dreams of parricide, incest,
and cannibalism that give expression to latent carnal wishes (*Republic*,
IX, 572). No longer, in Plato, are dreams so easily experienced as
divinely visionary and prophetic. They have been integrated into the
self as an important register of its reality. Lest we suppose that the
achievement of rationalism was peculiar to Plato, it is not difficult to
find evidence of an advance along a broad front.

In the *Poetics* Aristotle asserted that the tragic poet is able to gain
a more fundamental insight into the human condition than the historian because he need not concern himself, as must the historian, with
the accidental and adventitious. Aristotle also asserted that *Oedipus
Rex* was the most perfect example of tragedy. There is in these assertions an implicit translation of the machinery of the gods back into its
sources in the instinctual vicissitudes of men and women. Thucydides'
account of Pericles' funeral oration to the grieving Athenian parents of
the heroes of the first year of the Peloponnesian War reveals a profound acceptance of cruel reality, unmitigated by denials or projections
(Thucydides, 2, p. 116ff.).

Later, Epicurus conceived of an atomic universe that, among its
other considerable virtues, held out for Epicurus and his contemporaries the principal value of binding the gods and exiling them to a
remote province of the universe where they could live with such pleasure that they would have no interest in creating mischief for men out
of envy for man's poor and temporary happiness. Epicurus explained in
terms of the mechanical action of inanimate bodies natural phenom-

ena (eclipses, storms, earthquakes, plagues, etc.) that, in the earlier animistic culture, had been the objects of superstitious dread created by projections (Epicurus, "Letter to Herodotus," 766–771).

But it is essential not to oversimplify or dichotomize. Progress in civilization is intrinsically precarious, and no satisfaction or consolation once enjoyed is altogether renounced. Even Socrates the questioner, when faced with death, bethought himself of a dream in which he had received an injunction from the gods to make music and, being uncertain whether philosophy altogether qualified as music, sought to console himself and satisfy the gods by writing poetry (Plato, *Phaedo*, 60E). There is still an element of projection in Aristotle's ontology. The relationship between form and matter from which his cosmos is born remains a sexual one on the analogy of a (biologically misconceived) procreative relationship between men and women (he believed the male sperm to be the source of the active essence, or rational nature, whereas the female ovary contributed only the matter from which the fetus is formed). In Plato's metaphysics there is a no less narcissistic overestimation of the power of ideas, envisioned as archetypes according to which the cosmos is constructed. The purposive character of human mental processes was unquestioningly projected by both Plato and Aristotle onto inanimate nature; and although Democritus, Epicurus, and later Archimedes, Euclid, and no doubt the ingenious artisans of the time (I am convinced that Bacon, 1620, was correct in attributing to them a better grasp of reality than was common among the philosophers) had constructed a concept of matter that was stripped of earlier anthropomorphism and fundamentally adequate, for Plato and Aristotle a correct understanding of the nature of matter remained inaccessible. Nevertheless, the ontologies of Plato and Aristotle removed the gods from nature, and their epistemologies were reality bound even though the nature of reality was not adequately conceived. The ethics of Plato and Aristotle demanded the test of values by reason and implied individual responsibility for conduct. For these fourth-century Greeks the experience of self, society, and nature had changed in a fundamental way: The gods had died, were dying, or at least had departed.

To state this is not to assert that fourth-century Greeks had no religious beliefs or that they did not consult oracles or engage in cult observances, but rather that religious belief and practice had by then acquired approximately the same psychological character it has for most religious people today. Religion had become a question of belief rather than one of experience as it had been in pre-Homeric times. Perceptual experience had undergone an adaptation to reality. We would like to be able to understand the psychogenesis of this adaptation.

Psychic Structure and Reality Testing

Fundamental to the transformation we are considering is a modification of the psychic organizations and processes involved in self-awareness or self-experience. If we reflect once more on the description of Achilles' struggle with his wish to kill Agamemnon we see at once that the conflict between the murderous drive demand and the inhibiting agency was perceived by him as a conflict between himself and an admonishing hallucinatory figure that was able to influence him as might another person. Psychoanalysis has made us familiar with the fact that children, before the resolution of the Oedipus complex, form a narcissistic projective identification with their parents that gives the parents a godlike quality. Parents, therefore, act as surrogate egos for their offspring with respect to both morality and the definition of reality. Even if a child is unable to experience the world as his parents describe it, he "knows," because of this identification, that it is as it is said to be and not as it appears to him. This psychic dependency is necessary and adaptive because the child's capacities for instinct mastery and reality testing are still incompletely developed. We may assume, therefore, that the psychic structure of Homeric Greeks had reached a rudimentary stage of development but that maturation did not yet provide for any significant advance beyond this stage. The adult Homeric Greek continued to live to a large extent on the basis of narcissistic projective identifications. Hence, the transition from narcissistic dependency upon parents to psychic independence and autonomy was never quite accomplished, because it had to be achieved, not by the development of new psychic structures within the self, which could provide the basis for a more rational autonomy, but by repetitions of the projective identifications and by the substitution of hallucinatory figures of gods for the parents, who could no longer serve this function. Premonitory and admonitory hallucinations, therefore, occupied the place in psychic life that was later to be taken by conscience. The psychic organization that Homeric man had not yet adequately developed was an effective superego.

The formation of the superego provides for more than instinct mastery: It facilitates and consolidates the functions of self-observation and self-criticism. It thus allows for self-objectivity, autonomy, and responsibility (Waelder, 1934; Hanly, 1979), all of which are psychic qualities upon which rationality depends. The capacity for self-objectivity brings in its train a much more refined and powerful ability to differentiate what is subjective from what is objective in sense experience; hence, the ability to "objectify" objects is facilitated by the ability to objectify the self. Thus, the development of effective superego functioning was an important step in demystifying, undeifying, and deanthropomorphizing perceptual life.

Similarly the superego provides for autonomy, insofar as it brings self-evaluation and self-regulation within the grasp of the individual. The price to be paid for this acquisition is a consolidated realization of one's own motives and doings, as well as a more just and accurate recognition of self-limitations. The exercise of the autonomy that comes with the formation of a stable superego is incompatible both with the narcissistic grandeur, frenzy, mania, and elated triumph of the Homeric Greeks and with their dread, terror, and despair.

Responsibility depends upon a sagacious and tenacious self-observation that does not need to alienate from the self actions whose consequences may range from inconvenient to calamitous. Self-observation allows for a more accurate attribution of the motivation and causation of attitudes, wishes, and actions. It brings into existence a personality with a real capacity for self-honesty (whether that capacity is exercised or not) and the ability to be self-critical for failures of self-honesty. Responsibility, made possible by the formation of a stable superego, makes the individual accountable to himself no less than to others.

Yet it must be understood that Homeric man was also honest in his experience of self, of others, and of nature: To accuse him of dishonesty or inauthenticity would be like accusing a child of lying when he says he is afraid of the dark. It was the great achievement of post-Homeric Greece to bring into existence individuals who could develop stable, effective, internalized superegos as part of their maturation. This, however, is only one step toward a better understanding of the historical origins of modern man in ancient Greece. It raises a series of questions concerning the causes of this change, questions that can only be posed here; but two general points can be made.

We are entitled on theoretical grounds to ask whether some real reduction in the anxiety to which individuals were subjected must not have been an essential element in the historical process. There is no reason to believe that the subjective sources of anxiety deriving from constitutionally determined vicissitudes of instinctual life had declined in the post-Homeric period—or have declined even now. We must therefore assume that the ancient Greeks, exploiting the precarious protection afforded them by their archaic religious life, managed to bring about real improvements in their social and natural environment that enabled them progressively to abandon their projections and begin to take up the quest for self-understanding and self-mastery. (The achievement of the psychological conditions for a more rational life is reversible, and this achievement was in fact later reversed for many centuries until, during the Renaissance, propitious conditions once more arose. It was no accident that the men who again moved civilization forward did so by returning to the Greeks for inspiration.)

The hypothesis of this chapter can claim the merit of consistency with certain insights of the greatest of the Greek philosophers: Plato believed that, in order to know, the soul must be just—that is, harmoniously ruled by reason; Epicurus valued his atomic materialism because it banished the gods from nature and by rescuing man from religious anxiety offered him a better prospect of living with greater pleasure the only life he has; Aristotle taught that tragedy, by bringing about a catharsis of otherwise debilitating emotions, protected the homeostasis of psychic life necessary to a rational and civilized existence; and finally, Socrates believed that in order to know reality it is necessary to know oneself. No single statement could better summarize the argument of this chapter.

chapter ten

Psychopathology of the Trial Process

Any human process is vulnerable to the hazards of psychopathological disturbance: that is, a disturbance that distorts or inhibits some mental activity or behavior. Thus far individual development and family relationships have received most attention from psychoanalysis, and for an obvious reason—they are the ultimate determinants of psychopathology, wherever else it may be found in human relationships, and hence have been the focus of both scientific investigation and therapeutic intervention; but as the Greek poets and philosophers already preconsciously knew, psychopathology can make its influence felt in any area—the rise and fall of gods and kings, the choice of political leaders, or the preference for various forms of social and political order. In any case, it is reasonable to assume that the venerability and sanctity of the law do not immunize jurors, lawyers, and judges against the influence of unconscious processes while they are in court. The trial process is therefore vulnerable to psychopathological disturbance, with the result that justice may not be done, or it may be done by chance rather than by rational design. Any study of psychopathological aspects of the trial process has as many points of departure as there are principals in the courtroom action. This study concerns the jury. The term *psychopathology* is being used here in the sense of "psychopathology of everyday life."

Methodology

It is important at the outset to be clear about the limits inherent in the approach taken by the present study. The theoretical argument rests on several psychoanalytic principles that will be used as the basis for raising certain issues concerning trial procedures and typical events as they may affect the processes of thought, observation, memory, and feeling aroused in jurors during a trial that can be expected to have a significant influence on the jurors' decision. Given the constraints imposed on the collection of relevant data, the unconscious aspects of these processes can be inferred only on the basis of independently established psychoanalytic theories: Consequently anything said about them is probable only. Probable statements can, however, be useful in identifying and illuminating certain psychological issues inherent in the trial process.

In order to gain a somewhat greater degree of probability and provide reference to an actual trial, these psychoanalytic considerations have been linked to a particular trial, that of Stephen Truscott at Goderich, Ontario, Canada, in 1959.

In June 1959 a 12-year-old girl, Lynne Harper, was raped and strangled. Her body was found in a woodlot near the Royal Canadian Air Force (RCAF) station at Clinton, Ontario. She was the daughter of an officer at the station. The family lived in the married quarters on the base. Stephen Truscott, then 14 years old, the son of a warrant officer whose family also lived in the married quarters, was charged with the murder and subsequently, in September of the same year, found guilty by a jury at Goderich in Huron County, where the crime had been committed. He was sentenced to be hanged. An appeal to the Court of Appeal for Ontario was dismissed, but on the same day, his sentence was commuted to life imprisonment by the federal government. An application for leave to appeal to the Supreme Court of Canada was refused; but as a result of public concern aroused by a book about the case (LeBourdais, 1966) the federal cabinet in 1966 asked the Supreme Court of Canada to review the trial and, what was unusual, any further evidence it might wish to consider. The Supreme Court upheld the findings of the trial court with one judge, Mr. Justice Emmett Hall, dissenting (1967, S.C.R. 309). Stephen Truscott was released from prison on parole in 1969.

For this study parts of the trial transcript and the appeal books used in the Supreme Court of Canada were examined, and some of the jurors interviewed. These interviews had a number of unavoidable limitations. They relied on the memory of the jurors, refreshed occasionally by a rereading of material from the transcript during the interviews, and thus they were subject to the usual technical problems associated with remembering emotionally significant events of some 13 years before. There were two further problems: The trial, and especially the original sentence, had caused a sensation, horrifying liberal public opinion and prompting criticism of the trial; and subsequently LeBour-dais's book had been critical of the jury. These posttrial experiences made jurors defensive, expecting criticism and feeling obliged to justify their actions in order to forestall it. Of the seven jurors who were alive and well at the time of this study only four agreed to be interviewed.

It is not the intention of this study to make generalizations about the Truscott jury *per se*, but rather to use the Truscott trial to illustrate the kind of difficulties anyone must expect to encounter in carrying out the exacting obligation the law imposes on the jurors in a criminal trial.

There is also a problem of definition: What constitutes psychopathology in the context of a trial? In general, psychopathology refers to mental processes that make it difficult or impossible for an individual to deal adequately with reality. But how is reality to be defined in this context? It is assumed here that it is defined by the law governing the conduct of trials, the rules of evidence in particular, and the evidence that is presented to the court. These are the realities with which jurors have to cope in carrying out their duties. For example, the law requires that jurors deem the accused person to be innocent until his guilt has been established beyond a reasonable doubt. A juror's failure to function in this way might therefore be the result of a psychopathological disturbance, for such a juror would have failed to act according to the objective demands of the situation. (Of course, a juror may fail to carry out his work appropriately because he has been bribed or intimidated; but in this case different questions arise, concerning character pathology. There was no evidence of bribery or intimidation of jurors in the Truscott trial.) Again, the law requires that jurors base their findings on the evidence presented to the court and upon nothing else. Insofar as the jury finds on the basis of the evidence as presented, even though that evidence may turn out to have been incomplete or badly presented, there can be no question of psychopathology. The jurors will have dealt adequately with reality as defined by the legal context within which they must function. On the other hand, insofar as a juror systematically overlooks or denies certain important evidence, or arbitrarily denies it in favor of other evidence, we can reasonably suppose that his observing and thinking have been subject to the influence of a psychological disturbance.

Our interpretive and analytic procedure is thus premised on a clinical model. It is assumed that what is normal, adaptive, and constructive can be expressed in some rule of life. For example, it is assumed that an individual should be able to hold down a job that he wants, for which he is prepared, and at which he is successful. This rule specifies part of the content of what is meant by normality. There are, however, individuals who are made anxious by the prospect of success, who become depressed and engage in activities unconsciously aimed at frustrating their achievement. The depressive reaction and the inappropriate behavior can then be identified as abnormal not only by general standards of life but specifically in terms of the aims and capacities of the individual as recognized by himself. Rules of law or typical procedures are, to this study, what criteria of normality are to the clinical investigation of individuals. The concepts of "normal" and "abnormal" used here are, of course, not the same as their clinical counterparts in which "abnormal" denotes the presence of a neurosis or a psychosis. Abnormal is used here to mean only the temporary disturbance of a mental process. The question of the mental stability of jurors is important in itself, given that, statistically, one person in every five is likely to suffer from a significantly impairing neurosis (Hanly, 1970a).

The psychoanalytic concepts of unconscious motivation, of excitation and homeostasis, of drive development and fantasies, and of psychic defense mechanisms, are specifically applicable to the performance of the jury in relation to some rule of law, of evidence, or of practice. These concepts obviously do not constitute a summary of psychoanalytic theory: They have been selected for their applicability to specific psychological issues likely to arise for jurors, and consequently for the insight they afford into certain important psychodynamic aspects of trials. Williams (1963) has analyzed the intellectual and other conscious difficulties under which many jurors find themselves, such as boredom, reluctance to serve, difficulty in following complex and conflicting evidence over many days, and so forth. All the factors Williams identified would tend not only to facilitate but to reinforce the psychological factors to be identified here.

Although the general public may be aware that unconscious processes exist, it has little accurate understanding of their nature or of their influence on motivation. Unconscious mental processes take place in each of us, with a variety of effects—psychological errors, dreams, periodic mild depression, irrational attitudes, unrealistic beliefs, convictions, opinions, values, distorted self-images, and distorted images and perceptions of others. These unconscious processes thus make their influence felt in the lives of individuals who lack any significant neurotic symptoms (Freud, 1901). Everyone dreams; yet the dreamer's waking thoughts usually have no access to anything but the disguised manifest images and affects of the dream, should it even be recalled in waking hours: The source and significance of the dream remains a mystery. Similarly, if one is convinced that someone is guilty or not guilty of a crime, the reasons one presents to oneself for coming to that conclusion may disguise the thoughts and feelings that are the actual cause of one's conviction. Consequently it is not necessary to assume or seek to establish that there was anything peculiarly neurotic about the Truscott jurors in order to examine the Truscott trial from a psychoanalytic point of view: It is only necessary to assume that their frailties were the garden-variety frailties of mankind. What is certain is that any person called to do jury duty will bring with him his own unconscious mental life and that its influence may disturb his work as a juror.

Unconscious Thought Activity and the Juror's Obligation

In his preliminary instructions to the jury a judge enjoins its members to remove from their minds anything they may have heard or thought about the crime or the accused, so that they can base their finding on the evidence presented to the court and upon nothing else. This instruction is the expression of a legal ideal for which there is an obvious justification; but judges and lawyers know that this rule may not be followed in practice. In this respect the law seems to be based on concepts of mental functioning derived from 17th- and 18th-century rationalism: that the reasonable man can, by an act of will, make his mind a *tabula rasa* for the purpose of giving objective consideration to any matter. To be sure, the judge's psychological role as auxiliary superego (see below) supplies a powerful motive for compliance with his admonitions, but the existence of that motive already endangers the capacity of jurors to form independent opinions. Compliance may take the form of a temporary repression of a juror's pretrial reactions, ideas, and speculations, but it does not follow that these will not influence his evaluation of what is presented during the trial—only that the juror will be unaware of their influence upon him.

Observation of the four Truscott jurors was complicated by the fact that the public outcry against hanging a 15-year-old boy included criticism of the jury for finding him guilty at all when a finding of guilt meant a death sentence. The jurors were angrily indignant at this: They felt that they had discharged a difficult duty conscientiously. And they were defensive. One of the opening interview questions concerned the jurors' oath to find on the evidence alone. One juror anticipated this by launching into a defense of the jury's impartiality before the question could be asked, even though the scholarly, nonjudgmental, and publicity-free nature of the study had been made abundantly clear in advance. This juror, like others, assured the interviewer that he had not paid attention to the crime before the trial. He had, he said, been too busy following a course on television. A second juror responded to the question with a defense of the jury system: The fairest jury, he asserted, is one made up of people of the same social experience and education as the accused; experts should be called only in cases of "terrible crimes." Another juror said he had experienced no difficulties: He just did what the judge said. He then spoke glowingly of the judge, emphasizing his great height and bearing, despite which he "was not proud but just like everybody else" outside the courtroom. The fourth juror denied having formed any ideas about the crime during the sum-mer between its commission and the trial because he was thinking about a fishing trip to Quebec—but then contradicted this by stating that he thought "they had the wrong person." The accused was "too young to do it," judging by the 14-year-old boys in his village who would not be physically capable of the crime. He later stated, however, on the basis of his observation of a "stubby, developed" young female witness, that she had been the girlfriend of the accused and that "he had had her a couple of times before"; and that "he had been prodding lots of them" and "had been a stud around there." No evidence to this effect had been introduced into the trial. These fantasies were stimu-lated in the mind of the juror by the appearance of the accused and of a female witness of his own age, and by the fact that he seemed to relax when boys and girls from his school were in the courtroom as witnesses and that he had winked at the "stubby, developed" one when she was in the witness box.

Such an apparent paradox as that presented by the fourth juror's *volte face* on the subject of the capabilities of 14-year-old boys obvi-ously raises questions as to its psychological origins and their effect upon his objectivity as a juror; and the fourth juror was not alone in his opinion of Stephen Truscott's character. It seems to have been shared by many of the adults involved in the case, including even some Supreme Court justices who had never seen the accused.

When the Truscott case was reviewed by the Supreme Court of Canada the testimony of a juvenile witness, Jocelyn Godette, was cru-cial to the Court's decision. Godette had testified that both on the eve-ning of the crime and on the previous evening Stephen Truscott had asked her to go with him to a field beside Lawson's Bush (where Lynne Harper's body was found) to see two newborn calves, but not to tell anyone because Mr. Lawson "didn't want a lot of kids on his property."

The majority opinion of the Court, in upholding the trial verdict, concluded that these conversations were not a reflection on Stephen Truscott's character. At its worst, they wrote, it meant no more than that he had a tentative date arranged with Jocelyn Godette. He wanted a date that night and he turned to Lynne Harper when Jocelyn God-ette was not available. (The accused had been seen talking to Lynne Harper and later riding with her on the crossbar of his bicycle along the road leading to Lawson's Bush. He had admitted all of this, but said she had asked him to take her to the intersection of the side road and the highway, and that he had done so and seen her get into a car.) The majority opinion is no doubt correct in assuming that this is the worst construction that could be put on Godette's testimony by impartial legal experts; but that is not to say that jurors, who are certainly not legal experts and possibly not impartial, could not very easily be led to believe the further interpretation, for which there was no other evidence: that Truscott was a hardened, sexually rampant boy who coolly substituted Lynne Harper when Jocelyn Godette was unable to go with him to the woods (and to her death). The Crown attorney conveyed this interpretation to the jurors in a very provocative way. Jocelyn Godette had not been able to go with Truscott, because she had not had her supper. The Crown's gloss was: ". . . and I suggest to you, Gentlemen, that if they were late having their supper it was God's blessing to that girl." His gloss on Lynne Harper's ride on Truscott's bicycle was that she had been invited to see the newborn calves and "she went with him to the bush and to her doom." The interviews indicate that Godette's testimony, combined with the usually impassive Truscott's animation when Godette and his other schoolmates were in court, led some of the jurors to form an extremely ill opinion of him. A psychoanalytic perspective might have led jurors, if they wished to give him the benefit of doubt about his behavior, to wonder whether he may have needed to deny his misery and ward off feelings of humiliation before his peers, and so may have turned his pleasure at seeing them into an exaggerated bravado, which made him seem to be overexcited and callous. The majority of the Supreme Court may have considered only how *they* would have weighed the evidence had they been the jury, instead of attempting to identify with the jurors and imagine what meaning that evidence, in the context of the trial, would have for those nine men from Huron County.

The late Mr. Justice Hall stated in his dissent that the majority opinion "appears to ignore the reality of the situation when considered in the actual setting." My observations suggest that he was correct in this, at least concerning the reactions of some of the jurors to Godette's testimony. What part these reactions played in the jurors' final decision we are not privileged to know.

Sequestration, Homeostasis, and Anxiety

In the trial of a person accused of a violent crime, jurors are going to be subject to a series of powerfully provocative stimuli. Long before he has been called to jury duty the news of the crime will have made its impact on a prospective juror. As a juror he will be subjected to a fresh set of emotionally charged experiences: He will see the accused and will be charged with deciding his guilt or innocence. The human mental organism is subject to arousal into activity by stimuli received from the environment via the senses and by sources within itself as a result of the spontaneous action of the instincts. Once aroused, the mental organism has the task of resolving the arousal through gratification. Gratification may occur at once or be delayed; it may be direct and related to the object actually desired or feared, or indirect and related to a substitute object as a result of a defense mechanism. Dreams, for example, provide deferred substitute gratifications for wishes that are formed during waking hours but cannot be gratified because the gratificatory behavior would be in conflict with reality or with social or personal ethical norms. Thus, even in its sleeping state the mind is actively at work preserving its impulse life at tolerable levels of excitation (homeostatic balance) by the resolution of states of arousal. It is important to understand that, similarly, the human mind is always silently at work quite independently of the conscious will even though the individual may have as part of his self-image the (to him) self-evident belief that his will is the unique sovereign of his own thoughts, feelings, fantasies, motives, and actions.

The courtroom and the appearance of the robed judge seated above the court are likely to be strange and impressive, even awe inspiring, to many jurors. Jurors who are trying persons of grave crimes are apt to be anxious and highly stimulated. During the trial jurors are subject to a severe restriction. They have only one significant act to perform: to render a verdict of guilt or innocence. To this end they are supposed to be attentive, objective observers and thoughtful analysts of the events, testimony, and rulings unfolding before them in the courtroom. At the same time, at least until very recently, jurors have been cut off from the forms of intimate and recreational companionship that they would normally use to assist them in resolving highly charged emotional states and in working out successful adaptations to novel and demanding experiences.

Some of these factors will be considered later in the contexts of other psychoanalytic concepts, although they could also be discussed appropriately here; but perhaps two factors, the appearance of the lawyers (as distinct from their arguments) and the practice of sequestering the jury, will be sufficient to clarify the implications of the principle of homeostatic balance for our understanding of the psychology of the trial process.

The appearance of counsel may influence the outcome of the trial.

The jurors interviewed had retained a vivid impression of the court-room style of the two lawyers. They saw the Crown attorney as a rather bumbling, awkward individual, without much experience in the court-room or with its rules of procedure but shrewd and persistent in pre-senting his case despite having to be corrected by the judge on numer-ous occasions. They felt, without being able to explain precisely why, that the Crown was, despite his numerous courtroom errors, somehow very astute, and in this they were right. Although the Crown may not have set out deliberately to achieve this effect, his behavior enabled the jurors to identify with him. They saw the defense counsel, on the other hand, as masterful, clever, experienced, and able to dominate the wit-nesses, the courtroom, and themselves. They all avowed that if they were in trouble with the law they would want the services of the de-fense counsel, but nevertheless it was the Crown with whom they iden-tified. At least one juror developed such a strong animosity toward the counsel for the defense that he "sometimes wanted to reach out of the jury box and throttle him." However brilliant a lawyer's arguments, it is unlikely that they will convince a juror who feels such hostility to the person making them. In the pursuit of their own narcissistic gratifica-tions, lawyers can generate dramatics in the courtroom that, in their influence on the jurors' minds, vie successfully with the evidence they present. Paradoxically, the events during the trial that might have made the Crown secretly afraid that he was not presenting his case effectively were precisely those that benefited his case by facilitating the jurors' identification with him because they felt themselves similarly at sea.

Jurors will also be affected by the fact that they are sequestered and hence cut off from the relationships and actions they would nor-mally use to reduce anxiety and resolve feelings of anger, hostility, and excessive pity, and thus be able to maintain a high level of tolerance for uncertainty—which is the attitude of mind required for objectivity. The Truscott jurors interviewed all complained about sequestration. They felt imprisoned, frustrated by being unable to expose themselves to any sights, activities, or interests other than the trial. They were thrown into a dependency on one another in order to attain some measure of relief from the burden of responsibility under which they labored. Sequestering juries subjects them to a psychological predica-ment and also promotes a group identification that is itself usually regressive because it reduces the ability of each individual to observe and think for himself and thus form an independent opinion as to the guilt or innocence of the accused.

At the time of the Truscott trial a Canadian jury was not permit-ted to separate during the trial of a capital offense, but Parliament has since recognized the disadvantages of sequestration. Section 576 of the

Canadian Criminal Code was amended in 1972 to provide that the judge "may, at any time before the jury retires to consider its verdict, permit the members of the jury to separate." The trial judge is now responsible for weighing the hazards of a long period of isolation against the risk of extraneous influences upon the objectivity of jurors. The wise use of this discretion could go far toward removing the psychological liabilities of sequestration.

Unconscious Fantasies and Objectivity

In adults whose lives are quite exemplary the report of a sexual crime acts as a stimulus to unconscious memories, giving rise to an unsettling fascination with the crime and leading intrigued observers to ask why such model citizens should be so fascinated by this sordid crime. This question cannot usually be answered, because repression has silenced the memories, of adolescence and of the root instinctual experiences in the individual's childhood, that alone could yield an answer. The drives themselves impose severe demands upon the mental organism for homeostatic resolution. The instincts develop derivative impulses, aims, behavioral modes of gratification, and ideational representation, according to the major stages (phases) through which they pass in the course of individual physical and mental development. An aspect of this development that is important for this study is the tendency in small children to confuse sexual intercourse with violence when they observe it or fantasize it. This perception of sexuality is typically repressed, along with the repression of the Oedipus complex itself, at the onset of the latency period (which lasts from about the age of 5 or 6 to the onset of puberty). The confusion of sexuality with violence is commonly aroused into renewed activity with puberty as the result of either impulse fixation at, or instinctual regression to, one of the infantile sexual organizations; consequently adolescent boys and girls fantasize, dream, joke, and talk about intercourse as a form of violence. Three important corollaries follow from this: A pubescent boy is psychosexually equipped by his prepubescent development for acts of sexual violence; in the lives of almost all individuals this proclivity is not so strongly motivated that it cannot be satisfied by the production of a rich fantasy life focused upon this theme, associated with masturbation and followed by feelings of guilt; and adults, whether or not they are able to recall them, will have memories of such experiences.

Some of the jurors interviewed stated that before the trial they had had thoughts and discussions with others about the crime and the accused. The conscious thought some jurors had that "a 14-year-old boy isn't capable of raping and strangling a girl" may in fact have been the denial of a repressed thought to the opposite effect. The need to believe that adolescent children are innocent of aggressive sexual aims is the expression in conscious thought of the action of a defense against just such an impulse to rape in one's own adolescence. This is not to say that all pubescent boys teeter precariously on the brink of sadistic sexual crimes, or that memories of this Hydelike self are universally repressed. Psychoanalysis has shown that unconscious fantasies can function as the *psychological* equivalents of real experiences, producing in the ego the same guilt and anxiety that would be evoked by the actual occurrence. Memory thus holds the key to an appreciation of the psychological potential for sadistic sexual crime in any pubescent or adult male. A denial of this sort, if it were at work, would lay the groundwork for a subsequent projection of guilt upon the accused, which could in turn exert pressure in the direction of a finding of legal guilt. What is unconscious exerts a pressure for release, and it may be projected onto another in order to avoid the painful memory of having had such impulses. From a psychoanalytic point of view a juror could only be considered wholly immune to the tendency to project subjective guilt onto a person accused of sexual violence if he could recall, without distortion, his own adolescent and infantile sexual fantasies.

Defense Mechanisms and Objectivity

Twenty years after Lynne Harper's death one could still hear totally ungrounded speculations about the crime and the criminal congenial to the unconscious fantasies of the local gossips being repeated with an air of scandalized excitement in the living rooms of Huron County. What are the psychological factors at work in these preoccupations with sexual crime?

Psychoanalysis has identified the existence and described the operation of defense mechanisms that the psychic organism can use to maintain homeostatic balance and in particular to maintain anxiety at a tolerable level. Among these defense mechanisms are repression, projection, denial, sublimation, isolation, reaction formation, and identification. Of these, four are of particular interest to this study. *Repression* is the process that inhibits the recall of past experiences. It produces a psychogenetic amnesia, mild and temporary forms of which are familiar to everyone, for instance, in the inability to recall a known name. *Projection* is the process whereby qualities of self are attributed to something external, as in "childhood paranoia" when the child's aggressive impulses are projected into, for example, the bogeyman at the window of whom the child is genuinely terrified. *Denial* is the process whereby some unacceptable aspect of reality is set aside as though it did not exist, as when a small boy imagines himself to be Superman in order to deny the difference in size and strength between himself and his father. *Identification*, as a defense, is a process whereby an individual alienates some function or responsibility from himself and assigns it to someone else to exercise on his behalf while preserving the feeling that he is still exercising it himself; the aim is protection from the anxiety of having to perform some forbidding task.

In general, defense mechanisms work to maintain anxiety at a tolerable level and to ward off painful recognitions. Information about a violent crime, for example, will arouse anxiety, especially if the perpetrator has not been arrested. Added to this realistic anxiety there will, however, also be a subjectively originated anxiety because the information will reactivate old guilt-provoking memories and fantasies. Such memories are, however, very likely to have been repressed and therefore cannot be consciously recalled, however helpful they might be in finding a valid personal orientation toward the crime and the criminal. An example of this effect, combined with that of projection, is the blizzard of rumors and gossip that quickly surrounds the scene of a sensational sex murder.

These mental processes can also "find guilty" an accused person who, on the basis of the courtroom evidence alone, may not be so. Anyone charged with the responsibility for deciding the guilt or innocence of an accused person will have to deal in some way with his own unconscious reactions to the crime. If these are guilt-provoking there is always danger that an impartial assessment of the evidence presented for or against the accused will be impaired by an unconscious need to find him guilty. The defense mechanism at work in this event would be projection, which brings about the alienation of guilt feelings from the self and their transference to the accused. In this way unconsciously determined feelings of psychological guilt can influence decisions concerning legal guilt.

The point being made here is strictly theoretical: The interviews with the Truscott jurors afforded no observations that clearly indicated this type of psychopathology as a major influence upon the jurors' decisions. One feature in the reactions of the jurors interviewed, however, is consistent with this pattern. They were naturally keenly interested in the comportment of the accused, which they found to be impassive, defiant, belligerent ("He could stare you down"), or indifferent—except when young female witnesses appeared. Then he was observed by the jurors to respond with animation, winking and smiling at the witnesses. All the jurors interviewed interpreted this behavior as that of a tough, sexually depraved youth. One remarked ruefully that the accused seemed to be better endowed than he was himself. These ideas were not based on any evidence placed before the court. They can only be treated as fantasies, and, as such, they have the distinct appearance of a return of the repressed in a form disguised by projection. To the extent that this was the case, the jurors would be, unknown to themselves, biased against the accused and predisposed to find him guilty. It would be difficult for the juror to recognize such a bias in himself because the projection would make it appear to him self-evident that he was perceiving the guilt of the crime in the accused's own behavior—as one juror said, "plain as the palm of your hand."

This process should not be confused with something superficially akin to it—the entirely proper observation of the accused in order to form an impression of whether he is the kind of person who could commit the crime in question. (Even such impressions are hazardous, however, because of the effects that being accused of a crime, imprisonment, and the trial itself may have on the appearance and behavior of an accused person.)

It is of interest to note how obliquely pertinent to this issue is the dissent of Mr. Justice Hall in the Supreme Court of Canada judgment on the Truscott case. Mr. Justice Hall was of the opinion that Jocelyn Godette's testimony was inappropriately led by the prosecuting counsel, whose reference to it and interpretations of it had incited the jury against the accused by establishing in their minds that the accused had wanted to have sexual intercourse with the witness on the evening of the crime and, having been frustrated in that objective, turned to Lynne Harper as an alternative. In fact, however, although one juror repeated this prosecution theory, it was evident from the interviews that the jurors were primarily impressed by the *reaction* of the accused to the *appearance* of this witness rather than by anything she said or by any construction the prosecution placed upon it. Something in this reaction aroused in the jurors a sense of the guilt of the accused, as though they felt his courtroom behavior at this point to be precociously shameless and an implicit demonstration of guilt. It was on this perceived meaning (whether it was a projection or an objective perception) that the plausibility of the prosecution's case rested for the jury, not on the evidence, the counsel's use of it in substantiating their theories, or the judge's instructions to the jury concerning it.

The Supreme Court judges, including Mr. Justice Hall, as well as the lawyers presenting the case, would therefore seem to have been engaged in a complex, abstract game of legal moves and countermoves based on an unsubstantiated assumption that jurors follow this game with the degree of interest and understanding with which they would follow a game of hockey. These legal debates appear to take no account of the concrete psychological processes by which justice was done or not done in the courtroom. The law, from this point of view, turns a blind eye to the real course of justice because it assumes that the outcome of a jury trial is actually decided by the evidence presented by counsel, their arguments, and the instructions of the judge to the jury. These things indeed are the context for the jury's decision, but they are by no means always the basis for it. A powerful play of psychological factors and reactions, overlooked by the law, may have the decisive influence on the outcome.

These considerations bear on one of the legal issues raised by the Truscott trial: whether defense counsel should have sought a change of venue for the trial. LeBourdais (1966) strongly suggested in her examination of the trial that counsel for the defense, himself born and raised in the county, was naïve in thinking that the risk of prejudice against his client was insufficient to justify the cost to the family of a change of venue. A change of venue cannot remove the risk of emotional prejudice against someone accused of a violent sexual crime; jurors anywhere would have to deal with their own unconscious reactions to the crime and to the accused. Nevertheless, a change of venue might have removed two potential obstacles to an unbiased trial.

In the first place, the members of the community (any community) in which such a crime takes place are likely to be stimulated to form fixed opinions about the accused prior to his trial by the flood of information and misinformation circulating within the community itself. The immediate community will be in a higher state of excitement about it, and for a longer period, than will communities less directly involved. This generalization holds even if most of the Truscott jurors were in fact, as they claimed in interviews to have been, quite unoccupied by the crime over the summer (for personal reasons peculiar to each) until they were reminded of it by being called to jury duty.

Second, the accused in this case was a member of a distinct group within the county—the RCAF personnel and their families. There develops an extended kinship bond among members of a community who are born into it, raised within it, and share in it a common way of life, in this case that of an agricultural community. The psychological basis of this kinship bond is a common identification animated by a libidinal tie, which in turn is protected by the projection of hostile feelings onto an alien group (Freud, 1921). This kinship is fissured in many places by religion, politics, ethnic origin, and intracommunity vocational differentiation, but these splits can easily diminish in significance when a violent crime is committed. The permanent members of the community will want to believe that the guilty person is not one of them, and this wish, combined with the projection of unconscious hostile impulses onto the "outsiders" in their midst, causes a desire to believe that one of the "outsiders" is guilty. Many members of this rural community would therefore have heaved a sigh of relief when someone from the RCAF base was accused of the crime, and projected hostility would cause these same people to relish any fact or fantasy pointing in the direction of his guilt. Nevertheless, members of this community were not bereft of conscience or of the capacity to discriminate fact from fiction; and not a few members of the community, particularly among the townspeople, had associated with RCAF families and formed friendships with them. One would be committing the logical fallacy of division in attempting to deduce, from this demonstrable group phenomenon, anything about the attitudes of particular individuals. My own impression on the basis of interviews with the four available jurors is that they did, to a substantial degree, function as individuals, and as individuals they denied the validity of the allegation of group bias against the accused suggested by LeBourdais. One juror, for instance, had close associations with RCAF personnel at another base in the community. Nevertheless, the possibility of projection does provide an argument in favor of a change of venue in such cases.

Identification and the Alienation of Responsibility

The judge of the Truscott trial was viewed with awe by the jurors. They spoke of him in terms of reverential respect. One juror recalled his surprise at finding the judge to be so impressive and said he had not expected to have this feeling. All this means that the jurors, in addition to being consciously attuned to the instructions and admonitions of the judge, will have been unconsciously attuned to any slight, implicit, nonverbal as well as verbal communications bearing on his opinion about the guilt or innocence of the accused. How does this view of the judge relate to unconscious fantasy? What potential does it have for distorting the judgment of jurors? The judge can become an extension of each juror's sometimes primitive conscience, the superego.

The superego is a set of unconscious functions and contents within the ego itself (Freud, 1923a). These functions determine the moral and aesthetic responses of the individual, and are themselves governed by introjected parental images and admonitions. It is the superego that makes self-condemnation possible; it is the superego that punishes the ego with guilt when it fails to fulfill the demands of its imperatives; and it is the superego that requires the repression of impulses and wishes that demand gratification through morally or aesthetically unacceptable forms of behavior. Just as the instinctual unconscious is the source of fascination with a sensational crime, so the superego is the source of the reaction to it of moral horror.

Individuals often find it difficult to tolerate the burden of superego functioning, and consequently are content to enter into groups through which they can form a common identificatory idealization of a single individual to whom is assigned the role of providing moral leadership to the group. Religious organizations work in this way, and so do courts. The judge is the superego of the judicial process. The lawyers are to set out the facts, and the jury must find on them, but the judge regulates their presentation, decides what may or may not be admitted, rules on points of law, and generally imposes order on the proceedings. Most importantly, he summarizes the evidence for the jury, instructs them in the law, and it is for the judge to pronounce sentence. The language and the formalities of courtroom observance and even the architecture and furniture of the courtroom are designed to emphasize the superego role of the judge and enhance the awe surrounding him. This psychological role gives the judge a very great potential for influence upon the jury. To the authority of fact and reason and his knowledge of the law there is added the psychological authority of an auxiliary superego; consequently the judge can direct a jury psychologically as well as legally, and his psychological directions may be inappropriate even though his legal directions may be unexceptionable.

The role of the judge is therefore crucial. The psychological preconditions for the formation just described reside in the inevitable unfamiliarity of jurors with courts, court proceedings, and the law, combined with the authority the judge must exercise in all matters of law. He is the man whose decisions bind the conduct of the clever, highly educated, and well-to-do lawyers who contest the case for the Crown and the accused. In the court his word is law. His rulings may be challenged, but he decides whether to uphold or alter his ruling.

It is of course true that the jury alone bears the responsibility for deciding guilt or innocence. The judge instructs the jury very carefully on this point, but the instruction concerning the law is at odds in this respect with the psychology of his role under the law in the courtroom. Williams (1963) made the point that "the judge must not use such language as to lead the jury to think that he is directing them that they must find the facts in the way he indicates." Williams added, "Quite apart from any expression of opinion by the judge, the way in which he marshalls the facts and gets rid of irrelevancies may present a strongly persuasive argument for one side or the other" (p. 304). To this apt formulation our analysis must add that the judge may be quite unaware of the nature and extent of his influence because it is not only the legal and factual content of his summing up that is significant to the jurors but also the manner in which he delivers it. The jurors are therefore likely to experience a conflict within themselves between the verbal instruction, that the responsibility for their verdict is theirs alone, and the nonverbal psychological identity and function of the judge. It is not inconceivable that the judge's role identity in the mind of the juror may have a greater influence upon his thinking than the judge's words.

In the course of the Truscott trial some of the jurors developed an interest in the judge's opinion of the guilt or innocence of the accused. One juror felt that sometimes when the lawyers were arguing about technical legal points the judge "would be miles away figuring it out" (Truscott's guilt or innocence). "He [the judge] knew the truth." Another juror felt that the judge was impartial throughout and gave no sign of believing the accused guilty or innocent until his charge to the jury, but then, this juror felt, the judge had concluded that he was guilty. Another was uncertain about the judge's attitude—sometimes he felt the judge thought Truscott was guilty, at other times he did not know; but the jury had to go back to the judge for further instruction about part of the evidence, and as he gave it this juror was sure the judge thought the accused was guilty. At this point the defense counsel had objected, and the judge had ordered the relevant portion of the evidence to be read from the court record. In terms of the law nothing had gone amiss: The defense objection had been accepted, and the court record had been read; but the law does not take into account the effects of silent, unconscious processes in the minds of the jury that may be much more influential in forming a juror's opinion than the explicit verbal content of the courtroom procedure. An unconscious thought process may be at work such as "the judge thinks the accused is guilty, and if the judge thinks so it must be so." This process need never become conscious in the mind of the juror. From the security of the superego it can color the juror's assessment and appreciation of everything that has gone on in the court.

This influence is by no means confined to such obvious forms as a juror's perception that the judge is giving a tendentious reading of the evidence. An examination of the transcript of the Truscott trial reveals several examples of a less overt influence the significance and importance of which psychoanalysis enables us to understand and appreciate. When the judge instructed the jury regarding their assessment of the evidence pointing to the guilt of the accused, he appealed to superegoderived attitudes in the jurors. For example:

You must not permit the fact of his youth in any way to prevent you from bringing in a verdict in accordance with your *conscience*. Nor, on the other hand, ought you to allow the *revolting nature of the facts* surrounding this case in any way to influence you to bring in a verdict which is, in any way, shape or form, *contrary to the evidence*, or based on anything but the evidence . . . if the evidence raises a doubt in your mind, you will acquit him. When I say raises a doubt in your mind, I mean a reasonable doubt. Not a foolish doubt or a doubt because you are hesitant about doing your duty, and I am sure I need not say to a Jury of the County of Huron that I know you will accept your responsibilities in this matter, come what may, and that you will bring in a verdict according to your *conscience*.

Earlier, in the charge to them, the jury had been told:

Your churches may be the lid of respectability in the community but you, Gentlemen of the Jury, are the barometer of that respectability. You are the screws that hold the lid down in place. The whole character of your community depends on the way you do your *duty* in this case. (Friedland, 1974, p. 761ff., emphasis added)

The judge had thus, in effect, associated a guilty verdict with the performance of duty according to conscience. The last sentence quoted was especially provocative, no doubt without his consciously intending it to be so, because it evoked the theme of the goodness and safety of the community, suggesting perhaps the question "Would you want that boy living next door to your little girl?"

It was, on the other hand, the jurors' ego attitudes and feelings that the judge addressed when referring to their assessment of the evidence pointing to the innocence of the accused. He cautioned them, quite rightly, not to let the unpleasantness of the facts interfere with an impartial assessment of those facts and their implications; but embedded in his communications there is the unconscious assertion "What is moral in you will be on the side of a finding of guilt." Such a thought will communicate itself to the members of a jury without their being aware that they have received it and without their recognizing its influence upon their thinking. It will be felt only as a vague yet potent anxiety bound to the thought that an acquittal would be immoral.

In a slip of the tongue the judge quite possibly revealed his private opinion that the accused was guilty: "If, after you have decided in your minds what the facts are, you can think of any rational explanation of them inconsistent with the prisoner's innocence—I should say, inconsistent with the prisoner's guilt; or indeed, if you have any doubt about it, you must acquit him." The interfering repressed thought would appear to be the negative of the thought consciously uttered: "It will be hard for you to find a rational explanation of the facts that is inconsistent with his guilt." The jurors would have preconsciously detected the significance of this slip and been influenced by it. Writers from the earliest times have employed psychological errors to convey facets of the motives, feelings, and thoughts of fictional characters of which the characters are not yet aware, and jurors can be likened in this respect to spectators at a dramatic performance.

We have already considered the importance of the witness Jocelyn Godette and the Crown's interpretation that the accused was planning to rape and kill her. The judge took special interest in the testimony of this witness:

HAYES Q: Was there any more conversation between you then, on Tuesday?
A: Well, he just kept on telling me to "don't tell anybody to come with you, and that is all."
His LORDSHIP Q: Say that again. He just kept on telling me what?
A: Not to tell anybody.

Mr. Justice Hall of the Supreme Court fastened on this episode in his minority opinion, holding that it contributed to misleading the jury as to the import of the evidence in a way that prejudiced them against the accused. In fixing on this point Mr. Justice Hall was being guided by a feeling for the kind of factor we have been considering. A wise judge is like an intuitive creative writer: He has an instinctive prescientific sense of the workings of unconscious mental forces.

The judge's role is particularly important in the way he interprets court procedures for the jury. Jurors usually have very little knowledge of the legal process. Consider the problem that arose in the Truscott trial when the Crown attorney in his opening remarks made reference to a statement taken from the accused but not admitted as evidence: This left the jurors knowing that the accused had made a statement but not knowing what it contained—for instance, whether it was a confession or not. (Jurors who followed the subsequent controversy would have read that it was not.) Some of the jurors interviewed said they had been left at the time of the trial in a state of uncertainty about this and had followed the instruction to disregard it; but at least one juror did believe that the statement was a confession, that it was not admitted because it was not in the interest of the accused to have it presented to the jury, and that the court was protecting the interests of the accused. This juror, nevertheless, like the others said that he had followed the judge's instruction and disregarded the unknown statement in reaching his conclusion. Yet another juror said that he had no thought of the statement's being a confession, but in another context indicated he felt that any evidence rejected by the judge must be damaging. One must ask whether jurors are really able to resist being influenced by opinions of this kind.

This issue points to a psychological difficulty many jurors must encounter because of the unfamiliarity with the rules of evidence. When a person is deprived of an objective frame of reference in which to place an experience, that experience will still be interpreted, and there is every likelihood that it will be interpreted subjectively. For example, one of the Truscott jurors felt that the unadmitted statement cannot have been a confession because a confession would have made a trial unnecessary: In other words, he felt himself under a psychological constraint to form some interpretation of the significance of the statement. He was unable to rest content with simply not knowing. He had to form a surmise, in this case based on ignorance of the law.

This compulsion to interpret is readily understood from a psychoanalytic point of view. When the mind is subjected to a stimulus during sleep (e.g., a loud or unusual noise), unless it arouses him to form an objective opinion of its nature and source the sleeper will produce a dream that provides in its manifest content a context for the interpretation of the stimulus. Similarly the mind of ancient man, in the absence of an objective understanding of natural phenomena such as plagues, assigned to them the significance of divine retribution provoked by an unexpiated crime. The unconscious life of modern man still obeys the compulsion to interpret. The jurors' predicament in this situation may be likened to that of the sleeper or the ancient. Like the sleeper who is deprived of perceptions of reality by his sleeping state, the juror is denied access to reality by the rules of evidence—for example, in the Truscott case, access to the statement made by the accused. Like the ancient man whose mind was not supplied by his education with a scientific frame of reference in which to place his observations of nature, the juror must function without a thorough grounding in the law of trials, and consequently lacks the two best defenses against the formation of opinions produced by subjective thinking, which is peculiarly vulnerable to unconscious determination. The only objective indications available to the juror in the case we are considering were that the prosecution had made reference to an inadmissible statement and that it is the task of the prosecution to attempt to establish the guilt of the accused. Taken together, these indications would tend to open the door to the idea that there must be something damaging to the accused in the content of the inadmissible statement. The other defense available to the juror is the moral authority of the judge in support of the prohibition against considering the matter at all. Unfortunately this moral authority can easily be undermined by the thought that the judge is doing his best to protect the interests of the accused—a thought that is itself a distorted impression of the judge's work, which is to ensure that the trial is impartial: that is, to ensure that the rules of evidence are scrupulously observed. The distortion arises from the need to see the judge as a person who will do everything he can for a guilty person, a need likely to arise in the mind of any juror who is himself subject to guilt-arousing unconscious memories: That is, we are not dealing here with the objective meaning of the judge's actions but with their subjective significance to a juror. Such a notion, when combined in the juror's mind with the further impression that the judge believes the accused to be guilty, might disarm the juror's determination to make his own assessment of the evidence and cause him to underestimate the importance and significance of defense testimony.

Conclusion

There is no reason to think that the Truscott jurors functioned any differently from jurors generally. There is no reason to be particularly critical of them. There is reason, however, to believe that psychopathological factors were at work in the Truscott trial, and that they are usually at work in trials, with a potential to distort the legal process and, in certain cases, to subvert it.

This study has no evidence to offer concerning the guilt or innocence of Stephen Truscott. Methodologically it is limited to using his trial as an illustration of the kinds of insight psychoanalysis can bring to bear on this important social institution. It raises questions. It points out possible directions for empirical research into the work of juries, if legal impediments to such research were removed. The one qualified assertion about the trial that can be made is that if the jury reached the correct verdict it is possible that they did not do so for the right reason: that is, on the basis of the evidence as presented in court. Such a possibility arouses legitimate concern about the reliability of the judicial process and the jury system. Applied psychoanalysis could make useful contributions to the evaluation of alternative ways of deciding the guilt or innocence of persons accused of crimes of violence. This study has tried to identify some of the psychological factors that should be taken into account in such evaluations.

chapter eleven

Psychoanalysis and Values

The question of the relation between fact and value in psychoanalysis was raised at the end of Chapter One. It has been implicit in various guises in subsequent chapters: Can empirical psychoanalytic findings contribute to the philosophy of morals, or to aesthetics? Can interpretations of the psychology and motives of the characters in a play illuminate its formal beauty? Do the genetic arguments that contribute to the criticism of philosophical ideas (innateness of concepts, Platonism) have hidden value premises? Does a psychoanalytic account of an advance in culture from animism to rationalism make assumptions about values? And similar questions may be raised by the use of psychoanalytic principles to evaluate the way juries arrive at findings of guilt or innocence in courts of law.

More generally, a question of value arises in clinical psychoanalysis insofar as its aim is healthy psychic functioning (Hartmann, 1960). The relation of clinical findings to civilized morality was succinctly stated by Freud (1909c): "All who wish to be more noble-minded than their constitution allows fall victims to neurosis; they would have been more healthy if it could have been possible for them to be less good" (p. 191). Does psychoanalysis recommend trading off a certain amount of virtue for a greater amount of health? Has psychoanalysis its own set of moral values and its own moral doctrine, which it somehow derives from its clinical findings and the theories it bases upon them? If so, what is one to make of Freud's assertion that psychoanalysis is not a philosophy but a part of natural science?

Descriptive and Normative Statements

We are accustomed to making a distinction between descriptive and normative statements: Descriptive statements inform us about what is, and normative statements tell us about what ought to be. Descriptive statements state facts; normative statements express values. Empirical science is made up of descriptions, among them descriptions of regularities in nature and of the forces that cause them. Moral and cultural codes are made up of value statements that express moral principles, imperatives, ideals, cultural desiderata, norms of behavior, and the like. If psychoanalysis is an empirical science what, if any, place can values have in its theory and practice?

Psychoanalysis is not unlike philosophy in this respect (however different they may be in other ways). Philosophy does not tell us what we ought to do or what ideals we ought to live by; it seeks to understand the nature of truth, good, and beauty, and how we may know that nature, without informing us about *what* is true, good, and/or beautiful. Similarly, psychoanalysis provides an account of the psychogenesis of values, without advocating any particular set of values. It offers a descriptive account of the genesis of the normative. It can provide a natural history and an explanation of this genesis because of the way in which it integrates a developmental and a dynamic point of view.

The Pleasure Principle and the Genesis of Values

The pleasure principle is not in itself a moral principle. It describes the tendency of the human organism to discharge accumulating energies arising out of need through mechanisms of self-containment such as dreaming, or by diversion in neurotic symptoms and in behavior with objects. (A literary example of the self-containing and diversionary functions of neurotic symptoms can be found in Golding's (1954) *Lord of the Flies*: Simon's hysterical epilepsy enables him to know that the beastie the boys fear is in themselves, whereas the anxiety and aggression released by their abandonment and helplessness are projected by all the other boys into the dark places and the night of the island.) Such a discharge of energy gives rise to pleasure, the kind and intensity of which depend on the need and its urgency, and these experiences of pleasure confer value on the gratifying behavior and the gratifying object. The first such object is the breast, which feeds, and the mother who comforts the infant. It is biologically expedient that the infant should have no choice but to confer the highest value on this object and the activities associated with it—even if the object is not yet differentiated from self—for the infant's survival and well-being depend entirely upon them.

Intensification of need without discharge gives rise to pain. To say that the infant tries to avoid pain and to seek pleasure is to say that the infant seeks the object that changes pain into pleasure. It is pain that teaches the neonate not to be content with a hallucinatory substitute for the gratifying object, and thereby inaugurates the reality principle and the first beginnings of the ego. Although the drives are not intrinsically object related—in the sense that they arrive on the scene already acquainted with the gratifying object—they soon become profoundly bound to objects. For the most part it is suitable behavior with a suitable object that can give rise to unqualified phase-appropriate pleasure.

The adaptation and cultivation of the drives have therefore begun, motivated by the pleasure principle and guided by the reality principle. Moreover, the pleasure state becomes an end in itself as the infant discovers substitute activities (e.g., thumb sucking and its variants) that do not depend on the object and that are within its own reach by using parts of its own body to simulate the object and facilitate the pleasurable activity. This expedient is an infant's first development of a measure of autonomous self-control.

The strategy is valued as much for the pain it avoids as for the pleasure it yields, and therein lies its flaw. The substituted gratifying activity may impede—even dangerously—the search for an alteration in the world that would be more effective in removing the pain of need. Perhaps this perception contributes to the irritable anxiety that greets these manifestations in children, and their derivatives in adults. As well as reminding us of abandoned pleasures for which our desire has not been totally extinguished, they may also arouse envy for the narcissistic complacency with which the world and its difficulties have been abandoned, and anxiety at the risks incurred in the attendant denial. This problem, inherent in the "pure pleasure ego" (especially among those who most long for the state while denying it to themselves in any form), may contribute to the harshness with which some moralists condemn hedonism: That harshness may correspond to their fear of the strength of fixated wishes for pleasures that are no longer phase appropriate and thus can only be tolerated in some disguised form. The denigration of Epicurean ethics by classical and Christian moralists—misrepresenting its moral doctrines as recommending that life should be devoted to the delights of polymorphous perversity— probably owes not a little to this fear. The performance of duty for its own sake must replace the pursuit of pleasure; duty must be the only tolerable moral motive, as in Kant. Such moralists deceive themselves, however. They have only managed to substitute a subjective masochistic pleasure, or a narcissistic self-righteousness, for a more carnal pleasure with an object. One is reminded of Shakespeare's insight:

Thou rascal beadle, hold thy bloody hand!
Why dost thou lash that whore? Strip thine own back;
Thou hotly lust'st to use her in that kind
For which thou whip'st her.
(King Lear, IV, 6, ll. 159–162)

What is valued expands beyond the experience of satisfaction with the gratifying object to all of those things that are expedient for gaining and securing pleasure and avoiding pain. In the infantile psychic economy the ends are dictated by the drives and their governing pleasure principle; the means are slowly hit upon by the developing infantile ego, initially supported by any innate behavioral capacities at its disposal, and progressively, as cognitive capacities develop, by the reality principle. This law of the life of human beings has an unchanging core even though it undergoes many elaborations and modifications with maturation, as the drives, the behaviors they demand, and the objects that will satisfy them, all undergo vicissitudes, enrichments, and complications en route to adulthood. The demands of the drives may be deferred, or a substitute satisfaction may be found, but satisfied they must be.

The most effective way to control drives, if it is feasible, is their immediate and direct satisfaction. Deferral or substitution must be resorted to when immediate and direct satisfaction promises no less—or even more—pain than pleasure. There is thus a fundamental and unavoidable core of hedonism in human beings. It was this core to which Freud (1930) referred when he said that "one of the forms in which love manifests itself—sexual love—has given us our most intense experience of an overwhelming sensation of pleasure and has thus furnished us with a pattern for our search for happiness" (p. 82). It is this understanding of the nature of drive life in human beings that justifies Freud's (1930) assumption that the fundamental aim of human beings is the pursuit of happiness. Human nature confers on the state of happiness the highest value. Philosophers such as Epicurus, Hobbes, Hume, Locke, Mill, and others have given recognition to the importance of pleasure and pain as criteria of what is good and bad. Pleasure and pain are indicators of value.

The Pleasure Principle and Hedonism

Hedonism, as used in this context, needs clarification. In vulgar parlance, "hedonism" is the relentless and self-destructive pursuit of every sensual pleasure deemed meretricious by religious morality. The idea of hedonism in psychoanalysis is akin to philosophical hedonism, but also differs from it in that for psychoanalysis hedonism is not in itself a normative category but a descriptive one. Nevertheless, like utilitarianism (Mill, 1863), psychoanalytic hedonism includes a hierarchy of sexual and aggressive pleasures in their various forms: In psychoanalysis this hierarchy is defined primarily in terms of the developmental vicissitudes of instinct life in its course from infancy to maturity. Psychoanalytic hedonism includes the pleasures of love and work; indeed, mature (genital) love, and work toward the preservation and amelioration of life, is at the the top of the developmental hierarchy.

Psychoanalysis does not, as do philosophies, place a special moral value upon sublimated pleasures. For example, Plato (*Charmides, Symposium, Phaedrus*) held that the experiences and intellectual activities stimulated by sublimated homosexual love are superior to heterosexual, genital love. Although psychoanalysis does not underestimate the utility of sublimation as the best possible means of mastering unwanted motivations, indeed, gives it pride of place in the hierarchy of methods of drive mastery, the "ideal" motive is one that is sufficiently beneficial in its aim, action, and tendency, for the agent and for its object(s), to be directly expressed in action without defensive modification (*ideal* has no greater moral connotation in this context than in a description of Newton's laws of motion).

The psychoanalytic idea of hedonism also includes the need/wish to oppose powerfully motivated forms of sexual and aggressive pleasure seeking, for example, fratricidal impulses, incest, parricide, and so forth. Children are subject to a developmental predicament: Even with optimal parenting they will experience within themselves precocious drive demands that they are helpless to satisfy—they are not yet physically strong enough, or even capable of performing the desired act or comprehending its nature. The desires and imaginations of children easily outstrip their capacities, and they develop a fear of the strength of their instinct life because they have not yet developed a means of controlling it on their own. Their anaclitic bonds to their parents become invested with the need to have limits set and to be kept within them. Fortunate is the child whose parents are able to set the appropriate limits, to maintain them firmly, and to protect the child from provocation. The facts of psychic life and development, as uncovered by psychoanalysis, do not justify permissiveness, let alone the careless pursuit of pleasure. Regression to polymorphously perverse delights is no more recommended in psychoanalysis than in Homer's description of Circe's spell (*Odyssey*) or Spenser's (1590) "Bower of Bliss," where these regressions are evoked in symbolic form, but neither does psychoanalysis moralistically condemn these pleasures: It investigates the conditions under which such regressions or fixations occur and their consequences for psychic functioning. Freud (1915) recognized that pleasures once known can never be totally forgone. Early forms of sexual pleasure find their way into sexual play on the way to genital intercourse. The originally dominant oral pleasure is preserved both in the sensual pleasure of eating and in the sublimated, characterological form of pleasure in dependency. Psychoanalysis gives no preference to either puritanism or impulsive sensuality.

Psychoanalysis can provide a natural explanation of the genesis and role of values in human experience, but does such an explanation justify the use of the pleasure principle as a moral principle? That most of the members of some society believe in a certain deity does not establish the truth of their belief, and the conversion of all such a society's dissident members would make the belief universal but would not increase the probability of its truth. Similarly, the empirical statement that all persons are hedonists does not establish the moral statement that all persons ought to be hedonists: It only provides the basis for a prediction about how human beings do, on the whole, act. To explain the genesis of values does not in itself demonstrate their moral worth. That psychoanalysis has from the outset explored the manifold complexity of man's pursuit of pleasure—including the opposition to that pursuit, which develops naturally in the life of every normal person—only complicates the issue.

Freud (1895a) pointed out that in the first days of life the paths of discharge acquire a secondary function, that of giving expression to need—the beginnings of communication. He goes on to say that "the initial helplessness of human beings is the *primal source* of all *moral motives*" (p. 318). One aspect of this helplessness has been mentioned above (see also Grunberger, 1966, and Chasseguet-Smirgel, 1984), but there is a second. In the helpless cries of infants there is an imperative generated by the urgency of the need and the claim to its satisfaction. The infant cry expresses an entitlement that is the infant's only resource in dealing with its helplessness. In this there is an elemental, egoless transformation of need into obligation, the thought or verbal equivalent of which would be, if the infant could speak, "I ought to be nursed." From the experience of the reliable satisfaction of this demand there evolves, once the ability to identify with others has developed, the altruistic form of this imperative: the wish to help others who are in need. Here hedonism ceases to be egoistical; or rather, perhaps better, it comes to include care for the welfare of others because there is now pleasure in giving others pleasure. This imperative of affection does not, however, in itself involve conflict in the pursuit of pleasure, even though it arises from the resolution of such a conflict. The con-

flict is with the world. A wish that is frustrated gives rise to the hedon-
istic imperative: The wish ought to be fulfilled.

The Pleasure Principle, the Anaclitic
Bond, and the Conflict of Wants

As soon as the human infant can differentiate himself from his
mother, pleasure and pain become enriched and complicated by his
discovery that he is dependent upon his mother for his care, well-
being, and survival. The infant glorifies this mother with his love, a
love that is still saturated with omnipotence. This omnipotence is now
projected onto the mother, whose love exposes the infant to the realization that it is his mother's love for him that makes his mother minis-
ter to his needs and give him pleasure. The infant is now motivated to
please his mother in order to secure her love because this is the best
means of pursuing his own pleasure. The satisfaction of the wish to
please his mother allows the child to take pleasure in himself for two
reasons: It provides an assurance that when drive needs arise they will
be satisfied, and that their satisfaction will meet with approval. When
the child eats his porridge for breakfast he gains the satisfaction of a
drive demand, and he can feel secure in the knowledge that when
hunger returns its satisfaction will again be available; and he can bask
in the pleasure his mother takes in his eating. The child will experience himself as being good. On the other hand, when he angers or
disappoints his mother he may feel threatened in three ways: If he is
experiencing strong needs, as he is likely to be, he will suffer present
frustration; he will fear the loss of future satisfactions; and he will feel
disappointed with himself. He will experience himself as being bad in
his mother's eyes. The degree of threat will depend both on the
mother's anger and its expression and on whether the child has suffered prior trauma. His experience of being good or bad may also be
vicarious, insofar as it can feed upon mood changes in the mother,
which have nothing to do with the child but which the child, because
of his narcissistic belief in his own unique importance to his mother,
experiences as having been caused by himself. The child's evaluation of
himself thus becomes governed by his impressions and beliefs about the
value placed upon him by his mother. The anaclitic relationship and
the narcissistic projection conferred upon her by her child give the
mother a powerful influence on what the child considers to be good
and bad.

The structure of this relationship provides an important new value
experience: The child can now find himself urgently wanting to do

something that will give him pleasure but may give his mother pain and make her disapprove of him. This disapproval will in turn cause the child painful feelings of shame. He is not what he needs to be or ought to be. He ought to be loved by his mother. It is not difficult to see that need caused by helplessness is the agent of this second type of moral imperative. The wish to please the mother can conflict with a wished-for drive gratification; the demands of egoistic, reality-bound needs can conflict with the imperatives of desires.

Circumstances that can cause this conflict abound in childhood. There are the exigencies of everyday life that play a small part. There are the transitions from one infantile psychosexual organization to the next. A child's wish to retain a substitute form of oral gratification such as thumb sucking may precipitate a struggle with the mother. Incontinence, bed-wetting, and fears may do the same. Of greatest importance are the calamities of childhood (Brenner, 1982) of which, at the stage of development we are now considering, the loss of the object and the loss of the love of the object are germane. The 1- and 2-year-old whose mother replaces him as her baby by giving birth to a sibling is particularly vulnerable. The child will wish to remove the threat to his possession of the mother by getting rid of the sibling, who seems to him to have taken the mother away from him; and this wish in turn will make him fear the loss of the mother's love. Even this grossly oversimplified account indicates the profundity of the child's dilemma in these circumstances, for he is in a stage of life when his resources for autonomous conflict resolution are still woefully inadequate to the task imposed upon him. It is this very inadequacy, and the need it engenders, that is an essential part of the cause of his maternal dependency. This situation, in the absence of adequate parental care, can produce a traumatic conflict between the need to discharge envious anger and the need to preserve the mother's love.

This sort of experience, as well as others that are not traumatic, force upon the child the realization that some pleasures are better than others; that some pleasures are followed by pain, whereas others are not; that some pleasures are more important than others; and that the loss of the mother's love must be avoided at all costs. Pleasure and pain continue to assign value to actions and things, but they themselves begin to undergo evaluation. This evaluation is involuntary and undeliberated, except insofar as memories of past actions with the same or like objects exert an influence; with this exception it is governed by the relative strengths of the needs. This rudimentary evaluation of values is itself an expression of the work of the pleasure principle, for memories of past behavior and its results are called upon as a guide for choosing future behavior that will be as effective as possible in the pursuit of pleasure and the avoidance of pain. In this process there arises a powerful incentive to develop the ability to react with signals (Freud, 1926) of pleasure and pain to future objects, situations, and activities. This "calculus of pleasure and pain" is not always successful in leading to action. Small children become stuck in painful states of tantrum-generating indecision. Adults encounter equivalent difficulties, which plunge them into obsessional states of indecision or regression to dependencies that call upon others once more to make decisions for them.

Pre-Oedipal Fantasies of Punishment and Reward

Fantasies as well as memories help to form these choices, fantasies that condense experiences of pleasure and pain and the affective states and objects associated with them. They are the first beginnings of ideals that mark out what is to be pursued and what is to be avoided. Certain of them gradually come to represent agencies of condemnation and approval that can be substituted for the real parents in the inner experience of the child when the parents are not available. For example, a small boy who believes his father is enraged by something he has done, and who hides from his father to escape punishment, may not be able to escape from condemnation by an imaginary tribunal condensed from memories of his father and of other men of whom he has been afraid. This fantasy provides a measure of magical protection (denial) from the real punishment that he fears, and so helps the boy to leave his hiding place and return to the real world of his angry father. The fantasy punishment mitigates his fear insofar as it allows him to feel that he has already been punished, but he will also continue to feel afraid because he will be uncertain whether his father will accept the substitution. (A child of this age will not appreciate that his father could not possibly know of it.) These fantasies are a pre-oedipal form of self-punishment out of fear of punishment. They are the precursors of the fantasy of castration that forms the perverse core of the negative oedipal defense against the father's punishment. They sustain the common childish illusion that the parents' watchful approving or disapproving gaze follows them everywhere; for although the fantasies are altered by displacements and condensations they are modeled on the parents and on the child's relation to the parents, as are the idealized parents of the family romance. The fantasies provide a rudimentary capacity for self-evaluation and self-regulation, even though these are carried out under the illusion of parental rather than self-agency, and they thus prepare for the resolution of the Oedipus complex and for its structural effects; and, finally, they pave the way for acquisition of the self-surveillance required by autonomous moral functioning.

The pleasure (and hence value) conflicts considered thus far are contingent and accidental. To be sure, the pleasure principle is a fundamental law of psychic functioning that makes mandatory the pursuit of pleasure and the avoidance of pain; and to be sure it sets up a rudimentary sort of conflict with the world. The toddler discovers that some things he wants to do in his pursuit of pleasure—such as touching a hot object—in fact cause pain. These experiences can easily become "moralized." A father's raised voice, warning the child not to do something that would hurt him, can be experienced by the child as a loss of love and arouse in him a feeling of shame, of being bad. That children who are basically confident of parental love will protest, "I don't like Daddy's loud voice!" is a measure both of the vulnerability of children to such experiences and of their painfulness. Moreover, children can feel shame autonomously, as when they bungle a motor action of which they are particularly proud, as though they experience their inadequacy as a fall from the grace of parental admiration (Ferenczi, 1913). It is impossible to overestimate the extent to which, according to the rules of their own psychic life, the experience of children is value laden and moralized. This tendency is carried over into adult life. People who have been thrown out of work in a recession, through no fault of their own, will nevertheless become depressed and suffer feelings of worthlessness and inadequacy in addition to the other anxieties caused by unemployment. Unconsciously, they feel responsible for the economic accident that has befallen them.

The animism of childhood experience extends these moral attributes beyond children's own behavior to inanimate objects and processes generally. One of the tasks of reality testing, for children, is gradually to learn to differentiate between that which properly has moral attributes and that which does not. Furthermore, evolving drive life imposes special developmental tasks: As the pleasures of the oral stage give way to those of the anal stage, and eventually to the phallic stage, there occurs a biologically driven transvaluation of values that demands shifts to new forms of pleasure and the renunciation of former ones. These changes can be exceedingly difficult and painful, but they can also be substantially mitigated by good parenting, especially by good mothering, and hence although these transitions are inevitable their worst adversities are not. By contrast, the Oedipus complex is inevitable both in itself and in the suffering that it brings. The oedipal girl can turn neither to her mother nor to her father. She experiences her mother as her rival: To return to her anaclitic dependency on her would be a defensive regression from, and a betrayal of, the demands of her new sexual feelings; neither can she seek solace, let alone gratification, from her father without intensifying her anxiety that her mother will know how to punish her for it. The oedipal boy encounters a comparable dilemma: The Oedipus complex brings with it desires arising spontaneously within himself that hold out the promise of the most intense pleasures yet to be experienced, the perfect consolation for the abandoned oral and anal pleasures—but that cannot be gratified. Deprived of recourse to anaclitic solutions, children of both sexes are thrust toward an intrapsychic resolution. The girl intensifies her identification with her mother and her prohibitions; her wishes for her father lose their sexual character and become aim-inhibited love. The boy intensifies his identification with his father and his prohibitions, and his incest wishes change into aim-inhibited affection. These identifications form the nucleus from which individual conscience is formed. They provide the structural and functional basis in the individual psyche for the autonomous exercise of moral self-observation, self-judgment, and self-punishment (Waelder, 1934; Hanly, 1979). Through the resolution of the Oedipus complex children take a crucial step toward maturation: No longer are they so dependent upon their parents for these moral functions, despite and because of their continuing idealization of the parents. It is for this reason that the resolution of the Oedipus complex is the single most important developmental task.

The Oedipal Stage

From the perspective of the resolution of the Oedipus complex it becomes clear how profoundly compromised is the hedonic principle in psychoanalysis. Incestuous and parricidal desires arise spontaneously in the life of every individual. The pleasure of gratifying them must be permanently abandoned, and the desires themselves must be permanently inhibited. Here we have precisely the situation considered by Kant and the deontological school of moral philosophy to be paradigmatic of moral duty: A powerful murderous impulse must be repudiated in favor of a duty to treat one's parent with respect and obedience; a strong possessive sexual impulse toward the parent of the opposite sex must be replaced by affection. Freud (1923a) recognized this connection when he noted an affinity of the superego with the categorical imperative.

This human situation is powerfully evoked by Shakespeare in the speech with which Cordelia responds to Lear's demand for a testimony of her love for him. The heart of her reply is on one sentence:

I love your majesty
According to my bond; nor more, nor less.
(King Lear, I, 1)

Cordelia gives expression to a love for her father that has been constrained by the resolution of the Oedipus complex. It is a love constrained by her two obligations: one, presumably, to her absent mother, and one to her future husband to whom she wishes to give her sensual love as well as a large portion of her affection. Her love for her father therefore takes on the character of an obligation rather than an uncomplicated passion. She declares that she owes him affection according to the constraints imposed by an obligation to her mother (fear of her retribution) and by her wish to have a husband:

> *Good my lord,*
> *You have begot me, bred me, loved me: I*
> *Return those duties back as are right fit,*
> *Obey you, love you, and most honour you.*
> *Why have my sisters husbands, if they say*
> *They love you all? Haply, when I shall wed,*
> *That lord whose hand must take my plight shall carry*
> *Half my love with him, half my care and duty:*
> *Sure, I shall never marry like my sisters,*
> *To love my father all.*
> *(King Lear, I, 1)*

Cordelia's tragedy testifies to the power of the constrained love for her father. In the end, she had to try to rescue her father from her sisters. In general, the drives are enabled to override the constraints the ego imposes upon them either by a strengthening of the drives or by a weakening of the forces that constrain them. The notion of the will as an unconditional capacity for mastering drive demands, as found in Descartes, Kant, and others, is an illusion of moral narcissism. In this important respect there is no affinity between the superego and the categorical imperative. The sympathy that psychologically strong people can have for tragic or criminal lives is grounded in their preconscious realization that it is as much good fortune as any effort of their own that has made their lives different. They know and own in themselves the same motives that cause other lives to become tragic or criminal. They can acknowledge with gratitude those persons, relationships, and circumstances that have made it possible for their lives to be more fortunate.

Freud did not conceive of duty as an act of uncaused will. It is motivated by anxiety. Dutiful acts appear to consciousness to be un-

caused when they are performed in opposition to some felt desire because the anxiety that motivates them remains unconscious. Even when
the anxiety is conscious, in the form of a fear of the painful guilt that
acting on the desire would release, it has already undergone an affective
alteration: The original fear—of punishment by a vengeful parent of
the same sex—remains repressed, as do the memories and fantasies in
which that fear is embedded. Duty transcends neither psychic determinism, as some philosophers (Kant, 1785) have believed, nor the pleasure
principle, as Freud (1920) speculated (see Hanly, 1978); it follows the
dictates of the pleasure principle. Duty only overrides desire when fear
of the consequences of acting on a desire is even greater than the
anticipated pleasure of doing so. In this there is no diminution in the
moral or social worth of the ability to act from a sense of duty: Anyone
who cannot be thus guided by anticipated pain has, to that extent, a
morally and socially inferior, psychopathic character.

What is lost in the derivation of duty from the pleasure principle,
rather than from uncaused will, is the narcissistic illusion that human
beings are unique creatures in nature because of their capacity to perform willed actions. Descartes (1641), for example, considered the will
to be the signature of the deity upon his creation. It is, he thought,
the one mental faculty that has the divine character of infinity because
it is immune to causation and thus can be a law unto itself. (Those
who require this illusion will inevitably retain it in the face of this
argument and the facts of human nature on which it depends,
caused—obliged—to do so lest they lose the hope of regaining in another life the pleasure lost to morality in this one.)

Identification and Autonomy

Values are learned to some extent from experience, but the central values at the core of one's moral character are acquired, en masse as
it were, through identification with one's parents. These identifications
are powerful mechanisms for cultural inheritance. So powerfully identified with parental values do children become, and so thoroughly repressed are the experiences out of which they were formed, that some
philosophers (Plato, and others such as the Cambridge Platonists who
followed in his tradition) have become introspectively convinced that
morality is innate to the human mind. Freud (1915) noted the conservation of the instincts; there is also a conservation of these oedipal
identifications, which continue to influence the values by which a
person lives. The son who, in his teens and early manhood, becomes a
socialist in rebellion against the authority and values of his father, a

political conservative, often retains a predisposition to find his way back to conservatism—if not in his 30's, then in his 40's, or when his father dies.

The contribution of the individual to this process of value forma-tion must nevertheless be recognized. Identification is incorporative only metaphorically: It is with the image of the object that the ego identifies itself, even though the process is experienced as identifica-tion with the real parent. Affects that had previously been invested in the object come to cathect its image, and the relation to the object is modified in consequence. The relations a girl previously had only to her mother, and a boy to his father, are now established within them-selves. Whereas before they were only afraid of being punished or dis-approved of by their parents, they are now able to be afraid of being punished or disapproved of by themselves. Whereas before they de-pended entirely upon approval by their parents, they now are able to approve of themselves. The child has developed an autonomous moral capacity: the ability to be guided from within by considerations of what ought to be done and what ought not to be done. Although this development has its beginnings in the pre-oedipal stage in fantasies of punishment and reward, the capacity for moral autonomy acquires sta-ble psychic foundations with the identifications involved in the resolu-tions of the Oedipus complex.

But is this not an empty, illusory autonomy? Does not the psycho-analytic account of the genesis of morality imply that each generation is fated to be no more than the passive vehicle of the aspirations and inhibitions of the previous one? Psychoanalytic theory would indeed be defective if this were so: But it is not. Human beings are creative not only scientifically, technologically, and artistically; they are also mor-ally creative. Plato and Aristotle had no qualms of conscience over the enslavement of non-Greeks, nor had Jefferson over the enslavement of blacks, yet philosophers and statesmen of comparable humanity today would be unable to tolerate such attitudes in themselves. Moral creativ-ity is a fact of cultural and social history.

Value Testing and Moral Creativity

No doubt those who would rest moral creativity on uncaused choice will find the psychoanalytic account to be reductive and trivial-izing, as will those who wish to find in it evidence of spirituality and transcendence; but the long and troubled history of the acquisition of humane values—such as the equal right of all persons to life, liberty, and the pursuit of happiness—suggests, not the handiwork of moral beings exercising a sovereign will, but rather the gropings of a not always very rational animal largely dominated not merely by the pursuit of individual comfort and safety but often also by the lust for such power as might be used to shore up a denial of the accidental nature of human existence (Shakespeare, *King Lear*; Hobbes, 1651; Freud, 1927, 1930).

One source of moral creativity is the fact that it is not the object that becomes a constituent of the ego in identification, but rather the hypercathected image of the object. This circumstance allows for a certain amount of individual variation, for the image that is thus hypercathected is a synthesis of reality-bound perceptions of the parents and of fantasies about them. These fantasies owe their origin to the drive life of the individual, combining experiences with the parents and with the world. Among them are the family romance fantasies. For the most part they have the effect of exaggerating qualities found in the parents, but they can also include inventions of what the parents and the world should be like. Wishful fantasies can influence the images of the parents on which the identifications are built, and indeed these fantasy images may be better suited to the exigencies of life and the demands of the pleasure principle than reality-bound parental images would have been. In such cases the individual is exercising the human potential for moral creativity, at least insofar as the family is concerned; for individuals of unusual ego endowment, in favorable circumstances, this creativity may extend beyond the family to society. It would be naïve, however, to exaggerate this potential in individual human development for the amelioration of values, for it is often enough circumscribed by another factor that is no less important.

The identifications that we have been considering arise from a hypercathexis of parental images. The intensity of these investments is determined primarily not by the punitiveness of the parents but by the strength of the component drives of the Oedipus complex: For example, a boy's fear of his father is often much greater than is justified by either the father's actions or his feelings. If this fear remains untested, it will continue to be disproportionate, but the oedipal situation is not one that facilitates such testing. Inadequate parenting greatly exacerbates the problem. Children are typically—and, given the nature of the impulses and feelings they are struggling with, naturally—silent, withdrawn, or even secretive about their oedipal ideas and wishes. They find relief in sharing them with adults in the indirect, disguised form of fairy tales, stories, or accounts of current happenings, rather than by direct communication.

To the extent that the fear remains disproportionate it will lay down a predisposition to a degree of obedience to authority that is incompatible with the questioning and testing of values that is as necessary to their reform as it is to their rational, independent reaffirmation. In such a person safety and self-esteem depend upon unquestioning obedience. Moreover, if the task of self-regulation becomes too burdensome because the anxiety (guilt) it involves outweighs the pride (pleasure) it affords, the ego will regress to an earlier state in which the functions of the superego were carried out on its behalf by parents and their surrogates (Freud, 1921). Obedience to an external authority replaces self-criticism. The relief that ensues always has the effect not only of exaggerating the worth and reliability of the external authority but of causing the fantasy within the ego that this form of moral experience is not a regressive repetition but rather a wonderful new discovery. A condition of irresponsibility is denied by the feeling of being committed to a higher responsibility. This state of affairs has been considered by some philosophers to be an ideal: for example, Plato (*Republic*) and Hegel (1821).

When the degree of relief becomes elational, however, there comes about a morally perverse unification of ego and ego ideal in which the very sexual and aggressive impulses that the ego ideal was developed to master can be gratified, in disguised form, on behalf of "higher" purposes. The individual can feel it his duty, for instance, to carry out hostile acts against others who have done him no harm and who constitute no genuine threat: He will feel entitled to harm those identified for him as dangerous by his ego ideal (his leader). Such individuals voluntarily abandon their individuality, which they happily submit to serve a dictatorial, charismatic leader who offers them the needed opportunities for disguised, "higher," gratifications of unconscious libidinal and aggressive drive demands. The plasticity of psychic life that allows for moral progress also allows for moral regression.

With puberty and adolescence, the advent of sexual maturity brings with it a new opportunity for moral autonomy as well as a new risk. The opportunity is signaled in puberty by the first inner experience of self-identity: The individual begins to experience himself as belonging to himself rather than as primarily a son, for example. This self-experience is released by the maturation of the sexual drive, which now seeks for its satisfaction a person of the opposite sex, of the same age, and of a different family. Ideally, this development releases the youth from parental fear by releasing him from incest feelings. The values adopted with the identifications that originally contributed to the resolution of the Oedipus complex may lose enough of their sanctity to be subjected to reality testing and to the more rational considerations of self-interest and the welfare of others that philosophers have taken into account in constructing ethical theories (e.g., Mill, 1863). New experiences of sexual rivalry contribute to changing the old prohi-

bition against parricide and fratricide into a prohibition against homi-
cide. Parental political and social values previously taken as self-evident can be tested against alternatives and against the youth's own
perceptions of social reality. Just as youths will want to try out their
physical and intellectual capacities, so too will they want to make a
trial of inherited values and the beliefs used to justify them. In mature
personalities, what begins as healthy rebellion is likely to end, as
knowledge of others improves and self-knowledge deepens, in a stable
willingness to test values and the ways and means of satisfying their
demands.

This rational process of testing values by an examination of the
consequences, for self and others, of the actions demanded by those
values has been the focus of interest of philosophers like Hobbes and
Mill. The rationality of moral thought cannot, however, be taken for
granted. One of the flaws in Freud's (1900) topographical model was
that it failed to recognize, let alone account for, the pathology of
values. In the structural model Freud (1923a) made good this defi-
ciency by describing the genesis of the superego and the continuing
causal links between the instinctual unconscious and the superego. Motivation is therefore an important factor to the importance of which
our attention is called by philosophers like Kant; Kant, however, then
offers a completely spiritualized and fanciful account of moral motivation, which he limits to acting for the sake of duty alone—a psychological impossibility, no matter how conscious moral experience may
seem to authenticate such an account. Adolescent rebellion may be
healthy, or it may be unhealthy; moral thinking may be rational or it
may be irrational.

Adolescence is vulnerable to a resurgence of the demands of the
oedipal drive:

> No matter how resolutely the ego turns away from it and what the
> relative proportions of repression, sublimation, and "destruction" might
> be, in adolescence the Oedipus complex rears its head again, and so it
> does during later periods in life, in normal people as well as in neurotics.
> (Loewald, 1980, p.386)

The "salvation" from the Oedipus complex brought about at puberty
by the advent of procreative sexuality is never complete: The individual remains vulnerable to regression, and when regression occurs it
compromises the rebellion and renders it both noisy and ineffective.
Such adolescents will find it necessary to oppose parental injunctions
and prohibitions at every turn, whether these are in the individual's
best interests or not. Whatever the parents stand for, or are believed to

stand for, must be opposed at any cost. If the parents are monogamous, such adolescents will make a virtue of promiscuity. If the parents are promiscuous and self-indulgent, the adolescents will commit themselves to asceticism. These choices are at once impulsive and defensive: The reasons for them come later, as rationalizing justifications, and consequently no genuine testing of values is accomplished. No modification of the prohibitions and ideals of the superego is accomplished. The rebellion wears itself out without accomplishing anything.

This form of rebellion is driven by counterphobic reactions to the anxiety generated by resurgent oedipal impulses. The regression reinforces the identifications with the parents and the defenses they mobilize against aggression and sexuality. The restoration of the earlier power of these identifications threatens the adolescents' search for their own identity and the values that define and anchor it, and drives them toward a spurious identity built upon a negation of the earlier ones rather than a more genuine and workable identity based on their modification, improvement, adaptation, and integration. The predicament of such an adolescent is difficult in two respects. When there is a return to the negative Oedipus complex, sexual identity, which is not yet well established, is made especially precarious because of the risk of homosexuality inherent in cooperation, let alone obedience. What is tolerable for a latency child is extremely dangerous for a teenager, after the advent of procreative sexuality. The positive Oedipus complex is equally dangerous, and for the same reason. The child is more vulnerable to fantasy than an adolescent; but although the child's ambitions must end in humiliating disappointment because of his incapacity, that very incapacity is his protection. He could not have done it had he tried. Adolescents are less vulnerable to fantasy, but they are more at risk. A teenage girl, if she tried, might succeed in seducing her father and becoming pregnant. A teenage boy may be physically as strong or stronger than his father, and if he is not he can easily avail himself of weapons. These circumstances intensify anxiety, which secretly undermines and renders useless the adolescents' best efforts to find out for themselves what ideals to pursue and what obligations to honor. They will tend to be locked either into permanent rebellion or into repetition.

In reality this distinction between healthy and pathological rebellion is only ideal. There are many individual variations, and it is unlikely that any instance of an ideal rebellion is to be found among them. It is more likely that the achievement of moral maturity depends upon a second adolescent mastery of the Oedipus complex; it is also more likely that the reevaluation of values that makes moral creativity possible owes something to the competitive strivings promoted by the

Oedipus complex itself, albeit in a somewhat sublimated form. For young men the competition may, in part and unconsciously, be a repetition of the old rivalry with the father, although its conscious, sublimated purpose is to outstrip him morally: The existence of the former does not always preclude the achievement of the latter. A young woman, still angry about unnecessary disappointments at the hands of her mother, may seek to humiliate her mother and make her feel guilty by aggressively demonstrating her own superiority as a mother—and may therefore care for her own children better than she herself had been cared for.

Implications

A number of conclusions may be derived from this descriptive account of the development of the capacity for morality. Values are naturally occurring phenomena. Values originate in the drives as governed by the pleasure principle and in the defenses and identifications erected against the drives. These defenses and identifications continue to serve the pleasure principle, although they substantially complicate its work.

Psychoanalytic findings are inconsistent with the kind of bifurcations of psychic life to be found in moral philosophies such as those of Plato, Descartes, or Kant. Feelings of obligation, of duty, of prohibition, and the sense of being motivated by these feelings, originate in the biological and psychological processes by which the individual's identity is established. These inner experiences are not pure manifestations of a spontaneous moral will. The prohibition against murder, for example, is sanctioned by a number of groups of feelings: fear of retaliation at the hands of the victim's family and friends or of its surrogate, punishment by social authority (group one); fear of psychic punishment—guilt— (group two); fear of harming oneself in the other person insofar as one is able to identify with that person (group three). These are some of the ways in which "conscience does make cowards of us all."

The first group of feelings—fears of retaliation or punishment—are those identified by Hobbes as the basis of the social contract. They have the advantage of seeming to be reality bound, but from the point of view of morality this is their weakness, for their strength is diminished in proportion to the belief (whether realistic or not) that the act can be cloaked in secrecy as by the ring of Gyges and that retaliation or punishment can thus be avoided. The second group of feelings— fears of self-punishment through guilt—do not have this liability. An action prohibited by conscience cannot be hidden from conscience; its mere contemplation already arouses signal anxiety in the form of guilt (Freud, 1926). Freud (1923a) pointed to the extensive links between the id and the superego: One of these links is the cathected association that connects a later temptation to murder with the old parricidal and fratricidal temptations that have undergone repression, on account of castration and other anxieties. These charged, active memories lie behind and motivate a guilt and/or shame reaction to even the thought of killing anyone. The fear of self-punishment is more effective as a motive for duty (in this case, the duty not to act) than the fear of external punishment because, although it was originally a fear of an external authority (the father), the identification with the father and resolution of the Oedipus complex has transformed that fear. The authority that one inescapably fears is now oneself.

There is, however, a problem involved in the psychoanalytic account of the motivation for the duty to respect the life of another. The potential victim is neither one's father nor mother, sister nor brother. In healthy development the sexual drive can become guilt free insofar as the associative links to prohibited objects are broken by reality testing, the withdrawal of libido from them, and its investment in appropriate objects. May there not be a parallel process by which aggression is detached from the old objects of ambivalence—parents and siblings—and thus becomes free to carry out acts of aggression according to need, opportunity, and provocation? If the mother need not forever be the prototypical sexual object, why need the father be the prototype of every rival? The answer to these questions is not simple. Human nature, like nature generally, is not neatly organized for the purpose of human knowledge.

To the extent that the Oedipus complex is resolved, to that extent there occurs a diminution in spontaneous aggression toward others (Hanly, 1978). The oedipally resolved individual is able to be aggressive on behalf of his own interests and those of his loved ones and friends. He is not driven to advantage himself at the expense of others, although he may do so in circumstances that objectively make competition unavoidable. His preference is for cooperation. Such a person is better able to gratify his aggressive needs directly: He need not spend much energy on their inhibition and sublimation. His dutifulness will be based more on the first and third group of affects than on the second. To the extent that the Oedipus complex is not resolved, the parental images will continue to function as prototypes of guilt-producing inhibitions and shame-producing injunctions, and hence as motivations for the dutiful pursuit of obligations in the absence of other motives. As noted above, human motives are for the most part variable admixtures of these elements.

The tenacity and strength of these inhibiting forces are transparently evident in neurosis, and they are scarcely less evident in the punishment and anxiety dreams of healthy individuals. In its most severe form, duty is motivated by moral masochism—by taking pleasure in opposing ordinary satisfactions and in imposing privations on oneself: that is, by taking pleasure in psychic pain (see Grunberger, 1956; Chasseguet-Smirgel, 1985, 1986). Self-debasing submission offers such a pleasure to those who need to locate themselves in a hierarchy of power so that they can also experience the reverse, sadistic form of the pleasure, the imposition on others of the same self-debasing submission. Swift (1704) drew a brilliantly satirical caricature of the sadomasochism and the moral narcissism of the puritan.

The third group of feelings—identification or empathy with the victim of one's aggression—arises from aim-inhibited drives, including homosexual feelings, that are a part of the resolution of the Oedipus complex. The importance of homosexual feelings among them is evident in the preference that latency girls and boys have for their own sex until puberty. That these homosexual feelings are largely neutralized and have an affectionate rather than a sexual character is evident in the relative lack of interest that latency children have in sexual activity. These feelings provide for identification with peers. They provide a basis for sympathy and loyalty. They extend the wish to be treated well by others to the wish to treat others well. These affects and identifications open up an awareness that, just as one seeks the pleasure of need satisfaction and the avoidance of pain oneself, so do others. The identification assigns a value to the other that is comparable to the value that one attaches to oneself. Inherent in that identification is the recognition that, as long as one has the means to satisfy one's own needs, it is better that others have the same means available to them than to have these means all to oneself, for one has become identified with the other and the other's well-being. A latency child is able to share spontaneously, whereas the pre-oedipal or oedipal child really prefers to have the mother all to himself. This type of identification has a potential for infinite expansion and may culminate in the kind of brotherly love that Freud (1930) criticized. The relationship envisaged (no one can have a real relationship with more than a limited number of others) probably always has in some degree a narcissistic structure in which the individual contemplates providing for another what he wished might have been provided for himself.

This third group of feelings motivates what most people find to be the most congenial form of altruism: A kindness bestowed because one is liked and appreciated is usually preferred to one bestowed by someone who can find no motive for it but a duty to treat people in general decently. Even a psychoanalytically uninformed sense of the psychopathology of everyday morality and character is left chilled and puzzled by the second kind of altruism: The need to demonstrate altruism in that way indicates anxiety about hostility, just as the need to demonstrate sexual potency indicates anxiety about impotence. This third group of feelings, then, personalizes and hence humanizes actions that also owe their motivation to the avoidance of guilt. All three groups of feelings—self-interest, guilt, and affection—may work together in various ways to cause moral conduct.

Some theories of moral philosophy seem almost to have been derived from an exclusive emphasis on a single one of these genetically and functionally different motivations for moral conduct. One is tempted to find the seeds of Hobbesian contractarian ethics in the first group, of Kant's deontological ethics in the second, and of Mill's utilitarian principle of the greatest good of the greatest number in the third—although it can fairly be said of Mill's ethical theory that, as regarding motivation, it is inclusive rather than exclusive, and that for this as well as other reasons it is the most consistent with psychoanalytic findings of these three.

Morality, Responsibility, and Causality

A problem—essentially one of definition—implicit in this discussion of the motivation of moral behavior must now be explicitly addressed. Some philosophers would insist that by giving a causal explanation of the categorical imperative one destroys its moral significance because morality implies responsibility and responsibility requires uncaused choice. Is not this an example of the sort of reductionism that psychoanalysis is supposed to avoid? Is there not here a failure to distinguish between caused actions and actions—among them moral actions—motivated by reasons? Philosophers have criticized psychoanalysis for its failure to acknowledge this distinction in its theory, although it is sometimes claimed that it does so in its practice (Sartre, 1943; Merleau-Ponty, 1945; MacIntyre, 1958; Peters, 1958; Flew, 1970; Ricoeur, 1970) as have psychoanalysts such as Klein (1976), Kohut (1959), Kubie (1975), Gill (1976), Rycroft (1966), and Schafer (1976). One thing is certain: It is a psychoanalytic question about the answer to which there is no consensus in philosophy.

The issue has been no less controversial in philosophy than it has become in psychoanalysis. There are two schools of thought. Although they agree that responsibility requires choice, the incompatibilists hold that causality is incompatible with choice; the compatibilists hold that the causation of choice does not nullify responsibility, and hence have no difficulty with psychic determinism or with the psychological explanation of moral values and actions. Among the classical philosophers who were compatibilists are Epicurus, Hobbes, Spinoza, Hume, and Mill. Among the incompatibilists one can find Descartes, Locke, Kant, Berkeley, Hegel, and perhaps Plato and Aristotle and their medieval followers, although these are difficult to classify in this respect. Can the findings of psychoanalysis contribute anything to the controversy in philosophy, and hence to the resolution of the dispute in psychoanalysis?

Elsewhere (Hanly, 1979) I have attempted to explain how it comes about that introspective awareness perceives the executive capacities of consciousness as operating independently of causation. This "illusion of consciousness," as Spinoza might have called it, is contrary to the facts as uncovered by the psychoanalysis of the motivation of moral conduct (pp. 227–231). It is true that there is a psychological difference between an involuntary act and one that is voluntary, but the difference is not that involuntary actions are caused and voluntary actions are uncaused: The difference lies in the nature of their causation.

The woman who chooses to seek out socially inferior strangers for sex despite her fear of infection is acting very differently from a woman who has chosen sex with a man she has come to know and to love without fear. The first woman is subject to a compulsion that overrides a realistic fear. Here there is no doubt that the choice is caused by sexual desires, although she does not know why she must choose such men, or why, after having sex with such a man, she wants nothing further to do with him, or why he has come to seem pathetic and disgusting to her; but the choice of the second woman is no less caused by sexual desires than that of the first: The difference is that her sexual wishes are primarily mature and she has found a satisfying man. The sexual wishes of the first woman are primarily immature, and they prevent her from forming a healthy relationship with a suitable man. Sexual wishes are both caused and causal in the lives of men and women. What differs is the nature of the wishes, and what is true of human sexuality is no less true of human morality.

Psychoanalysis and Values

Psychoanalysis provides an explanation of the psychological process by which the lives of human beings come to be governed by values—that is, a naturalistic explanation of morality. This achievement is comparable in its philosophical importance, and to man's understanding of himself and of his place in nature, to Darwin's discovery of the mechanism of evolution. Psychoanalysis does not advocate any specific set of values, moral rules, or political, judicial, or social systems as being best for mankind. Psychoanalysis traces the contribution to morality made by the formation of the superego as a reaction formation against the Oedipus complex. It explains how the prohibition against killing the father acts as a foundation for duty and dutiful conduct. Psychoanalysis does not say that one ought not to kill one's father; rather, it describes how it comes about that in the course of development individuals normally become subject to an inner prohibition against harming the parent of the same sex, and the consequences of failure to form such a prohibition. It is not the task of psychoanalysis to reform or to advocate values. To quote Hartmann (1960): "psychoanalysis as a science cannot be expected to provide us with ultimate moral aims, or general moral imperatives; these cannot be deduced from its empirical findings" (p. 60).

Neither has applied psychoanalysis a basis for adjudicating the controversy concerning form and content in art, although it can illuminate the psychological origins of that controversy: It can remind formalists of the importance of thematic material; it can clarify psychological aspects of both form and content in art and literature; and it can cast light upon the relation of the artist or writer to his or her work. Nor is psychoanalysis subject to special values or aims that guide its analysis, for example, of beliefs in the innateness of ideas. (Freud actually upheld a version of innateness that is as vulnerable to criticism as any other.) Consistency with the well-established findings of science is the one constraint extrinsic to the clinical testing of theories by the method of free association. To be sure, a genetic account of an idea may undermine its credibility. If an idea has a genetic psychological explanation, we can understand how it could arise and acquire conviction even in the absence of objective evidence. Nevertheless, a genetic explanation does not in itself prove the idea in question to be false without other invalidating evidence. In its application to the humanities and social sciences, psychoanalysis has no philosophical objectives other than those of natural science generally.

It may also appear that the genetic-developmental approach of psychoanalysis to the study of the history of civilization, and its comparisons of certain stages of cultural development with stages of individual mental development, presupposes an implicit preference for the values of modern, technological, secular society; however, in describing differences in the adaptation to reality between ancient and modern people applied psychoanalysis does not require as a premise either that there must be no difference or that, if a difference exists, ancient peoples ought to have had the same beliefs and affective attitudes as moderns.

Some contemporary cultural anthropologists, influenced by the theories of Levi-Strauss (1958), or by an extreme egalitarianism that requires that all differences be effaced, consider that any description or explanation of cultural differences between ancient and modern man is in itself an act of hostility toward the ancients that must be motivated by a condescending, paternalistic, complacent preference for modernity. But to differentiate the "demonological" morality of the pre-oedipal child, based on narcissistic projection, from the more autonomous morality of the postoedipal child, based on repression and sublimation, does not imply that pre-oedipal children ought not to rely upon the defense of projection to the extent that they do; nor is such a judgment implied by stating that postoedipal children are less dependent on their parents and more able to test the values received from them, and hence are better able to carry out reality testing than pre-oedipal children. Similarly to find, on the basis of evidence, that ancient peoples were less able to carry out reality testing than moderns does not imply that they ought to have held the beliefs of moderns and had modern methods for testing those beliefs. Such a finding is rather an evolutionary description and an attempt to understand the contribution of animism, for example, to human cultural development as a whole.

Certainly a researcher may be so narcissistically vulnerable as to need to wrest a feeling of superiority from a factual difference. Such a need will find some subtle form of expression in the work itself. (The reader of this work is invited to scrutinize it, with this and other questions in mind, for motives that could distort either description or inference.) But those investigators who must establish that every difference hides a deeper functional similarity, who need to assert that the demonologies of animistic cultures are on a par with the quirks and quarks and black holes of modern physics, are vulnerable to an equal and opposite psychological error, one motivated by idealization as a defense against the very hostility and narcissism they attribute to the evolutionists. Between this Scylla and that Charybdis observation and understanding that would reach the truth of the matter must find their way. One must always remember that motivations that influence what an investigator wants to find, or what can or cannot be taken into consideration, have a greater opportunity to distort findings and conclusions in applied psychoanalysis, in the humanities, and in clinical psychoanalysis, than in those natural sciences that are able to employ quantifiable experiment in their search for knowledge.

Applied psychoanalytic studies in the social sciences can investigate the psychological processes involved in the choice of political leaders (Rangell, 1980), racial prejudice (Traub-Werner, 1984), war and peace (Steinberg, 1991), and so forth, without advocating the choice of a particular leader, social policy, or defense strategy. Applied psychoanalytic studies can clarify the range of psychological possibilities for the decision makers who have to practice the art of the possible. One can show, as I have attempted to do in the chapter on a criminal jury, the factors that caused individual jurors to reach a decision and to compare them with factors on the basis of which an ideal jurisprudence would reach such decisions. Even when such a comparison reveals disparities, however, it does not necessarily follow that the actual finding in the case was wrong, only that the finding was not based on the reasons on which it could or should have been based. Such a conclusion does, of course, raise a question about the reliability of juries; but many considerations, among them legal as well as political considerations, must be taken into account in any proposal for changing the jury system. Applied psychoanalysis can contribute to the study of the psychological factors that may interfere with objectivity on the part of the jurors, and those that will promote as much objectivity as possible.

Psychoanalysis cannot accept the utilitarian account of the proof of the criteria of moral goodness as presented by Mill (1863). If it could do so it could also lay claim to providing the foundation of morality no less (although no more) than does utilitarianism. Mill's argument was that a thing is desirable only because people desire it, that the happiness of all is desirable because each person desires his own happiness, and that the happiness of all is simply the sum of these individual desires for happiness. From a psychoanalytic point of view, however, not only what people desire but what they fear must be taken into account in order to arrive at an adequate conception of happiness. Psychoanalysis can offer abundant evidence that pleasure does not always lead to happiness, and that individuals may be confused about what would make them happy or, if not confused, still be unable to carry out the actions that would attain their ends. Mill's purview was restricted to conscious desires; when unconscious desires are taken into account the contribution of fear to the outcome of the pursuit of pleasure must also be given its due, as it is in human nature. If such a naturalistic ethic is viable, however, it might be argued that psychoanalytic findings concerning the nature of human desires and fears could provide the psychological foundation for a moral theory. The complexity of this issue does not permit its consideration here.

Even if psychoanalysis cannot tell us what we ought and ought not to do, it can still shed light on how we come to form such beliefs and to act on them or fail to do so, and by so doing it can contribute to the demystification of values and morality by removing them from the Olympian heights of spirituality and locating them in the lives of men and women, where they belong and where their capacity to serve human needs can be tested. Psychoanalysis can also contribute to the evaluation of needs through the exploration of their development, of the consequences when they remain unsatisfied when they are phase appropriate, and of the consequences of their continuing to demand satisfaction when they have ceased to be phase appropriate. More generally, psychoanalysis can enrich our ability to estimate the nature of character and the psychological consequences of actions. For example, psychoanalytic knowledge has contributed to the decriminalization of homosexuality, to a more understanding and humane parenting, and to a more enlightened attitude toward crime and a more realistic attitude toward its prevention. Psychoanalysis has strengthened the rational evaluation of moral values and imperatives by adding improved psychological knowledge to those deliberations.

Even though it does no moral teaching or indoctrination clinical psychoanalysis can nevertheless have an effect on the values of patients. For example, a patient of mine wanted to see criminals hanged by their thumbs in public: For her, men were criminals. Men made her feel humiliatingly inferior and envious. Any among them who qualified for social retribution should be subjected to public torture. When during her analysis she began to be able to enjoy her sexuality and to esteem herself and her femininity, these vengeful feelings subsided; her punishment fantasy became a memory and ceased to govern her attitude toward criminality. A measure of compassion replaced her sadism. Although it can thus strengthen an individual's capacity for rational moral thought, it would be unrealistically sanguine to expect that the availability or use of psychoanalysis would ever be sufficient to bring about any significant improvement in general moral enlightenment. Only the gradual amelioration of the quality of the relations between parents (and their surrogates) and children can achieve such an improvement.

Truth is the one value that psychoanalysis is obliged to pursue. The pursuit of truth in the clinical situation demands an uncommon degree of self-honesty on the part of both analyst and patient because, if the truth about the patient's life is to be uncovered, it will be found to include matters about which the patient previously had to engage in self-deception. One of the encouraging things that psychoanalysis has found about human nature is that there appears to be an inherent linkage between self-honesty, psychological health, and good character.

It is the task of applied psychoanalysis to use the resources of psychoanalysis in two ways. The first is to interpret and explain the psychological aspects of a subject according to the best available psychoanalytic findings and theories while taking into account the best available scholarship on the subject in question. This aspect of the work is psychoanalytic in the knowledge that is brought to bear on the subject, but it must share the general methods of the humanities and social sciences: scholarly, historical, empirical fact-finding, evaluation of evidence, and reasoning from it. The second way is to use self-analysis to become aware of the unconscious memories and fantasies evoked by the subject under study, in an attempt to see it as it is rather than as one would wish it to be. At best this avoids, or at least minimizes, the distortions caused by defenses; and it may enrich the knowledge of the subject insofar as it enables the interpreter to consider more objectively whether the unconscious memories and fantasies evoked by the subject may have something to contribute to its understanding. Knowledge, as distinct from personally, culturally, or ideologically conditioned interpretation, is no less difficult to achieve in applied psychoanalytic studies than in the humanities and social sciences generally.

I have chosen Ariadne's thread to symbolize the search for objectivity in the labyrinth of subjectivity that is the psychic life of man and in which even the most conscientious scholar can become lost. Psychoanalysis has two strengths to offer the bespectacled Theseus who dares to brave the labyrinth: first, the orientation to unconscious psychic life it offers, and the knowledge that has already been gained by means of it; second, the self-knowledge it makes possible. It is also reassuring to know that in this labyrinth there is no Minotaur. There is only the risk of having mistaken a semblance of oneself for the object one would study.

References

Abend, S. (1989). Countertransference and psychoanalytic technique. *Psychoanal. Q.* 58: 374–395.

Abend, S., M. Porder, & M. Willick. (1983). *Borderline Patients: Psychoanalytic Perspectives.* New York: International Universities Press.

Adam, J. (1902). *The Republic,* 2 vols. 2nd ed. Cambridge, Eng: Cambridge University Press, 1963.

Aristotle. *Poetics.* Trans. G. M. A. Grube. Library of the Liberal Arts. Indianapolis & New York: Bobbs-Merrill, 1958.

Arlow, J. A. (1961). Ego psychology and the study of mythology. *J. Amer. Psychoanal. Assn.* 9: 371–393.

Arlow, J. A. (1979). Metaphor and the psychoanalytic situation. *Psychoanal. Q.* 48: 363–385.

Arlow, J. A. (1982). The poet as prophet: A psychoanalytic perspective. *Psychoanal. Q.* 55: 53–68.

Arlow, J., & D. Beres. (1974). Fantasy and identification in empathy. *Psychoanal. Q.* 43: 26–50.

Bacon, F. (1620). Novum Organum. In *The English Philosophers from Bacon to Mill,* ed. E. A. Burtt. New York: Modern Library, 1939, pp. 5–123.

Bell, C. (1914). *Art.* New York: Stokes.

Berkeley, G. (1710). The principles of human knowledge. In *Berkeley,* ed. M. W. Calkins. New York: Scribner's, 1929, pp. 99–216.

Bernard, E. (1920). *La méthode de Cézanne.* Paris: Mercure de France.

Bonaparte, M. (1933). *The Life and Works of Edgar Allan Poe: A Psychoanalytic Interpretation.* Trans. J. Rodker. New York: Humanities Press, 1971.

Bonaparte, M. (1939). A defence of biography. *Int. J. Psycho-Anal.* 20: 231–240.

Bradley, A. C. (1904). *Shakespearean Tragedy.* London: Macmillan, 1937.

Bradley, F. H. (1897). *Appearance and Reality.* London: Swan & Sonnenschein.

Brenner, C. (1976). *Psychoanalytic Technique and Psychic Conflict.* New York: International Universities Press.

Brenner, C. (1982). *The Mind in Conflict.* New York: International Universities Press.

Brenner, C. (1985). Countertransference as compromise formation. *Psychoanal. Q.* 54: 155–163.

Brès, Y. (1968). *La psychologie de Platon.* Paris: Presses universitaires de France.

Broad, C. D. (1930). *Five Types of Ethical Theory.* London: Routledge & Kegan Paul.

Broad, C. D. (1952). *Ethics*. Dordrecht: Martinus Nijhoff, 1985.

Brooke, N. (1963). *Shakespeare: "King Lear."* London: Edward Arnold.

Calef, V., & E. Weinshel. (1981). Some clinical considerations of introjection: Gaslighting. *Psychoanal. Q.* 50: 44–66.

Camus, A. (1942). *The Stranger*. Trans. S. Gilbert. New York: Random House, 1946.

Carpenter, R. (1921). *The Aesthetic Basis of Greek Art of the Fifth and Fourth Centuries B.C.* Rev. ed. Bloomington: Indiana University Press, 1962.

Chasseguet-Smirgel, J. (1984). *Creativity and Perversion*. New York: Norton.

Chasseguet-Smirgel, J. (1985). *The Ego Ideal: A Psychoanalytic Essay on the Malady of the Ideal*. New York: Norton.

Chasseguet-Smirgel, J. (1986). *Sexuality and the Mind*. New York: New York University Press.

Coleridge, S. T. (1818). *Lectures and Notes on Shakespeare*. Collected by T. Ashe. London: George Bell & Sons, 1890.

Colie, R. L. (1974). The energies of endurance: Biblical echo in King Lear. In *Some Facets of King Lear*, ed. R. L. Colie & F. T. Flahiff. Toronto: University of Toronto Press, pp. 116–144.

Coltrera, J. (1965). On the creation of beauty and thought: The unique as vicissitude. *J. Amer. Psychoanal. Assn.* 13: 634–703.

Cornford, F. M. (1957). *From Religion to Philosophy*. New York: Harper & Bros.

Descartes, R. (1641). Meditations on first philosophy. In *Philosophical Works of Descartes*, Vol. 1, trans. E. S. Haldane & G. R. T. Ross. New York: Dover, 1955, pp. 133–199.

Devereux, G. (1967). *From Anxiety to Method in the Behavioural Sciences*. Paris: Mouton.

Devereux, G. (1970). The structure of tragedy and the structure of the psyche in Aristotle's *Poetics*. In *Psychoanalysis and Philosophy*, ed. C. Hanly & M. Lazerowitz. New York: International Universities Press, pp. 46–75.

Devereux, G. (1972). *Ethnopsychanalyse complémentariste*. Paris: Flammarion.

Dodds, E. R. (1963). *The Greeks and the Irrational*. Berkeley: University of California Press.

Donnelly, J. (1953). Incest, ingratitude and insanity: Aspects of the psychopathology of King Lear. *Psychoanal. Rev.* 40: 149–155.

Dostoevsky, F. (1866). *Crime and Punishment*. Trans. C. Garnett. New York: Random House, 1978.

Drake, S. (1978). *Galileo at Work: His Scientific Biography*. Chicago: University of Chicago Press.

Einstein, A. (1921). *The Meaning of Relativity: Four Lectures Delivered at Princeton University*. Trans. P. Adams. London: Methuen, 1922.

Eissler, K. R. (1961). *Leonardo da Vinci: Psychoanalytic Notes on the Enigma*. New York: International Universities Press.

Eissler, K. R. (1963). *Goethe: A Psychoanalytic Study*. Detroit: Wayne State University Press.

Eissler, K. R. (1965). *Medical Orthodoxy and the Future of Psychoanalysis*. New York: International Universities Press.

Eliot, T. S. (1919). Tradition and the individual talent. In *The Sacred Word*. New York: Barnes and Noble, 1960, pp.47–59.

Epicurus. *Epicurus, the Extant Remains*. Trans. C. Bailey. Westport, CT: Hyperion Press, 1988.

Fenichel, O. (1945). *The Psychoanalytic Theory of the Neuroses*. New York: Norton.

Ferenczi, S. (1913). Stages in the development of the sense of reality. In *First Contributions to Psycho-Analysis*. London: Hogarth Press, 1952, pp. 213–239.

Feuer, L. (1968). God, guilt and logic: the psychological basis of the ontological argument. *Inquiry*. 11: 257–281.

Feuer, L. (1970). Lawless sensations and categorical defenses: The unconscious sources of Kant's philosophy. In *Psychoanalysis and Philosophy*, ed. C. Hanly & M. Lazerowitz. New York: International Universities Press, pp. 76–123.

Feyerabend, P. (1965). Problems of empiricism. In *Beyond the Edge of Certainty: Essays in Contemporary Science and Philosophy*, ed. R. G. Colodny. Englewood Cliffs, NJ: Prentice-Hall, pp. 145–260.

Fitzpatrick, M. A. (1984). 'Projection' in Alice Munro's *Something I've Been Meaning to Tell You*. In *The Art of Alice Munro: Saying the Unsayable*, ed. J. Miller. Waterloo, Ont.: University of Waterloo Press, pp. 15–20.

Flew, A. (1970). Psychoanalysis and free will. In *Psychoanalysis and Philosophy*, ed. C. Hanly & M. Lazerowitz. New York: International Universities Press, pp. 126–154.

Freud, S. (1895a). Project for a scientific psychology. *Standard Edition* 1: 295–343.

Freud, S. (1895b). Studies in hysteria. *Standard Edition* 2: 145–260.

Freud, S. (1897). Extracts from the Fliess papers. *Standard Edition* 1: 177–280.

Freud, S. (1900). The interpretation of dreams. *Standard Edition* 4–5.

Freud, S. (1901). The psychopathology of everyday life. *Standard Edition* 6: 1–279.

Freud, S. (1905a). Fragment of an analysis of a case of hysteria. *Standard Edition* 7: 1–122.

Freud, S. (1905b). Three essays on the theory of sexuality. *Standard Edition* 7: 135–245.

Freud, S. (1907). Delusions and dreams in Jensen's *Gradiva*. *Standard Edition* 9: 7–95.

Freud, S. (1908). Creative writers and day-dreaming. *Standard Edition* 9: 143–153.

Freud, S. (1909a). Analysis of a phobia in a five-year-old boy. *Standard Edition* 10: 5–149.

Freud, S. (1909b). Family romances. *Standard Edition* 9: 237–241.

Freud, S. (1909c). Notes upon a case of obsessional neurosis. *Standard Edition* 10: 155–318.

Freud, S. (1910a). The antithetical meaning of primal words. *Standard Edition* 11: 155–161.

Freud, S.(1910b). Leonardo da Vinci and a memory of childhood. *Standard Edition* 11: 63–137.

Freud, S. (1912a). A note on the unconscious in psycho-analysis. *Standard Edition* 12: 260–266.

Freud, S. (1912b). Observations on transference-love. *Standard Edition* 12: 159–171.

Freud, S. (1912c). Recommendations to physicians practising psycho-analysis. *Standard Edition* 12: 111–120.

Freud, S. (1913a). The theme of the three caskets. *Standard Edition* 12: 289–330.

Freud, S. (1913b). Totem and taboo. *Standard Edition* 13: 1–162.

Freud, S. (1914). On narcissism: An introduction. *Standard Edition* 14: 69–102.

Freud, S. (1915). Instincts and their vicissitudes. *Standard Edition* 14: 111–140.

Freud, S. (1917a). Introductory lectures on psycho-analysis. *Standard Edition* 16: 243–496.

Freud, S. (1917b). Letter to Abraham, 11 Nov. 1917. In *A Psycho-Analytic Dialogue: The Letters of Sigmund Freud and Karl Abraham, 1907–1926.* Trans. B. Marsh & H. C. Abraham. New York: Basic Books, 1965, pp. 261–262.

Freud, S. (1918). From the history of an infantile neurosis. *Standard Edition* 17: 3–122.

Freud, S. (1919a). 'A child is being beaten': A contribution to the study of the origin of sexual perversions. *Standard Edition* 17: 179–204.

Freud, S. (1919b). The uncanny. *Standard Edition* 17: 219–256.

Freud, S. (1920). Beyond the pleasure principle. *Standard Edition* 18: 7–64.

Freud, S. (1921). Group psychology and the analysis of the ego. *Standard Edition* 18: 69–143.

Freud, S. (1923a). The ego and the id. *Standard Edition* 19: 3–66.

Freud, S. (1923b). Remarks on the theory and practise of dream-interpretation. *Standard Edition* 19: 109–121.

Freud, S. (1924a). The economic problem of masochism. *Standard Edition* 19: 159–179.

Freud, S. (1924b). The loss of reality in neurosis and psychosis. *Standard Edition* 19: 183–187.

Freud, S. (1925). Negation. *Standard Edition* 19: 235–239.

Freud, S. (1926). Inhibitions, symptoms and anxiety. *Standard Edition* 20: 87–174.

Freud, S. (1927). The future of an illusion. *Standard Edition* 21: 5–56.

Freud, S. (1930). Civilization and its discontents. *Standard Edition* 21: 64–145.

Freud, S. (1933). New introductory lectures on psycho-analysis. *Standard Edition* 22: 157–182.

Freud, S. (1937). Analysis terminable and interminable. *Standard Edition* 23: 216–254.

Freud, S. (1939). Moses and monotheism: Three essays. *Standard Edition* 23: 7–137.

Freud, S. (1940). An outline of psychoanalysis. *Standard Edition* 23: 144–207.

Friedland, M. (1974). *Cases and Materials on Criminal Law and Procedure.* 4th ed. Toronto: University of Toronto Press.

Frosch, J. (1970). Psychoanalytic considerations of the psychotic character. *J. Amer. Psychoanal. Assn.* 18: 24–50.

Fry, R. (1924). *The Artist and Psycho-Analysis.* London: Hogarth Press.

Frye, N. (1957). *The Anatomy of Criticism.* Princeton, NJ: Princeton University Press.

Gardner, H. (1967). *King Lear.* John Coffin Memorial Lecture. London: Athlone Press.

Gauthier, D. (1982). Three against justice: The foole, the sensible knave, and the Lydian shepherd. *Midwest Studies in Philosophy.* 7: 11–29.

Gay, P. (1985). *Freud for Historians.* New York: Oxford University Press.

Gay, P. (1988). *Freud: A Life for Our Time.* London: J. M. Dent & Sons.

Gedo, J. (1987). Interdisciplinary dialogue as a lutte d'amour. In *Psychoanalytic Perspectives in Art,* Vol. 2, ed. M. M. Gedo. Hillsdale, NJ, & London: Analytic Press, pp. 223–235.

Gill, M. M. (1976). Metapsychology is not psychology. In *Psychology versus Metapsychology: Psychoanalytic Essays in Memory of George S. Klein,* ed. M. M. Gill & P. Holzman. *Psychological Issues,* Monograph 36. New York: International Universities Press, pp. 71–105.

Giovacchini, P. (1960). On scientific creativity. *J. Amer. Psychoanal. Assn.* 8: 407–426.

Glover, E. (1950). *Freud or Jung.* London: Allen & Unwin.

Goldberg, A. (1976). A discussion of the paper by C. Hanly and J. Masson, 'A critical examination of the new narcissism.' *Int. J. Psycho-Anal.* 57: 67–70.

Goldberg, A. (1988). *A Fresh Look at Psychoanalysis: The View from Self-Psychology.* Hillsdale, NJ: Analytic Press.

Goldberg, S. L. (1974). *An Essay on 'King Lear.'* London: Cambridge University Press.

Golding, J. (1959). *Cubism: A History and an Analysis 1907–1914.* Rev. ed. Boston: Boston Book & Art Shop, 1968.

Golding, W. (1954). *The Lord of the Flies.* New York: Putnam's, 1962.

Greenacre, P. (1955). *Swift and Carroll: A Psychoanalytic Study of Two Lives.* New York: International Universities Press.

Grunbaum, A. (1984). *The Foundations of Psychoanalysis.* Berkeley: University of California Press.

Grunberger, B. (1956). Psychodynamic theory of masochism. In *Perversions: Psychodynamics and Therapy,* ed. S. Lorand & M. Balint. New York: Random House, pp. 183–208.

Grunberger, B. (1966). Narcissism and the Oedipus complex. In *Narcissism.* New York: International Universities Press, 1979, pp. 265–281.

Habermas, J. (1971). *Knowledge and Human Interests.* Trans. J. J. Shapiro. Boston: Beacon Press.

Hacker, F. J. (1953). On artistic production. In *Explorations in Psychoanalysis,* ed. R. Lindner. New York: Julian, pp. 128–138.

Hall, E. (1967). Dissenting opinion. *Supreme Court of Canada. [1967] S.C.R.* 309.

Hanly, C. (1967). Secularization of Western society. *Proceedings of the Seventh Inter-American Congress of Philosophy.* Québec: La presse de l'université Laval.

Hanly, C. (1970a). *Mental Health in Ontario.* Toronto: The Queen's Printer.

Hanly, C. (1970b). On being and dreaming. In *Psychoanalysis and Philosophy,* ed. C. Hanly & M. Lazerowitz. New York: International Universities Press, pp. 155–187.

Hanly, C. (1972). Wittgenstein on psychoanalysis. In *Ludwig Wittgenstein: Philosophy and Language,* ed. A. Ambrose & M. Lazerowitz. London: Allen & Unwin, pp. 73–94.

Hanly, C. (1978). Instincts and hostile affects. *Int. J. Psycho-Anal.* 59: 149–156.

Hanly, C. (1979). *Existentialism and Psychoanalysis.* New York: International Universities Press.

Hanly, C. (1982). Narcissism, defence and the positive transference. *Int. J. Psych-Anal.* 63: 427–444.

Hanly, C. (1983). A problem of theory testing. *Int. Rev. Psychoanal.* 10: 393–405.

Hanly, C. (1984). Ego ideal and ideal ego. *Int. J. Psych-Anal.* 65: 253–261.

Hanly, C. (1985). Logical and conceptual problems of existential psychiatry. *J. Nerv. Ment. Dis.* 173: 263–281.

Hanly, C. (1986). Review of *The Assault on Truth: Freud's Suppression of the Seduction Theory* and *In the Freud Archives. Int. J. Psych-Anal.* 67: 517–519.

Hanly, C. (1987). Le schématisme narcissique et le cas-limites. *Psychothérapies.* 1: 19–28.

Hartmann, H. (1950). The application of psychoanalytic concepts to social science. *Psychoanal. Q.* 19: 385–392.

Hartmann, H. (1960). *Psychoanalysis and Moral Values.* New York: International Universities Press.

Hawking, S. (1988). *A Brief History of Time.* New York: Bantam Books.

Hazlitt, W. (1817). Characters of Shakespeare's plays. In *The Complete Works of William Hazlitt,* Vol. 4. London & Toronto: J. M. Dent & Sons, 1930.

Hegel, G. W. (1821). *Philosophy of Right.* Trans. T. M. Knox. New York: Oxford University Press, 1942.

Heimann, P. (1950). On counter-transference. *Int. J. Psycho-Anal.* 31: 81–84.

Heimann, P. (1977). Further observations on the analyst's cognitive process. *J. Amer. Psychoanal. Assn.* 25: 313–333.

Hensen, R. (1979). What Kant might have said: Moral worth and the overdetermination of dutiful action. *Philos. Rev.* 88: 39–54.

Herodotus. *The Histories of Herodotus of Halicarnassus.* Trans. H. Carter. London: Oxford University Press, 1962.

Hesiod. Theogony. In *The Presocratic Philosophers*, ed. G. S. Kirk & J. E. Raven. Cambridge, Eng.: Cambridge University Press, 1962, pp. 24–37.

Hirn, Y. (1900). *The Origins of Art: A Psychological and Sociological Inquiry*. London: Macmillan.

Hobbes, T. (1651). *Leviathan*. Ed. M. Oakeshott. Oxford: Blackwell, n.d.

Homer. *Iliad*. Trans. E. V. Rieu. Harmondsworth, Eng.: Penguin, 1950.

Homer. *The Odyssey of Homer*. Trans. Samuel Butler. New York: Walter J. Black, 1944.

Hospers, J. (1952). Free will and psychoanalysis. In *Readings in Ethical Theory*, ed. W. Sellars & J. Hospers. New York: Appleton-Century-Crofts, pp. 560–575.

Hunter, G. K. (1972). Introduction. In *Shakespeare: King Lear*. Harmondsworth, Eng.: Penguin Books.

Johnson, S. (1765a). Notes on the plays. In *Johnson on Shakespeare*, ed. W. Raleigh. London: Oxford University Press, 1952, pp. 64–206.

Johnson, S. (1765b). Preface to Shakespeare. In *Johnson on Shakespeare*, ed. W. Raleigh. London: Oxford University Press, 1952, pp. 9–63.

Johnson, S. (1779). The life of Cowley. In *Samuel Johnson: Rasselas, Poems and Selected Prose*, ed. B. H. Bronson. New York: Holt, Rinehart & Winston, 1971, pp. 353–365.

Jones, E. (1949). *Hamlet and Oedipus*. New York: Norton.

Jones, E. (1953–1957). *The Life and Work of Sigmund Freud*, Vols. 1–3. New York: Basic Books.

Jones, E. (1957). *Sigmund Freud: Life and Work: Vol. 3. The Last Phase, 1919–1939*. London: Hogarth Press.

Jung, C. G. (1936–1954). The archetypes and the collective unconscious. In *Collected Works* 9(1). New York: Pantheon, 1959.

Kant, I. (1781). *Immanuel Kant's Critique of Pure Reason*. Trans. N. K. Smith. London: Macmillan, 1950.

Kant, I. (1785). *Groundwork of the Metaphysic of Morals*. Trans. H. J. Paton. London: Hutchinson, 1947.

Kant, I. (1790). *Kant's Critique of Judgement*. Trans. J. C. Meredith. Oxford: Clarendon Press, 1952.

Kant, I. (1795). *Perpetual Peace: A Philosophical Essay*. Ed. L. W. Beck. Indianapolis: Bobbs-Merrill, 1957.

Kernberg, O. (1970). A psychoanalytic classification of character pathology. *J. Amer. Psychoanal. Assn.* 18: 800–822.

Kitteridge, G. L. (1940). Introduction. In *The Tragedy of King Lear*. Boston: Ginn, pp. vii–xiv.

Klein, G. S. (1976). *Psychoanalytic Theory: An Exploration of Essentials*. New York: International Universities Press.

Kohut, H. (1959). Introspection, empathy, and psychoanalysis: An examination of the relationship between mode of observation and theory. In *The Search for the Self: Selected Writings from Heinz Kohut*, Vol. 1, ed. P. H. Ornstein. New York: International Universities Press, 1978, pp. 205–232.

Kohut, H. (1960). Beyond the bounds of the basic rule. *J. Amer. Psychoanal. Assn.* 8: 567–586.

Kohut, H. (1966). Forms and transformations of narcissism. In *The Search for the Self: Selected Writings from Heinz Kohut, 1950–1978*, vol. 1, ed. P. H. Ornstein. New York: International Universities Press, 1978, pp. 427–440.

Kohut, H. (1977). *The Restoration of the Self*. New York: International Universities Press.

Kris, A. (1982). *Free Associations*. New Haven, CT: Yale University Press.

Kris, E. (1952). *Psychoanalytic Explorations in Art*. New York: International Universities Press.

Kris, E. (1953). Psychoanalysis and the study of creative imagination. In *The Selected Papers of Ernst Kris*. New Haven, CT: Yale University Press, 1975, pp. 473–493.

Kubie, L. S. (1975). The language tools of psychoanalysis: A search for better tools drawn from better models. *Int. Rev. Psycho-Anal.* 2: 11–24.

Kuhn, T. S. (1970). *The Structure of Scientific Revolutions*. 2nd ed., enlarged. Chicago: University of Chicago Press.

Lacan, J. (1966). *Écrits: Le champ freudien*. Paris: Éditions du seuil.

Lamb, C. (1808). On the tragedies of Shakespeare. In *The Complete Works and Letters of Charles Lamb*. New York: The Modern Library, 1935, pp. 289–303.

Langer, S. (1942). *Philosophy in a New Key*. Cambridge, MA: Harvard University Press.

Langer, S. (1953). *Feeling and Form*. London: Routledge & Kegan Paul.

Langer, W. L. (1958). The next assignment. *American Historical Review*. 63: 283–304.

Laswell, H. (1930). *Psychopathology and Politics*. Chicago: University of Chicago Press.

Lazerowitz, M. (1955). *The Structure of Metaphysics*. London: Routledge & Kegan Paul.

Lazerowitz, M. (1964). *Studies in Metaphilosophy*. London: Routledge & Kegan Paul.

Lazerowitz, M. (1968). *Philosophy and Illusion*. London: Allen & Unwin.

LeBourdais, I. (1966). *The Trial of Stephen Truscott*. Toronto: Prentice-Hall.

Leites, N. (1947). Trends in affectiveness. *Amer. Imago* 4: 89–112.

Leites, N. (1963). The stranger. In *Art and Psychoanalysis*, ed. W. Phillips. New York: Meridian Books, pp. 247–267.

Little, M. (1953). Counter-transference and the patient's response to it. *Int. J. Psycho-Anal.* 32: 32–40.

Lévi-Strauss, C. (1958). *Anthropologie Structurale*. Paris: Plon.

Lévi-Strauss, C. (1962). *La pensée sauvage*. Paris: Plon.

Levy-Bruhl, L. (1910). *Fonctions mentales dans les sociétés inférieures*. Paris: Alcan.

Locke, J. (1690). *An Essay Concerning Human Understanding*. In *The English Philosophers from Bacon to Mill*. New York: Modern Library, 1939, pp. 238–402.

Loewald, H. (1980). The waning of the Oedipus complex. In *Papers on Psycho-analysis*. New Haven, CT: Yale University Press, 1980, pp. 384–404.

MacIntyre, A. C. (1958). *The Unconscious: A Conceptual Analysis*. London: Routledge & Kegan Paul.

Masson, J. L., & D. D. Kosambi. (1970). *Avimaraka*. New Delhi: Motilal Banarsides.

May, R. (1958). Contributions of existential psychotherapy. In *Existence: A New Dimension in Psychiatry and Psychology*, ed. R. May. New York: Simon & Schuster, 1967, pp. 37–91.

Mazlish, B. (1975). *James and John Stuart Mill*. New York: Basic Books.

Merendino, R. (1985). On epistemological functions of clinical reports. *Int. J. Psycho-Anal.* 12: 327–336.

Merleau-Ponty, M. (1945). *Phenomenology of Perception*. Trans. C. Smith. London: Routledge & Kegan Paul, 1962.

Mill, J. S. (1863). *Utilitarianism*. London: Longmans Green, 1907.

Munro, A. (1986). Fits. In *The Progress of Love*. Toronto: McClelland & Stewart, pp. 106–131.

Noy, P. (1972). About art and artistic talent. *Int. J. Psycho-Anal.* 53: 243–250.

Noy, P. (1979). Form creation in art: An ego-psychological approach to creativity. *Psychoanal. Q.* 48: 229–256.

Parker, D. H. (1924). *The Analysis of Art*. New Haven, CT: Yale University Press.

Parsons, T. (1950). Psychoanalysis and the social structure. *Psychoanal. Q.* 19: 371–384.

Paton, H. (1936). *Kant's Metaphysic of Experience*, 2 vols. London: Allen & Unwin.

Pauncz, A. (1952). Psychopathology of Shakespeare's King Lear. *Amer. Imago* 9: 57–78.

Peters, R.S. (1958). *The Concept of Motivation*. London: Routledge & Kegan Paul.

Plato. Charmides. In *Laches and Charmides*, trans. R. K. Sprague. Indianapolis & New York: Bobbs-Merrill, 1973.

Plato. *Epistles*. Trans. G. R. Morrow. New York: Liberal Arts Press, 1962.

Plato. *Ion. Two Comic Dialogues*. Trans. Paul Woodruff. Indianapolis: Hackett, 1983.

Plato. *Phaedo*. Ed. R. Hackforth. New York: Cambridge University Press, 1972.

Plato. *Meno*. Trans. B. Jowett. New York: Bobbs-Merrill, 1949.

Plato. *Phaedrus*. Trans. W. C. Helmbold & W. G. Rabinowitz. Indianapolis & New York: Bobbs-Merrill, 1956.

Plato. *Republic*. Trans. B. Jowett. New York: Liberal Arts Press, 1948.

Plato. *Symposium*. Trans. W. C. Helmbold & W. G. Rabinowitz. New York: Bobbs-Merrill, 1956.

Plato. *Timaeus*. Trans. Benjamin Jowett. New York: Macmillan, 1949.

Popper, K. (1966). *The Open Society and Its Enemies*, Vol. 1. London: Routledge & Kegan Paul.

Pruyser, P. W. (1983). *The Play of Imagination: Toward a Psychoanalysis of Culture*. New York: International Universities Press.

Putnam, H. (1981). *Reason, Truth and History*. Cambridge, Eng.: Cambridge University Press.

Racker, H. (1953). A contribution to the problem of counter-transference. *Int. J. Psycho-Anal*. 34: 313–324.

Rangell, L. (1980). *The Mind of Watergate: A Study of the Compromise of Integrity*. New York: Norton.

Rangell, L. (1988). The future of psychoanalysis: The scientific crossroads. *Psychoanal. Q*. 57: 313–340.

Rank, O. (1909). *The Myth of the Birth of the Hero*. New York: Vintage Books, 1952.

Reed, G. (1982). Towards a methodology for applying psychoanalysis to literature. *Psychoanal. Q*. 51: 19–42.

Reed, G. (1985). Psychoanalysis, psychoanalysis appropriated, psychoanalysis applied. *Psychoanal. Q*. 54: 234–269.

Renik, O. (1978). Neurotic and narcissistic transferences in Freud's relationship with Joseph Popper. *Psychoanal. Q*. 47: 398–418.

Ricoeur, P. (1970). *Freud and Philosophy*. New Haven, CT: Yale University Press.

Ricoeur, P. (1974). *The Conflict of Interpretations*. Ed. D. Idhe. Evanston, IL: Northwestern University Press.

Ricoeur, P. (1981). *Hermeneutics and the Human Sciences*. Trans. J. B. Thompson. New York: Cambridge University Press.

Roheim, G. (1947). *Psychoanalysis and the Social Sciences*. New York: International Universities Press.

Roheim, G. (1950). *Psychoanalysis and Anthropology*. New York: International Universities Press.

Rose, G. J. (1980). *The Power of Form: A Psychoanalytic Approach to Aesthetic Form*. Psychol. Issues, Monograph 49. New York: International Universities Press.

Rycroft, C. (1966). Introduction: Causes and meaning. In *Psychoanalysis Observed*, ed. C. Rycroft. London: Constable, pp. 7–22.

Ryle, G. (1949). *The Concept of Mind*. London: Hutchinson's University Library.

Sartre, J.-P. (1943). *Being and Nothingness*. Trans. H. E. Barnes. New York: Philosophical Library, 1956.

Schafer, R. (1976). *A New Language for Psychoanalysis*. New York: Yale University Press.

Schafer, R. (1978). *Language and Insight*. New Haven, CT: Yale University Press.

Schur, M. (1972). *Freud: Living and Dying*. New York: International Universities Press.

Shakespeare, W. (1604–1605). *King Lear*. New York: Cambridge University Press, 1968.

Sharpe, E. F. (1946). From King Lear to the Tempest. In *Collected Papers on Psycho-Analysis*. London: Hogarth Press, 1968, pp. 214–241.

Shengold, L. (1974). More about the meaning of 'nothing.' *Psychoanal. Q.* 43: 116–119.

Shengold, L. (1988). *Halo in the Sky: Observations on Anality and Defense*. New York: Guilford Press.

Siomapolous, G. (1977). Poetry as affective communication. *Psychoanal. Q.* 46: 499–513.

Sophocles. Oedipus Rex. In *The Theban Plays*. Trans. E. F. Watling. Harmondsworth: Penguin, 1947, pp. 25–73.

Sparshott, F. (1963). *The Structure of Aesthetics*. Toronto: University of Toronto Press.

Spence, D. (1982a). *Narrative Truth and Historical Truth: Meaning and Interpretation in Psychoanalysis*. New York: Norton.

Spence, D. (1982b). Narrative truth and theoretical truth. *Psychoanal. Q.* 51: 43–69.

Spenser, E. (1590). The faerie queene. In *Spenser Poetical Works*. London: Oxford University Press, 1912, pp. 1–406.

Steinberg, B. (1991). Psychoanalytic concepts in international politics: The role of shame and humiliation. *Int. Rev. Psycho-Anal.* 18: 65–86.

Stompfer, J. (1960). The catharsis of King Lear. *Shakespeare Survey* 13: 1–10.

Storr, A. (1972). *The Dynamics of Creation*. London: Secker & Warburg.

Swift, J. (1704). *A Tale of a Tub*. London: Oxford University Press, 1949.

Swinburne, A. C. (1876). *A Study of Shakespeare*. London: Chatto & Windus, 1902.

Thucydides. *The Peloponnesian War*. Trans. R. Warner. Harmondsworth, Eng.: Penguin Books, 1954.

Tolstoy, L. (1896). *What Is Art? and Essays on Art*. Trans. A. Maude. London: Oxford University Press, 1925.

Traub-Werner, D. (1984). Toward a theory of prejudice. *Int. Rev. Psycho-Anal.* 11: 407–412.

Trilling, L. (1950). *The Liberal Imagination*. New York: Viking Press.

van Frassen, B. (1984). To save the phenomena. In *Scientific Realism*, ed. J. Leplin. Berkeley: University of California Press, pp. 250–259.

Véron, E. (1878). *Aesthetics*. Trans. W. H. Armstrong. London: Library of Contemporary Science, 1879.

Viderman, S. (1970). *La construction de l'espace analytique*. Paris: Denoel.

Viderman, S. (1972). Comme un miroir, obscurément. . . . *Nouv. rev. psychanal.* Paris: Gallimard.

Waelder, R. (1926). Schizophrenic and creative thinking. In *Psychoanalysis: Observation, Theory, Application*. New York: International Universities Press, 1976, pp. 42–56.9

Waelder, R. (1930). The principle of multiple function: Observations on over-determination. In *Psychoanalysis: Observation, Theory, Application*. New York: International Universities Press, pp. 68–83.

Waelder, R. (1934). The problem of freedom in psychoanalysis and the problem of reality testing. In *Psychoanalysis: Observation, Theory, Application*. New York: International Universities Press, 1976, pp. 101–120.

Waelder, R. (1965). *Psychoanalytic Avenues to Art*. The Freud Anniversary Lecture Series. New York: International Universities Press.

Wallace, E. R. (1985). *Historiography and Causation in Psychoanalysis*. Hillsdale, NJ: Analytic Press.

Wallerstein, R. S. (1988). One psychoanalysis or many? *Int. J. Psycho-Anal.* 69: 5–21.

Wangh, M. (1950). Othello: The tragedy of Iago. *Psychoanal. Q.* 19: 202–212.

Warton, J. (1754). *The Adventurer, Vol. 2, No. 122*. New York: AMS Press, 1968.

Weinshel, E. (1986). Perceptual disturbances during analysis: Some observations on the role of the superego in reality testing. In *Psychoanaly-sis: The Science of Mental Conflict*, ed. A. D. Richards & M. S. Willick. Hillsdale, NJ: Analytic Press, pp. 353–374.

Williams, G. (1963). *The Proof of Guilt*. 3rd ed. London: Stevens & Sons.

Winnicott, D. W. (1953). Transitional objects and transitional phenomena: A study of the first not-me possession. In *Collected Papers: Through Pediatrics to Psycho-Analysis*. New York: Basic Books, 1958, pp. 229–242.

Winnicott, D. W. (1971). *Playing and Reality*. New York: Basic Books.

Woodbury, L. (1958). Parmenides on names. *Harvard Stud. Classical Philol.* 63: 145–160.

Zak, W. (1984). *Sovereign Shame*. London & Toronto: Associated Universities Press.

Index

Aesthetic values
  and identification, 101
  and psychoanalysis, 101
Aesthetics
  and catharsis, 88–90
  and content, 87, 91, 92
  and form, 86–87, 90, 93
  and psychoanalysis, 86, 87–88, 101–102
Ahend, S., 40, 157
Allegory of the cave, 149–150
  interpretation, 150–151
  and rebirth, 149
Altruism, motivation of, 209–211
Anal sadism
  in Goneril and Regan, 116–117
  and narcissism, 119
Analyst and neurosis, 44
Animism
  in Ancient times, 157–158
  in childhood, 157
  and conaturality of self with objects, 58
  and conaturality of words with objects, 58
  and formal regression in dreams, 59
  in modern adults, 59, 158
  and power of words, 64
Applied psychoanalysis
  and clinical psychoanalysis, 30, 51
  and conjectures, 130
  and contradiction, 103, 105
  contributions to psychoanalytic theory, 31–32
  and critical idealization of Lear, 107, 116, 118, 120
  and evaluation of art, 101
  and evidence, 35–37, 38, 105, 106, 141–142
  and falsifiability, 31, 156
  forms of, 46–49
  and interdisciplinary studies, 46, 155
  points of departure for, 35, 50, 103
  and testing interpretations, 30, 106, 144–142, 144–151, 156
Archaic residues, 48, 67

Aristotle, 32, 47, 89, 90, 105, 122, 134, 154, 212
Arlow, J., 40, 44, 90, 92, 94, 144, 149
Art
  and autobiography, 126, 132–133
  and catharsis, 100
  and content, 97, 98, 99
  and form, 90, 126
  and imitation, 90, 91
  and poetic truth, 90, 91, 131
  and psychic interpretation, 100
  and science, 99
  and universality, 133, 134
Artist and neurosis, 44

B

Bacon, F., 12
Bell, C. 86
Beres, D., 40, 44, 92
Berkeley, G., 212
Bernard, E., 97
Bonaparte, M., 46
Borderline personality, 157
  and ancient man, 157
  and childhood, 157
Bradley, A. C.,106, 110
Brenner, C., 5, 40, 44, 80, 197
Brès, Y., 152
Broad, C. D., 78
Brooke, N., 119

C

Calef, V., 32
Camus, A., 103, 130
Carpenter, R., 87
Catharsis, 100
  in art, 87
  in Aristotle's poetics, 89
  and content in art, 92
  and dreaming, 89–90